"In this deeply thoughtful and enlighte
Christian dogmatic theology, Rosario R(
argument that the methods of thinkers like Tillich and Barth do not easily translate into the twenty-first century. Drawing from a rich variety of
contemporary theologians, he calls us to the urgent task of asking, how
can we bridge differences for the sake of true community? Who is my
neighbor? He suggests that the biblical stories of Babel and Pentecost
may be keys to getting at this important question in theology today."
—Amy Marga, Associate Professor of Systematic Theology,
Luther Seminary

"This is a challenging and daring book. It dares ask two axial questions
that organize and guide the author's reflections: What happens to doctrinal language when we accept theological diversity as normative? And
what happens when we stop viewing theological pluralism as a problem
to be solved (Babel) and embrace it as a gift of the Spirit (Pentecost)?
Rosario Rodríguez's tour de force is insightful and brilliantly argued. I
recommend this volume without hesitation."
—Orlando O. Espin, University Professor of Theology
and Religious Studies, University of San Diego

"Attentive to tradition and sensitive to recent developments, *Dogmatics after Babel* is a provocative and wide-ranging contribution to
conversations about how to speak about God with truth and humility
in a cultural situation that seems to make such speech impossible."
—Matthew Lundberg, Professor of Religion, Calvin College

"In the cacophony of a theological Babel, Rosario Rodríguez provides
us with an inclusive pneumatological path forward—one that embraces
our theological diversity. Skillfully moving beyond normative Eurocentric revelational and anthropological theological approaches, he leads
toward a liberative spirituality capable of preserving human dignity and
emancipating the oppressed. A must-read for those seeking harmony."
—Miguel A. De La Torre, Professor of Social Ethics
and Latinx Studies, Iliff School of Theology

"Deeply researched, carefully argued, richly ecumenical and Abrahamic, this book both reviews the most important Christian theological arguments of the last few centuries and stakes out new ground by suggesting the outlines of an interfaith, pneumatological, liberation theology. I highly recommend this book and look forward to the good fruit it will bear."

—David P. Gushee, Distinguished University Professor of Christian Ethics and Director, Center for Theology and Public Life, Mercer University

"Rosario Rodríguez addresses head-on the question of how we may have meaningful faith while at the same time honoring and engaging the plurality of religious convictions that surround us. After surveying an impressive range of thinkers, schools of thought, and resources, he suggests that attending to the work of the Spirit gives us ways of making personal connections to what we believe while avoiding what he identifies as 'theological totalitarianism.' Rosario Rodríguez's book will benefit anyone who wants to understand better the state of the question, How might we speak about God from out of our own particular traditions and experiences while at the same time recognizing that God lives and acts beyond what we know, including in the histories and experiences of others?"

—Cynthia L. Rigby, W. C. Brown Professor of Theology, Austin Presbyterian Theological Seminary

"In this book, Rubén Rosario Rodríguez develops an elegant and compelling account of the challenges facing contemporary theology and outlines a constructive way in which these challenges can be met. In doing so, he threads the needle between a postliberal concern for the self-revelation of God given in Scripture and mediated through the Christian tradition and a postcolonial concern for the contextual and power-laden nature of all speech about God as well as the need for theology to attend to non-Western, non-Christian, and marginalized voices."

—Luke Bretherton, Professor of Theological Ethics and Senior Fellow at the Kenan Institute for Ethics, Duke University

Dogmatics after Babel

Dogmatics after Babel

Beyond the Theologies of Word and Culture

Rubén Rosario Rodríguez

WESTMINSTER
JOHN KNOX PRESS
LOUISVILLE · KENTUCKY

First edition
Published by Westminster John Knox Press
Louisville, Kentucky

18 19 20 21 22 23 24 25 26 27—10 9 8 7 6 5 4 3 2 1

Book design by Drew Stevens
Cover design by Lisa Buckley Design

Library of Congress Cataloging-in-Publication Data

Names: Rosario Rodríguez, Rubén, 1970– author.
Title: Dogmatics after Babel : beyond the theologies of word and culture / Rubén Rosario Rodríguez.
Description: First edition. | Louisville, KY : Westminster John Knox Press, 2018. | Includes
  bibliographical references and index.
Identifiers: LCCN 2018007905 (print) | LCCN 2018029104 (ebook) | ISBN 9781611648836
  (ebk.) | ISBN 9780664261658 (pbk. : alk. paper)
Subjects: LCSH: Dogma. | Theology—Methodology.
Classification: LCC BT28 (ebook) | LCC BT28 .R598 2018 (print) | DDC 230—dc23
LC record available at https://lccn.loc.gov/2018007905

Most Westminster John Knox Press books are available at special quantity discounts when purchased in bulk by corporations, organizations, and special-interest groups. For more information, please email SpecialSales@wjkbooks.com.

"Words mean something."
Bernhard Asen (1944–2016)

Contents

Acknowledgments   ix

Introduction   xi

1. Contextualizing The Conversation   **1**

  1.1 The Enlightenment's Break with the Past   1

  1.2 Kierkegaard's Defense of Scriptural Authority   4

      1.2.1 Truth as Existential Appropriation   6

      1.2.2 Revelation as a Historical Possibility   9

      1.2.3 Faith not Fideism   12

  1.3 From Neo-orthodoxy to Narrative Theology   14

  1.4 Narrative Theology as Public Discourse   20

  1.5 Reconciling Revelational and Anthropological Approaches   31

2. Two Sides of the Same Coin   **35**

  2.1 The Postwar Crisis in Intellectual Discourse   35

  2.2 Barth and Tillich on the Doctrine of Revelation   38

  2.3 What Is Scripture? Some Competing Perspectives   49

  2.4 Past the Impasse: A Pneumatological Proposal   60

3. Postmodern Babylon   **65**

  3.1 Beyond the Theologies of Word and Culture   66

  3.2 Sallie McFague's Metaphorical Theology   71

  3.3 John Milbank's Transcendental Ontology   83

  3.4 Miguel De La Torre and the Politics of *Jesús*   95

  3.5 Embracing an Exilic Theology   106

4. Dogmatic Claims in Pluralistic Context   **109**

    4.1 Dogmatic Theology in Interdisciplinary Context   110

    4.2 Analogical Apprehension of the Hidden God   119

    4.3 The Dogmatic Burden: "What We Cannot
           Speak About"   127

    4.4 The Hiddenness of God as Hermeneutical Principle   131

    4.5 A Trinitarian Perspective on Religious Pluralism   140

5. Pneumatology—Revelation as Sacramental Encounter   **145**

    5.1 Scriptural Conceptions of Spirit   147

          5.1.1 Spirit in the Tanakh   148

          5.1.2 Spirit in the New Testament   157

          5.1.3 Spirit in the Qur'an   164

    5.2 Liberation as the Historical Experience
           of the Spirit   168

    5.3 The Sacrament of History   175

Conclusion: From Babel to Pentecost   187

Bibliography   197

Index of Subjects and Authors   217

Acknowledgments

In a perfect world this book would have been written and published before my second book, *Christian Martyrdom and Political Violence* (Cambridge University Press, 2017); but while this might be the best of all possible worlds (Leibniz), things rarely go according to plan. In *that* book I employed methodological directions explored more fully in this book—specifically an analysis of the hiddenness of God in all three "Abrahamic" religions as limiting the scope of dogmatic claims, and the centrality of God's preferential option for the poor, powerless, and oppressed in the sacred scriptures of Judaism, Christianity, and Islam—in order to develop a comparative theology of martyrdom in conversation with Judaism and Islam. In *this* book the comparative methodology is front and center, since in the radically pluralist twenty-first-century context, theological construction *demands* dialogue and cooperation with other religions. Consequently, there are some areas of overlap linking both books. My hope is that readers will read and engage this volume first, in which I more thoroughly engage the methodological concerns that necessitate a comparative approach in theological construction, before reading the book on martyrdom, in which I apply the methodological insights encountered herein.

I want to thank my editor at Westminster John Knox Press, Robert Ratcliff, for encouraging me to write this book, since the germ of an idea that eventually became this book was born from a conversation I had with him many years ago when I was a graduate student and he was providing editorial feedback to the Hispanic Theological Initiative dissertation fellows. In many ways, this is a book I have wanted to write ever since I left the pastorate and began doctoral work in systematic theology at Princeton Theological Seminary. Without Bob's encouragement, insightful feedback, and abiding patience, this book could not have been completed. I also want to thank my former department chair at Saint Louis University, James Ginther, for a course reduction in the spring of 2015 that allowed me to make significant progress toward completing the book, as well as my graduate assistants at Saint Louis

University over the past three years, Sam Walk, Chad Kim, Robert Johnson, and Josh Sturgeon, for their assistance tracking down articles, retrieving books from the library, proofreading early drafts, formatting endnotes, and compiling the subject index. Special thanks to my former student, Creighton Coleman—a Pentecostal theologian with a passion for political theology—for his vital insights and contributions to the fifth chapter. I am also extremely grateful to my colleagues in the Department of Theological Studies at Saint Louis University, Jack Renard and Dan Finucane: Jack for continuing my education about Islam and pointing me to various sources I would not have encountered on my own, and Dan for his careful and close reading of this book from beginning to end in its various drafts. Without Dan's feedback, wisdom, and encyclopedic knowledge of Christian theology, this would be a much poorer book.

A short word about the dedication of this book: Bernhard Asen was my colleague at Saint Louis University for twelve years. He was a beloved Bible professor whose course on the Hebrew Prophets was legendary and revealed his deep love for the Word of God. When my son was diagnosed with leukemia and underwent several years of grueling chemotherapy, Ben always made an effort to inquire about my son's health, offer words of encouragement, and reassure me that many people were praying for his recovery. Unbeknown to me, Ben had been quietly fighting his own battle with cancer, a battle he finally lost on May 6, 2016. Many of the ideas in this book were sounded out in conversations with Ben, and the epigraph on the dedication page, "Words *mean* something," is a mantra often repeated by Ben. These words speak to the urgency motivating me to write a book about the possibility of making dogmatic claims after Babel.

As always, thanks to my wife, Elizabeth Blake, and our children, Isabella and Raphael, for their love and support when I get lost in the world of "theology-blah-blah."

Introduction

"And because we are so prideful and so despondent, we build ourselves a Tower of Babel. Therefore the righteousness of God, which we have already seen and touched, has been transformed in our clumsy hands into a whole variety of human righteousness."

—Karl Barth[1]

The tale of the tower of Babel (Gen. 11:1–9), with origins in the mythic prehistory of ancient Israel, continues to fascinate and confound the imagination.[2] Argentinian short story writer, poet, and essayist Jorge Luis Borges (1899–1986) envisioned an eternal and spatially infinite library in his short story, "The Library of Babel," whose vast collection contains every book ever written translated into every language. However, because of its immense size and completely random ordering, the library is in effect useless—one could spend a lifetime searching for an elusive text never to find it—which brings its librarians to the brink of suicidal despair: "For every rational line or forthright statement there are leagues of senseless cacophony, verbal nonsense, and incoherency."[3]

1. Karl Barth, *The Word of God and Theology*, trans. Amy Marga (London: T. & T. Clark International, 2011), 8.
2. Literary critic George Steiner's landmark work on the problems of translation, *After Babel: Aspects of Language and Translation*, 2nd ed. (Oxford: Oxford University Press, 1992), contends that different cultures develop their own distinct languages as an expression of their desire for secrecy and privacy. Accordingly, translation is at the heart of all human communication, even within one's own native language and culture, as all interpretation is itself an act of translation. Also see Jeffrey Stout, *Ethics after Babel: The Languages of Morals and their Discontents* (Princeton: Princeton University Press, 2001), and Bernard S. Phillips, *Beyond Sociology's Tower of Babel: Reconstructing the Scientific Method* (New York: Aldine de Gruyter, 2001). Beyond the realm of academic discourse, Pieter Bruegel (1525–1569) titled an oil painting "The Tower of Babel," and M. C. Escher (1898–1972) titled a woodcut the same name; Ray Bradbury makes reference to the Tower of Babel in *Fahrenheit 451* (New York: Ballantine Books, 1953), 38, as does Russian novelist Victor Pelevin, *Babylon*, trans. Andrew Bromfield (London: Faber and Faber, 2000), 37. The British pop group Squeeze recorded the album *Babylon and On* (1987) and Elton John recorded the song "Tower of Babel" for the album *Captain Fantastic and the Brown Dirt Cowboy* (1975). The title of this monograph is an homage to Stout's monumental work in ethics in an effort to focus this monograph's analysis of the distinctive language of dogmatics given the diverse but confused state of academic theology today.
3. Jorge Luis Borges, "The Library of Babel," in *Collected Fictions*, trans. Andrew Hurley (New York: Penguin Books, 1998), 114.

In whatever permutation one encounters it, the myth of Babel stands as a cautionary fable about human arrogance in defiance of God leading to the confusion of tongues: an apt metaphor for the state of Christian theology early in the twenty-first century.

As Reformed theologian Douglas F. Ottati has noted, "we live at a time of radical plurality (if not downright confusion)."[4] Citing Gordon D. Kaufman who opined, "That the contemporary theological scene has become chaotic is evident to everyone who attempts to work in theology,"[5] Ottati concludes that the current state of theology is, if anything, even "more chaotic since Kaufman wrote that."[6] Within North American Christianity (primarily Roman Catholicism and Protestantism in all its different permutations), this confusion of tongues has manifest itself in a variety of cultural clashes over the church's stance on issues like the use of inclusive language for God, ordination of LGBTQ persons, same-sex marriage, reproductive rights, women's ordination, religious pluralism, humanity's responsibility for environmental degradation, and the relationship of faith to science.[7] This scattering and division of humanity in terms of culture and language (Gen. 11:9) is intensified within academic theology, where the seminary and university curricula include courses on patristic theology, Latin American liberation theology, historical theology, black liberation theology, medieval theology, feminist theology, orthodox theology, gay and lesbian theology, neo-orthodox theology, transgender theology, Radical Orthodoxy, mujerista theology, modern theology, womanist theology, *mestizo* theology, political theology, eco-theology, postcolonial theology, public theology, decolonial theology, postmodern theology, and so forth and so on, *ad infinitum*. For some within the church, this proliferation of theological perspectives is positive—a flowering of the Spirit—while for others it signals a failure of doctrinal and ecclesial unity.

Despite this plethora of competing movements within the Western Christian tradition, especially in Europe and North America, two distinct methodological approaches came to dominate the theological

---

4. Douglas F. Ottati, *Theology for Liberal Protestants: God the Creator* (Grand Rapids, MI: Wm. B. Eerdmans Publishing Co., 2013), 25.

5. Gordon D. Kaufman, *An Essay on Theological Method*, rev. ed. (Missoula, MT: Scholars Press, 1979), ix.

6. Ottati, *Theology for Liberal Protestants*, 25n1.

7. See John L. Allen Jr., *The Future Church: How Ten Trends Are Revolutionizing the Catholic Church* (New York: Image, 2009) in which religion journalist John L. Allen identifies ten cultural trends that will transform the Catholic Church into the next century, arguing that the church will have to adopt fundamental changes in order to adapt to these cultural shifts. Key trends identified by the author include the global character of the church, the spread of Islam, the forces of globalization, the ecological crisis, and rapid advances in biotechnology. Though the author speaks from a Catholic context, his analysis is applicable *mutatis mutandis* to Christianity in its various confessional forms.

landscape in the twentieth century under whose long shadow all contemporary efforts at theological construction still stand: (1) the *anthropological* approach embodied in Paul Tillich's (1886–1965) theology of
culture[8] and (2) the *revelational* approach originating in Karl Barth's
(1886–1968) critical retrieval of orthodoxy.[9] In Tillich's analysis, the
"theologian of culture" begins with an examination of the historical
and social context of the believing community, then seeks to ascer-
tain the meaning of God's message for the present human situation
through a method of correlation by which the universal concerns of
the human condition find expression in the particular symbols of the
Christian faith. By contrast, the "church theologian" eschews the particularities of human culture, focusing primarily on God's transcendent
message as revealed in Scripture (and to a lesser extent, confessional
traditions) before addressing the culture in which the church is located.
The critique raised by the anthropological model about the revelational
approach is that it perpetuates a "supranaturalist" theology in which
Scripture stands outside of culture, thus shielded from criticism by
culture,[10] while the critique of the anthropological approach by more
church-centered theologians is that, in its efforts to make the Christian
faith relevant to the surrounding culture, theologies of culture undermine the uniqueness of God's self-revelation in Jesus Christ.[11] In the
North American context, theologians of culture influenced by Tillich's
correlational method include David Tracy, Sallie McFague, Rosemary
Radford Ruether, and Gordon Kaufman, while proponents of a more

8. See Paul Tillich, "On the Idea of a Theology of Culture" and "What Is Wrong with the 'Dialectic' Theology?"
in *Paul Tillich: Theologian of the Boundaries*, ed. Mark Kline Taylor (Minneapolis: Fortress Press, 1991), 35–54,
104–16; and *Systematic Theology*, 3 vols. (Chicago: The University of Chicago Press, 1951, 1957, and 1963).

9. See Karl Barth, *The Epistle to the Romans*, trans. Edwyn C. Hoskins (Oxford: Oxford University Press, 1968);
"No! Answer to Emil Brunner," in *Karl Barth: Theologian of Freedom*, ed. Clifford Green (Minneapolis: Fortress
Press, 1991), 151–67; and *Church Dogmatics*, 13 vols. eds. G. W. Bromiley & T. F. Torrance, trans. various (Edin-
burgh: T. & T. Clark, 1936–1969).

10. See David Tracy, *The Analogical Imagination: Christian Theology and the Culture of Pluralism* (New York:
Crossroad, 1981); Sallie McFague, *Metaphorical Theology: Models of God in Religious Language* (Philadelphia: For-
tress Press, 1982); Rosemary Radford Ruether, *Sexism and God-Talk: Toward a Feminist Theology* (Boston: Beacon
Press, 1983); and Gordon D. Kaufman, *In Face of Mystery: A Constructive Theology* (Cambridge, MA: Harvard
University Press, 1993).

11. See Hans W. Frei, *The Eclipse of Biblical Theology: A Study in Eighteenth and Nineteenth Century Hermeneutics*
(New Haven, CT: Yale University Press, 1974); *Types of Christian Theology*, ed. by George Hunsinger and William
C. Placher (New Haven, CT: Yale University Press, 1992), and *The Identity of Jesus Christ: The Hermeneutical Basis
of Dogmatic Theology* (Philadelphia: Fortress Press, 1975); George A. Lindbeck, *The Nature of Doctrine: Religion and
Theology in a Postliberal Age*, 25th anniversary ed. (Louisville, KY: Westminster John Knox Press, 2009); Stanley
Hauerwas, *Character and the Christian Life: A Study in Theological Ethics* (South Bend, IN: University of Notre
Dame Press, 1994); John Milbank, *Theology and Social Theory: Beyond Secular Reason* (Oxford: Blackwell Publishers
Ltd., 1990); David B. Burrell, *Analogy and Philosophical Language* (New Haven, CT: Yale University Press, 1973);
also see *Postliberal Theology and the Church Catholic: Conversations with George Lindbeck, David Burrell, and Stanley
Hauerwas*, ed. John Wright (Ada, MI: Baker Academic, 2012), and *Why Narrative? Readings in Narrative Theology*,
ed. Stanley Hauerwas and L. Gregory Jones (Eugene, OR: Wipf & Stock Publishers, 1997).

Scripture-centered theology include Hans W. Frei, George A. Lind-beck, Stanley Hauerwas, David B. Burrell, and John Milbank.

Is Babel a problem to be solved? Human hubris creates a plurality of competing perspectives all claiming to be "the word of God" yet all suffering from the same myopia. As Karl Barth has argued: "Isn't our religious righteousness, too, a product of our pride and despair, a Tower of Babel, which the devil laughs about louder than about anything else!?"[12] Barth's critique of religion rejects theological pluralism as an act of human arrogance, pride, and rebellion in no uncertain terms: "It is high time to openly confess and gladly admit with relief that *this* god, to whom we have built the Tower of Babel, is not a god. He is an idol. He is dead."[13] Barth's theological contemporary, Paul Tillich, also thought the myth of Babel apropos for describing the challenge of theological plu-ralism: "Perhaps the story of the Tower of Babel, telling of man's desire to be united under a symbol in which his finitude is overcome and the divine sphere reached, is nearest to our own situation."[14] Admittedly, Tillich viewed theological pluralism in a more positive light than Barth, suggesting that the broken communion caused by the sin of Babel finds redemption in the story of Pentecost in which the "disciples' ecstatic speaking with tongues was interpreted as the conquest of the disruption of mankind as symbolized in the story of the Tower of Babel."[15] Still, despite their differences, both Barth and Tillich viewed the discord and lack of doctrinal agreement within modern Christianity as an undesir-able state; one promulgated by the human drive to overcome what Til-lich terms the "ambiguity of freedom" through an imposition of one's own values as normative over against alternative points of view by means of a theological totalitarianism.[16] This book dares ask the question: What if Babel is the future of global Christianity? In other words, what

12. Barth, *The Word of God and Theology*, 10.
13. Ibid., 11. While committed to using gender-inclusive language throughout this work, all quotations reflect the culturally and historically bound perspectives of the original author.
14. Paul Tillich, *Systematic Theology*, vol. 3, *Life and the Spirit, History, and the Kingdom of God* (Chicago: The University of Chicago Press, 1963), 73.
15. Ibid., 151.
16. See Rubem Alves, *Protestantism and Repression: A Brazilian Case Study*, trans. John Drury, reprint ed. (Eugene, OR: Wipf & Stock Publishers, 2007), for an analysis of this kind of theological totalitarianism within Protestantism, which he terms "Right-Doctrine Protestantism," referring to those churches unable to adapt to the rising multiplicity of "ways of articulating the faith" for whom theological pluralism proved catastrophic and who responded to these changes by forcefully reestablishing "the authority and rule of their traditional ideological and theological discourse" by "inaugurating inquisitional practices, the function of which was to eliminate the divergent discourses classified as heretical" (2). In the North American context, this reaction to the rise of liberal Christianity in the nineteenth century gave birth to Protestant fundamentalism, out of which the modern evangelical movement was born. See Harriet Harris, *Fundamentalism and Evangelicals* (Oxford: Clarendon Press, 1998), and George M. Marsden, *Fundamentalism and American Culture: The Shaping of Twentieth Century Evangelicalism, 1870–1925* (Oxford: Oxford University Press, 1980).

happens to doctrinal language when we accept as normative the theological diversity described above? What happens when we stop viewing
theological pluralism as a problem to be solved (Babel) and embrace it
as a gift of the Spirit (Pentecost)?

More often than not, many of the ideological conflicts shaking up
the church can be distilled into a debate over how to read and interpret Scripture.[17] At this moment in history a plurality of perspectives
is unavoidable, and methods of reading and applying sacred Scripture
that disregard the cultural and historical location of *all* interpretations
ring false. Yet underlying the Christian doctrine of revelation is the
assumption that in and through these culturally conditioned human
texts the redeeming grace of God somehow enters human history in
order to ground and redirect human existence. How do we avoid making false idols of our own particularities? How do we reclaim scriptural
assertions of transcendent truth that are neither above nor beyond but
somehow comprehensible *in the midst* of history?

Every believer—whether implicitly or explicitly—employs a distinct
methodology in the reading, interpretation, and contemporary application of sacred texts and traditions. The discipline of theology, broadly
defined by St. Anselm's classical affirmation *faith seeking understanding*, guides Christian reflection on the Word of God and the Christian tradition by establishing criteria for identifying and evaluating
sources and for determining what authority past doctrinal formulations still have for present and future theological construction. If God's
self-revelation is the ultimate "object" of theological study, then doctrine is the medium by which knowledge of God is communicated.
Granted, an important goal of Christian doctrine is "conveying what
is common to Christianity through the ages, its core beliefs, and foundational identity,"[18] but of more fundamental importance, as Katherine Sonderegger reminds us, is the nature and being of God: "Who is
God? And what is God? (*Qui sit et quid sit Deus*). These are the questions of an entire lifetime."[19] Closely related to the question "who is
God" lies the question "what does God command," questions that,

17. See Jack Rogers, *Claiming the Center: Churches and Conflicting Worldviews* (Louisville, KY: Westminster John Knox Press, 1995); N. T. Wright, *Scripture and the Authority of God: How to Read the Bible Today*, rev. exp. ed. (New York: HarperOne, 2013); Craig Blomberg, *Can We Still Believe the Bible? An Evangelical Engagement with Contemporary Questions* (Ada, MI: Brazos Press, 2014); and Christena Cleveland, *Disunity in Christ: Uncovering the Hidden Forces That Keep Us Apart* (Downers Grove, IL: InterVarsity Press, 2013).

18. Christine Helmer, *Theology and the End of Doctrine* (Louisville, KY: Westminster John Knox Press, 2014), 5–6.

19. Katherine Sonderegger, *Systematic Theology*, vol. 1, *The Doctrine of God* (Minneapolis, MN: Fortress Press, 2015), xi.

though couched in the language of belief, have universal relevance for the human condition. Consequently, though recent history has consigned doctrine to the margins of academic and public discourse, the discipline of theology still has a responsibility to speak its distinctive discourse *extra muros ecclesiae* ("beyond the walls of the church"). At the same time, questions of theological method expose seemingly irreconcilable fault lines between different Christian traditions, highlighting the historical brokenness of the one, holy, catholic, and apostolic church, further undermining the relevance of the church's internal discourse for the broader society.

The dominant narrative concerning modern theology in Europe and North America not only prioritizes the task of apologetics in order to make theological claims understandable and palatable to an increasingly secular culture, it also presents "liberalism and Neo-orthodoxy—and, more recently, their respective contemporary heirs, revisionism and postliberalism" as the only "two theological options; other possibilities tend either to be interpreted as variants or combinations of these two or else marginalized."[20] Admittedly, after the Second World War the discourse between these two dominant approaches became so polarized that theological consensus seemed untenable. However, this narrative can only be sustained by ignoring the historical shift that has taken place in global Christianity post–World War II, in which the church in Europe and North America faced increasing secularization and decreasing cultural relevance, while Africa, Asia, and Latin America underwent a Christian resurgence.[21] These changes within world Christianity underscore the fact that, despite methodological differences, both the anthropological and revelational schools of thought are located within the First World, Western intellectual tradition, and both are responding to the post-Enlightenment atheistic rejection of Christianity manifested in the works of Ludwig Feuerbach, Karl Marx, Sigmund Freud, and Friedrich Nietzsche.[22] Therefore, while the dominant

20. Hugh Nicholson, *Comparative Theology and the Problem of Religious Rivalry* (Oxford: Oxford University Press, 2011), xi.

21. See Dana L. Robert, "Shifting Southward: Global Christianity Since 1945," in *International Bulletin of Missionary Research* 24, no. 2 (April 2000): 50–58; Alister E. McGrath, *The Future of Christianity* (Oxford: Blackwell Publishers, 2002); and William R. Burrows, Mark R. Gornik, and Janice A. McLean, eds., *Understanding World Christianity: The Vision and Work of Andrew F. Walls* (Maryknoll, NY: Orbis Books, 2011). This latter work, in honor of missiologist Andrew Walls, documents well the transition from a Eurocentric model of "Christendom" toward a more nuanced understanding of Christianity as a "world" movement.

22. See Ludwig Feuerbach, *The Essence of Christianity*, trans. George Eliot (New York: Harper Torchbooks, 1957); Karl Marx (with Frederick Engels), *Contribution to the Critique of Hegel's "Philosophy of Right," Economic and Philosophic Manuscripts of 1844, Theses on Feuerbach,* and *Manifesto of the Communist Party,* in *The Marx-Engels Reader,* 2nd ed., ed. Robert C. Tucker (New York: W. W. Norton & Company, 1978), 16–25, 66–125, 143–45, 469–500; Sigmund Freud, *Moses and Monotheism,* trans. Katherine Jones (New York: Vintage Books, 1955), *The*

theological traditions of the West have, until recently, played a normative role in defining doctrine and practice for world Christianity, the emergent theologies of the late twentieth century in Asia, Africa, and Latin America—as well as marginalized theologies within Europe and North America—defy the hegemony within academic and ecclesial discourse by articulating contextual and local theologies resistant to the notion of a singular Christian tradition.[23] By affirming that particular experiences, cultural contexts, and traditions of interpretation play crucial roles in theological construction,[24] these nascent theological movements demonstrate how the driving concerns of Europe and North America—atheism and secularization—are not a priority for the majority of Christians in the world. Furthermore, by reclaiming Scripture as a locus of divine revelation, these new theologies might perhaps open a door to a "second naiveté" by which the Bible can once again "function as a unifying force just insofar as it provides the basic grammar, so to speak, that shapes the Christian vision of the world" in all its mosaicked variety.[25] The challenge for the church becomes articulating a distinctly Christian discourse without becoming irrelevant to the broader culture or dissolving into fideistic solipsism.

Christine Helmer traces the development of the nineteenth- and twentieth-century Protestant theologies most responsible for the methodological impasse described above in order to argue that doctrine has lost its referential point of contact with the divine:

<hr/>

Future of an Illusion, trans. James Strachey (New York: W. W. Norton & Company, 1975), and *Civilization and Its Discontents*, trans. James Strachey (New York: W. W. Norton & Company, 1961); Friedrich Nietzsche, *On the Genealogy of Morality*, ed. Keith Ansell-Pearson, trans. Carol Diethe (Cambridge: Cambridge University Press, 1994, 2007) and *Beyond Good and Evil: Prelude to a Philosophy of the Future*, ed. and trans. Walter Kaufmann (New York: Vintage Books, 1989).

23. A sampling of the various theological movements resisting European and North American cultural domination include Latin American liberation theology, black liberation theology in the United States, feminist theology in Europe and North America, African theology, Korean *minjung* theology, and Latino/a theology in the United States. See Gustavo Gutiérrez, *A Theology of Liberation: History, Politics and Salvation*, rev. ed., ed. and trans. Sister Caridad Inda and John Eagleson (Maryknoll, NY: Orbis Books, 1988); Rubem A. Alves, *A Theology of Human Hope* (St. Meinrad, IN: Abbey Press, 1972); Juan Luis Segundo, *The Liberation of Theology*, trans. John Drury (Maryknoll, NY: Orbis Books, 1976); *Liberation Theology: A Documentary History*, ed. Alfred T. Hennelly (Maryknoll, NY: Orbis Books, 1990); James H. Cone, *Black Theology and Black Power* (1969; repr., Maryknoll, NY: Orbis Books, 1997); *A Black Theology of Liberation* (1970; repr., Maryknoll, NY: Orbis Books, 2010); *Black Theology: A Documentary History, 1966–1979*, ed. Gayraud S. Wilmore and James H. Cone (Maryknoll, NY: Orbis Books, 1979); Mary Daly, *The Church and the Second Sex* (New York: Harper & Row, 1968), *Beyond God the Father: Toward a Philosophy of Women's Liberation* (Boston: Beacon Press, 1973); Rosemary Radford Ruether, *Sexism and God-talk: Toward a Feminist Theology* (1983; repr., Boston: Beacon Press, 1993).

24. For an introduction to the issues regarding the contextual character of theology see Stephen B. Bevans, *Models of Contextual Theology* (Maryknoll, NY: Orbis Books, 1992), 11–22; Robert J. Schreiter, *Constructing Local Theologies* (Maryknoll, NY: Orbis Books, 1985), 1–21, 75–94; and Stephen B. Bevans and Roger P. Schroeder, *Constants in Context: A Theology of Mission for Today* (Maryknoll, NY: Orbis Books, 2004), 32–72, 239–80, 348–95.

25. Mark I. Wallace, *The Second Naiveté: Barth, Ricoeur, and the New Yale Theology* (Macon, GA: Mercer University Press, 1995), xi. Also see Justo L. González, "Metamodern Aliens in Postmodern Jerusalem," in *Hispanic/Latino Theology: Challenge and Promise*, ed. Ada María Isasi-Díaz and Fernando S. Segovia (Minneapolis, MN: Fortress, Press, 1996), 340–50.

What troubles me about this is the loss of doctrine's connection to its subject matter. To look ahead to my conclusion, in my view such a move to elevate the linguistic doctrinal formulations to the status of norms for a Christian worldview cuts doctrine off from a living connection to the reality of God. If theology is to describe and explain divine reality in relation to persons living in their worldly environments, as I believe it ought to do, then it must be oriented to an understanding of doctrine that opens up this aspect of reality to human intellectual and existential practices.[26]

In other words, whether it is the reactionary fideism of neo-orthodoxy and postliberal theology or the cultural accommodation of Protestant liberalism and theologies of culture, most contemporary theologies lack the adequate vocabulary to speak rationally about divine presence and agency in the world in terms nonbelievers would accept as reasonable—even if epistemologically uncertain. According to Helmer's thesis, George Lindbeck's (1923–2018) use of Ludwig Wittgenstein's (1889–1951) philosophy of language and Clifford Geertz's (1926–2006) cultural anthropology to articulate a cultural-linguistic theory of religions[27] has—despite its intended goal of facilitating ecumenical dialogue—reduced doctrine to the distinctive "grammar" of a particular religious worldview and in doing so "led to the decoupling of doctrine from its role as witness to a transcendent reality."[28] Lindbeck's cultural-linguistic model views doctrine as a social construction arising within the language and praxis of particular confessional communities, which suggests that in order to understand the *nature* of doctrine across different traditions one first needs to understand the concrete *role* doctrine plays in living communities of faith. The glaring unresolved tension in Lindbeck's conception of doctrine is the question of how to evaluate the truth-claims made by distinct religious worldviews, especially when there is disagreement over authoritative and normative sources or when competing religions posit contradictory claims.

In a similar vein to Helmer, Miroslav Volf challenges the academy to embrace a "theological" reading of sacred texts grounded in the Christian community's internal discourse about God but warns against limiting theological reflection to the church's discrete grammar. In other words, theological discourse is ultimately *about* God: "I take it that theology is not simply reflection about how communities of faith use

---

26. Helmer, *Theology and the End of Doctrine*, 61.
27. See Lindbeck, *The Nature of Doctrine*, 65–70.
28. Helmer, *Theology and the End of Doctrine*, 150.

language about God—not 'critical talk about talk about God.' God, not just human talk about God, is the proper object of theology."[29] As such, theological narrative traditions have wide cultural relevance because at bottom they attempt to say something meaningful about God. Given God's desire for communion with all humankind as *imago Dei* (Gen. 1:26–28), theology ought to proceed in an interdisciplinary manner, addressing multiple publics (à la David Tracy) rather than resting solely on the internal coherence of the church's private language (à la Lindbeck) by striving for intelligibility across multiple cultures and rationalities.[30] Theology's internal conversation concerning "truth claims about God means also to be interested in how beliefs about God and God's relation to the world *fit* among themselves and with what other beliefs human beings hold."[31] Accordingly, our beliefs bring us into conversation with other confessional traditions, different religions, not to mention secular and scientific modes of reasoning.

29. Miroslav Volf, *Captive to the Word of God: Engaging the Scriptures for Contemporary Theological Reflection* (Grand Rapids, MI: Wm. B. Eerdmans Publishing Co., 2010), 57.
30. See J. Wentzel van Huyssteen, *The Shaping of Rationality: Toward Interdisciplinarity in Theology and Science* (Grand Rapids, MI: Wm. B. Eerdmans Publishing Co., 1999).
31. Volf, *Captive to the Word of God*, 58.

1

Contextualizing the Conversation

"The Bible is a document both of the divine self-manifestation and of the way in which human beings have received it."

–Paul Tillich[1]

1.1 THE ENLIGHTENMENT'S BREAK WITH THE PAST

The breakdown of ecclesial and biblical authority leading to the current cacophony of competing theological voices occurred gradually over time as, brick by brick, Western Christianity built and ascended its very own Tower of Babel. The dissonance and diversity characterizing twenty-first-century academic theology traces its origins to an earlier age. Renaissance humanism and the Protestant Reformation contributed to the erosion of the centuries-long dominance of premodern Biblical hermeneutics in Western thought, once embodied by St. Augustine's seminal *De doctrina christiana*, "a mainstay of the theological curriculum for most of the thousand years after Augustine's death,"[2] by fracturing the unity of Scripture and tradition through which the Magisterium of the church had long maintained "one right reading."[3] In light of the Protestant-Catholic polemics of the sixteenth

1. Paul Tillich, *Biblical Religion and the Search for Ultimate Reality* (Chicago: The University of Chicago Press, 1955), 4.
2. Paul L. Allen, *Theological Method: A Guide for the Perplexed* (London: T. & T. Clark International, 2012), 49.
3. See Mary Ann Donovan, *One Right Reading? A Guide to Irenaeus* (Collegeville, MN: Liturgical Press, 1997) for an interpretation of apostolic succession and the exegesis of Scripture in Irenaeus in which the Scriptures are both formative and normative for the Church's self-understanding in such a way that any valid exegesis of these Scriptures must be congruent with the lived faith of the community (*sensus fidelium*). In practical terms this "rule of faith" is maintained by the office of bishop, whose responsibility it is to maintain doctrinal orthodoxy. In *Against Heresies* III.1–5, Irenaeus argues that one right reading demands one true teacher—Jesus Christ—whose teaching is available to all by the power of the Holy Spirit *through* Christ's designated successors. The church is the location for authoritative teaching and the teaching of the apostles is handed on through the bishops who are, in effect, speaking for God.

and seventeenth centuries, Scripture and tradition became rival sources of knowledge of God, each vying for normative authority in cross-confessional theological battles. Yet, within Western theology, it was the rise of Enlightenment rationalism that most utterly and completely undermined biblical authority. During the Enlightenment ecclesial and biblical authority became targets of derision as new philosophical perspectives challenged traditional beliefs and sought to ground all knowledge—including knowledge of God—on an objectively verifiable rational foundation. The sixteenth- and seventeenth-century "wars of religion" that followed the Protestant Reformation flung Europe into a state of seemingly unending war, during which nearly a third of Germany's population was killed.[4] Though the political realities motivating these wars were varied and complex, it became commonplace to blame differences of religion for Europe's troubles, despite the fact that Protestants and Catholics often fought on the same side, or that at one point Francis I of France even allied himself with the Ottoman Empire.[5]

Regardless, doctrinal disputes between Protestants and Catholics were blamed for the bloodletting that left Europe politically and religiously divided, with Germany partitioned into Roman Catholic, Reformed, and Lutheran regions, England undergoing civil war, and Catholic France fighting the Hapsburg dynasty over control of the Holy Roman Empire (sometimes by allying itself with Protestants). In this setting, where matters of doctrine exacerbated political divides that became life-threatening international conflicts, people began to question the previously unchallenged teachings of revealed religion. French philosopher, scientist, and mathematician René Descartes (1596–1650) developed a methodological skepticism that examined all beliefs and accepted as true only those that could be demonstrated with the same clear and certain knowledge attained by a mathematical proof. Though a devout Catholic, who included a critique of atheism in his *Meditations on First Philosophy* (1641), Descartes contributed to the erosion of biblical and ecclesial authority by subjecting all previously held beliefs to rational scrutiny. This method gave impetus to a growing cultural attitude that the seventeenth- and eighteenth-century Enlightenment was an era of unmatched human progress,

4. See Mark Konnert, *Early Modern Europe: The Age of Religious War, 1559–1715* (Toronto: University of Toronto Press, 2008), 99–112, 145–62, 297–312; Steven Gunn, "War, Religion, and the State," in *Early Modern Europe: An Oxford History*, ed. Euan Cameron (Oxford: Oxford University Press, 1999), 102–34.
5. See Mack P. Holt, *The French Wars of Religion, 1562–1629*, rev. 2nd ed. (Cambridge: Cambridge University Press, 2005); and Daniel Goffman, *The Ottoman Empire and Early Modern Europe* (Cambridge: Cambridge University Press, 2002).

as evidenced by great scientific and technological advances (including Descartes's own contributions to lens making and the science of optics),[6] in which reason eclipsed religion as the basis for organizing human societies.

Inevitably, this enshrinement of reason over tradition had an impact on the discipline of theology, especially in nineteenth-century Germany, where a battle was fought over the role historical truths played in the process of coming to religious belief, further undermining the reliability of theological claims. In fact, the cultural tensions that gave rise to the neo-orthodox rejection of nineteenth century liberalism continue to dominate academic theology in the West well over one hundred years later. The leading figure of the German Enlightenment, philosopher Immanuel Kant (1724–1804), defined this age of reason as "man's release from his self-incurred tutelage. Tutelage is man's inability to make use of his understanding without direction from another. . . . 'Have courage to use your own reason!'—that is the motto of enlightenment."[7] Within Kant's epistemological critique, human rationality was categorized into pure, practical, and aesthetic reason, with religious belief lacking the self-evident clarity displayed by the necessary truths of mathematical logic therefore consigned to the realm of practical reason alongside political philosophy and ethics. As the Bible began to be read with critical acumen, with scholars no longer limited by the church's one authoritative interpretation, doubt was cast upon those parts of the biblical narrative that seemed to contradict the discoveries of modern science (Copernicus, Galileo, Newton), such as the creation story in the opening chapters of Genesis. Furthermore, literary and historical analysis of the biblical texts raised questions of authorship (could Moses have written the first five books of the Hebrew Bible?), and eventually reduced the canon of Scriptures to a collection of ancient religious texts lacking any unique claim to divine authorship. In this context, Friedrich Schleiermacher (1768–1834) defended Christianity against the assault of scientific reason and historical criticism by grounding the truths of theology within the believer's subjective experience of divine reality:

6. See D. Graham Burnett, *Descartes and the Hyperbolic Quest: Lens Making Machines and their Significance in the Seventeenth Century*, Transactions of the American Philosophical Society no. 95 (Philadelphia, PA: American Philosophical Society, 2005).

7. Immanuel Kant, "What Is Enlightenment?" in *Immanuel Kant: Philosophical Writings*, ed. Ernst Behler (New York: Continuum, 1986), 263. Though every effort is made to use gender inclusive language throughout this monograph, historical sources reflect the cultural prejudices and biases of their day and age, so they will not be edited to reflect contemporary practices.

Wherefore it is a life in the infinite nature of the Whole, in the One and in the All, in God, having and possessing all things in God, and God in all. Yet religion is not knowledge and science, either of the world or of God. Without being knowledge, it recognizes knowledge and science. In itself it is an affection, a revelation of the Infinite in the finite, God being seen in it and it in God.[8]

This approach, itself a variant of the Kantian "turn to the subject" that placed limits on what can be known by appeals to reason alone, sidesteps the question of historical veracity by locating knowledge of God in the psychological awakening of a God-consciousness, turning Jesus into an exemplar of God-directed self-awareness whose life is the source of doctrine. However, this source can be "entirely traced back to inner experience and simply describes and clarifies this experience."[9] Accordingly, human religiousness replaces God as theology's proper object of study, with doctrines becoming narratives about communally shared "religious" experiences rather than propositional claims about the nature of God, "because such teachings are simply an expression of inner experiences, the result being that one who has these experiences automatically belongs to that sphere, but one who does not have these experiences does not even enter into that sphere at all."[10] In other words, Schleiermacher's treatment of Christian doctrine says very little *about* God while speaking volumes about the human *experience of* God. His impact on both the theologies of culture and the theologies of the Word cannot be overstated, and the fact that both approaches remain captive to Enlightenment modes of thought is in great part the result of his methodological "turn to the subject" in defending faith against its "cultured despisers."

1.2 KIERKEGAARD'S DEFENSE OF SCRIPTURAL AUTHORITY

Schleiermacher was not the only nineteenth-century Christian thinker to question the primacy of historically verifiable truths as a criterion for making doctrinal claims. Søren Kierkegaard (1813–1855), in reaction to Hegelian views about historical truths serving as

---

8. Friedrich Schleiermacher, *On Religion: Speeches to Its Cultured Despisers*, trans. John Oman (Louisville, KY: Westminster John Knox Press, 1994), 36.

9. Friedrich Schleiermacher, *Christian Faith: A New Translation and Critical Edition*, vol. 2, trans. Terrence N. Tice, Catherine L. Kelsey, and Edwina Lawler, eds. Catherine L. Kelsey and Terrence N. Tice (Louisville, KY: Westminster John Knox Press, 2016), 625–26.

10. Ibid., 626.

contingent expressions of Infinite Spirit, reduced the Christian gospel to its bare essence:

> Even if the contemporary generation had not left anything behind except these words, "We have believed that in such and such a year the god appeared in the humble form of a servant, lived and taught among us, and then died"—this is more than enough. The contemporary generation would have done what is needful, for this little announcement, this world-historical *nota bene*, is enough to become an occasion for someone who comes later, and the most prolix report can never in all eternity become more for a person who comes later.[11]

Kierkegaard's point is that contemporaneity to the events of the Bible is no guarantee of faith, so whether one is an eyewitness to the miracles attributed to Jesus or one is two thousand years removed from those events, historical truths cannot provide the necessary foundation for belief. At most, historical truths can provide evidence in support of faith, establishing the reasonableness of certain beliefs, but Cartesian absolute certainty remains an unattainable standard for evaluating theological claims. Accordingly, the quality of available historical evidence is not the ultimate deciding factor in coming to faith; rather, the work of God's Spirit in transforming the believer is the font of faith and the very means by which the Bible is accepted as a reliable source of knowledge of God by believers.

Still, Kierkegaard's hyperbole notwithstanding, the generation of believers contemporary with Jesus left us much more than a mere fragment describing God's salvific work in Jesus of Nazareth. Consequently, historical investigation remains a vital component of the modern subject's coming to faith, as evidenced by the continuing interest in the Jesus of history. Despite its commitment to a persistently skeptical historical method, the current (or "third") quest for the historical Jesus has succeeded in correcting some of the extremes of nineteenth century German historical criticism. For example, biblical scholars are now more willing to read canonical texts as historical sources, to consider the Pauline Epistles important source material for interpreting the Synoptic Gospels, and to apply the same level of hermeneutical suspicion toward non-Christian sources (Josephus, Tacitus, Celsus, Marcus Aurelius, etc.) previously reserved only for Christian canonical sources

---

11. Søren Kierkegaard, *Philosophical Fragments*, ed. and trans. Howard V. Hong and Edna H. Hong, 2nd printing (Princeton: Princeton University Press, 1987), 104.

in their reconstructions of early Christian history.[12] This methodological openness to previously "suspect" canonical sources is attributable to the interdisciplinary character of the most recent quest for the historical Jesus: "It is no longer merely New Testament scholars and historians who are wading into the rushing waters of the quest, but an entire cadre of interdisciplinary explorers, each bringing their own distinctive disciplinary methods, tools and insights to the historical study of Jesus and the Gospels."[13] The conversation is no longer limited to historians, philologists, and biblical scholars but now includes theologians who interpret source texts as explicitly confessional narratives in their original historical context while also locating the contemporary hermeneutical task within living faith traditions that have arguably preserved a history of interpretation in diachronic unity to these source materials, and therefore contain insights of value to the historian.[14] Still, the current quest for the historical Jesus is far removed in method, scope, and intent from its eighteenth- and nineteenth-century origins.

1.2.1 Truth as Existential Appropriation

G. W. F. Hegel's (1770–1831) philosophical project, a universal, all-embracing system of thought that attempted to account for all aspects of human experience—religion included—subsumed theology under philosophy, placing reason above faith. According to Hegel, the absolute truths of reason are imperfectly represented in theological narratives, such as the Christian doctrine of the Trinity, which for Hegel is symbolic of the tripartite universal dialectic constitutive of human reasoning (thesis, antithesis, synthesis). By this schema, the whole of history—the evolution of the human species, the rise and fall of cultures, everything contained in the material universe—is a manifestation of Spirit (*Geist*) in Nature, creating an apparent contradiction that is

---

12. For a brief introduction to the quest for the historical Jesus see James K. Beilby and Paul Rhodes Eddy, eds., *The Historical Jesus: Five Views* (Downers Grove, IL: InterVarsity Press, 2009), 9–54. The authors trace the quest's origins to Enlightenment rationalism; its first wave dating to the late eighteenth-century posthumous publication of an anonymous manuscript written by Hermann Samuel Reimarus (1694–1768); the "no quest" period during the post–World War I ascendency of neo-orthodoxy linked to the work of figures as diverse as Karl Barth, Emil Brunner, Paul Tillich, and Rudolf Bultmann; its second wave in the mid-twentieth century instigated by students of Bultmann; and finally, the third quest originating in the late-twentieth century running to the present and identified with the work of such figures as N. T. Wright, John Dominic Crossan, E. P. Sanders, and Géza Vermes.

13. Ibid., 41.

14. On the role of transmitted traditions for historical study see Hans-Georg Gadamer, *Truth and Method*, 2nd rev. ed., trans. Joel Weinsheimer and Donald G. Marshall (London: Bloomsbury, 2004). For an analysis of hermeneutics as formation and communal wisdom, see Anthony C. Thiselton, *The Hermeneutics of Doctrine* (Grand Rapids, MI: William B. Eerdmans Publishing Company, 2007), 81–115.

ultimately overcome by the historical emergence of conscious minds participating in a rational process of dialectical self-realization until Finite mind (humanity) becomes fully identified with Infinite mind (God/Spirit), a philosophical reality prefigured in the Christian dogma of the incarnation. Thus, according to Hegel, God is imperfectly represented in all religions since every historical religion makes universal claims for its particular point of view, suggesting that dogmatic claims are better understood as mythical language for underlying philosophical truths: "Therefore, the content of religion proclaims earlier in time than does Science, what *Spirit is*, but only Science is true knowledge of itself."[15] Though Schleiermacher is opposed to Hegel's systematization in many ways, both ultimately stand on similar ground insofar as their respective discussions of the content of Christian dogmatic claims is thoroughly anthropocentric, focusing almost exclusively on the human awareness and experience of God rather than God alone.

By contrast, the Kierkegaardian understanding of the Christian doctrine of revelation emphasizes the divine act of communication as a suprarational—but not irrational or antirational—event that makes human knowledge of God possible *by an act of God*. Referencing Feuerbach, Kierkegaard argues that ignoring this infinite qualitative difference between God and humanity[16] is tantamount to proclaiming "all theology is anthropology,"[17] giving rise to his critique of Hegelianism as a religion of immanence contrasted to Christianity as a religion of transcendence. While Kierkegaard demonstrates there can be no direct objective ("historical") relationship to God with the affirmation "truth is subjectivity,"[18] he does not posit an unquestioned fideism in place of verifiable empirical claims but reconceptualizes truth as an act of existential appropriation of revealed knowledge:

> If Christianity is essentially something objective, it behooves the observer to be objective. But if Christianity is essentially subjectivity, it is a mistake if the observer is objective. In all knowing in which it holds true that the object of cognition is the inwardness of the subjective individual himself, it holds true that the knower must be in that state. But the expression for the utmost exertion of subjectivity is the infinitely passionate interest in its eternal happiness. . . . With

15. G. W. F. Hegel, *Phenomenology of Spirit*, trans. A. V. Miller (Oxford: Oxford University Press, 1977), 488.
16. Kierkegaard, *Philosophical Fragments*, 41–46.
17. Søren Kierkegaard, *Concluding Unscientific Postscript to Philosophical Fragments*, vol. 1, ed. and trans. Howard V. Hong and Edna H. Hong, 2nd printing (Princeton: Princeton University Press, 1992), 579.
18. Ibid., 189–251.

the infinite, passionate interest in his eternal happiness, the subjective individual is at the extreme point of his exertion, at the extreme point, not where there is no object (an imperfect and undialectical distinction) but where God is negatively present in the subjectivity that with this interest is the form of the eternal happiness.[19]

So, while this relationship to God is described in terms of "absolute paradox"—emphasizing incommensurability between an infinite God and finite human cognition[20]—some basis for making informed decisions between competing beliefs is possible by appeal to practical reason. Understanding that Kierkegaard's claim "truth is subjectivity" applies only to a certain kind of knowledge—what he calls "eternal happiness" but modern philosophers might describe as a worldview or religious outlook (and Tillich termed "ultimate concern")[21]—it is nonetheless illustrative to look at a more mundane analogy in order to better understand what is meant by existential appropriation.

Riding a bicycle is something most adults are able to do yet rarely give much thought to. Nevertheless, it is possible to objectively describe in great detail every aspect of riding a bicycle without being able to ride one. Intellectually, it is possible to conceive the act of applying force to the pedals to create forward motion while balancing upon a metal frame resting on two wheels that one steers with handlebars; it is possible to predict with quantitative exactness the amount of force required to create forward momentum or brake to a stop; it is even possible—with the aid of optical motion capture cameras and a personal computer—to create a real-time three-dimensional model of a bicyclist's full body motion in order to better grasp the mechanics of riding a bicycle. Yet, despite this overabundance of objective empirical data about the act of riding a bicycle, no amount of theorizing, or study and analysis of these quantitative descriptions, enables one to ride a bicycle. In the end, it is the painful task of actually sitting astride a bicycle and taking a few tumbles that leads to learning how to ride a bicycle. In other words, no amount of objective knowledge replaces the subjective process of acquiring the necessary skills to ride a bicycle—this is what Kierkegaard means by "truth is subjectivity," that the process of existential appropriation itself *is* the knowledge gained. Nowhere is this subjective process more essential to the knowledge gained than in understanding revealed religion.

---

19. Ibid., 53.
20. Kierkegaard, *Philosophical Fragments*, 37–48.
21. Paul Tillich, *Dynamics of Faith*, reprint (Grand Rapids, MI: Zondervan, 2001), 4.

1.2.2 Revelation as a Historical Possibility

The incarnation as an event in human history lies at the heart of Kierkegaard's articulation of Christianity as a revealed religion. Still, it is important to differentiate what Kierkegaard means at different times by the term "historical," especially in relation to the act of divine revelation, because unlike Schleiermacher and Hegel, Kierkegaard is most concerned about "the possibility of being related to God in time."[22] According to Kierkegaard, the Christian understanding of revelation is at its core a divine-human encounter *in* history. In other words, Kierkegaard rejects Schleiermacher's understanding of the historical mediation of grace, which, while proceeding from "the divine activity of Christ" is also "everywhere conditioned by the ongoing development of the natural and historical world."[23] For Kierkegaard, such mediation subsumes revelation to the category of historically immanent and necessarily contingent events: "Precisely by coming into existence, everything that comes into existence demonstrates that it is not necessary, for the only thing that cannot come into existence is the necessary, because the necessary *is*."[24] Divine self-disclosure, on the other hand, is both eternal and necessary, and as such better understood as a *breach* of the immanence and continuity characteristic of the Hegelian view of history as the evolution of Spirit (both divine and human) over time: "But a believer who believes, that is, believes against the understanding, takes the secret of faith in earnest and does not dally with understanding but is aware that curiosity about glimpsing is unfaithfulness and betrays the task."[25] Mark C. Taylor describes the difference between the Kierkegaardian conception of divine transcendence and the Hegelian understanding of God as immanent in the historical process:

> Kierkegaard conceives God as a radically transcendent and completely free acting subject, whose omnipotent will is the ultimate ground of reality. Unlike the Hegelian God, who is incomplete apart from the world and hence is internally and necessarily related to finitude, the Kierkegaardian God, who is possessed of perfect aseity, is externally related to the world he infinitely transcends. The relation between the infinite and the finite depends upon divine

22. Steven M. Emmanuel, *Kierkegaard and the Concept of Revelation* (Albany, NY: State University of New York Press, 1996), 64.
23. Kevin M. Vander Schel, *Embedded Grace: Christ, History, and the Reign of God in Schleiermacher's Dogmatics* (Minneapolis, MN: Fortress Press, 2013), 117.
24. Kierkegaard, *Philosophical Fragments*, 74.
25. Kierkegaard, *Concluding Unscientific Postscript*, 569.

freedom instead of divine need, and therefore is contingent rather than necessary.[26]

In the *Philosophical Fragments* (1844), Kierkegaard explores how it is possible for a finite, historically located individual to have knowledge of an eternal reality, while also questioning how the historical event of encountering the eternal in time can have more than a mere historical (thus necessarily contingent) significance in the life of the individual. At stake is the claim that a historical event—specifically the incarnation of God in Jesus the Christ—is necessary for Christian faith and "eternal happiness."

The underlying question in the *Philosophical Fragments* is whether or not Schleiermacher and Hegel are correct that "self-knowledge is God-knowledge."[27] Writing as the pseudonym Johannes Climacus,[28] Kierkegaard presents the *Fragments* as a "thought experiment" designed to clarify the crucial distinction between a rational religion of immanence and a suprarational religion of revelation. Arguing that Christianity is properly understood as the latter, Climacus observes that the believer cannot possess knowledge of God prior to an act of divine self-revelation, otherwise "we return to the Socratic, even though we think we are going further."[29] While Taylor provides a balanced study of Kierkegaard's pseudonymous authorship that respects the distinct identity of Kierkegaard's various pseudonyms yet argues for a unifying coherence to the whole pseudonymous corpus, he does not adequately relate the pseudonymous works to Kierkegaard's eponymously authored texts. Taylor argues that in the pseudonymous authorship Kierkegaard presents Christian faith as an internal subjective state: "The self's faith, as Jesus' divinity, is inward and cannot be outwardly expressed."[30] This book critiques Taylor's position by drawing upon Kierkegaard's whole authorship (including unpublished journal entries) to argue for an understanding of Christian faith as an existential commitment to a certain kind of concrete action (praxis) rather than a mere "inward" psychological state. Kierkegaard affirms Climacus's position that Christian faith is a gift from God and thus intrinsically different from philosophical speculation in his self-penned religious discourses: "no one can learn this from another, but each one

26. Mark C. Taylor, *Journeys to Selfhood: Hegel & Kierkegaard* (New York: Fordham University Press, 2000), 126–7.
27. Kierkegaard, *Philosophical Fragments*, 11.
28. For the landmark study of Kierkegaard's pseudonymous authorship, see Mark C. Taylor, *Kierkegaard's Pseudonymous Authorship: A Study of Time and the Self* (Princeton: Princeton University Press, 1975).
29. Kierkegaard, *Philosophical Fragments*, 28.
30. Taylor, *Kierkegaard's Pseudonymous Authorship*, 367.

individually learns it only from and through God."[31] Accordingly, it is safe to assume—despite the hermeneutic intricacies that come with navigating Kierkegaard's pseudonymous authorship—that Climacus, like Kierkegaard, is making a philosophical argument in defense of Christianity as a revealed religion over against a Hegelian view of Christianity as a religion of immanence. Climacus clearly states these intentions on the very title page of the *Philosophical Fragments*: "Can a historical point of departure be given for an eternal consciousness; how can such a point of departure be of more than historical interest; can an eternal happiness be built on historical knowledge?"[32]

The first part of this question asks whether it is possible for a finite, historically bound human consciousness to have genuine knowledge of an infinite, unbound, eternal consciousness. Then Climacus asks whether the historical event of discovering this eternal consciousness (revelation) is more than a mere historical accident, which leads to the final question as to whether it is possible to base one's eternal happiness (salvation) on just such a historical act.

Climacus develops his argument by contrasting Christianity as a revealed religion with the Socratic perspective, which can be equated with the Hegelian view of Christianity, through a discussion of the Platonic theory of recollection found in Plato's dialogue the *Meno*. In this dialogue Socrates is able to guide a slave boy with no formal education to solve a mathematical problem with minimal prompting, demonstrating how "a man cannot try to discover either what he knows or what he does not know? He would not seek what he knows, for since he knows it there is no need of the inquiry, nor what he does not know, for in that case he does not even know what he is to look for."[33] The implication for revealed religion—and Christian faith in particular—is that the knowledge gained by means of the historical event of revelation is something "the learner does not and cannot possess," hence he or she "cannot merely recover it via introspection."[34] Unlike Socrates, who did not impart new knowledge to the slave boy but merely helped him recall knowledge already in his possession simply by virtue of being human (a "rational animal" in the Aristotelian sense), the teacher in revealed religion "must bring it [knowledge] to him, but not only that.

---

31. Søren Kierkegaard, *Eighteen Upbuilding Discourses*, trans. Howard V. Hong and Edna H. Hong (Princeton: Princeton University Press, 1990), 28.

32. Kierkegaard, *Philosophical Fragments*, 1.

33. Plato, *Meno*, in *Greek Philosophy: Thales to Aristotle*, 3rd ed., ed. Reginald E. Allen, trans. K. C. Guthrie (New York: The Free Press, 1991), 120.

34. Emmanuel, *Kierkegaard and the Concept of Revelation*, 62.

Along with it, he must provide him with the condition for understanding it."[35] According to Climacus, such a teacher is much more than the occasion for recollection, as in Socratic understanding; such a teacher is more properly understood as God and Savior:

> The teacher, then, is the god himself, who, acting as the occasion, prompts the learner to be reminded that he is untruth and is that through his own fault. But this state—to be untruth and to be that through one's own fault—what can we call it? Let us call it *sin.*
>
> The teacher, then, is the god, who gives the condition and gives the truth. Now, what should we call such a teacher, for we surely do agree that we have gone far beyond the definition of a teacher. . . . What then should we call such a teacher who gives him the condition again and along with it the truth? Let us call him a *savior,* for he does indeed save the learner from unfreedom, saves him from himself.[36]

Recalling that Climacus is conducting a "thought experiment"—that he is not describing the Christian understanding of revelation but simply describing the conditions under which the claims of a revealed religion like Christianity can be accepted as reasonable—his argument "cannot be seen as intended to convince the non-Christian that Christianity is true . . . but rather that the question cannot be decided without a 'new organ,' namely faith."[37] In other words, given that religious faith is not "objective truth" but is better understood as a certain kind of "subjectivity," Climacus has not offered an objective historical argument to counter Christianity's "cultured despisers"; instead he has provided a phenomenological description of Christian faith, which Climacus has described as a "new organ"[38]: that is, a new way of encountering the eternal in history radically different from the religion of immanence insofar as it does not subsume revelation to the natural historical process but posits Christianity as a transcendent truth that "could not have been discovered apart from a revelation."[39]

1.2.3 Faith not Fideism

Having articulated a rational alternative to Schleiermacher's and Hegel's more anthropocentric view of Christianity, Kierkegaard advocates for

35. Kierkegaard, *Philosophical Fragments,* 14.
36. Ibid., 15, 17.
37. C. Stephen Evans, *Passionate Reason: Making Sense of Kierkegaard's* Philosophical Fragments (Bloomington: Indiana University Press, 1992), 41.
38. Kierkegaard, *Philosophical Fragments,* 111.
39. Evans, *Passionate Reason,* 45.

an understanding of God and divine revelation as an objective reality encountered in history that, from an epistemological perspective, is experienced as the Absolute Paradox.[40] Granted, this eternal truth is appropriated subjectively since it is not objectively evident to all, but to claim "truth is subjectivity" is not to posit that God lacks objective reality distinct from humankind's experience and consciousness of God. Rather, for Kierkegaard the historical event of revelation is of prime importance since it is the foundation of the divine-human encounter in time, the medium in which human reason receives the "new organ" of faith, though admittedly this explanation treads dangerously close to an irrationalist fideism. Still, recognizing that Climacus undertakes a rational defense of revealed religion in the *Philosophical Fragments*, it seems counterintuitive to then conclude that fideism—the belief that faith is independent of, to the point of rejecting, reason—is the alternative he offers in place of the Socratic position. The term fideism originated in the nineteenth century, attributed by some to the French Protestant theologian Louis Auguste Sabatier (1839–1901), to "denote the view that (as Kant has demonstrated) reason could not prove the truths of religion and that therefore believers could rely upon faith, which was a kind of religious experiencing."[41] According to this view, as embodied in the theology of Friedrich Schleiermacher, religious dogmas are "symbolic expressions of religious feelings."[42] Lumping Kierkegaard in with this brand of fideism misses the very distinction between immanent and revealed religions he was trying to identify via the pseudonymous works of Johannes Climacus. Advocating some form of the religion of immanence as delineated by Climacus eradicates the possibility of a historical encounter between finite human beings and the eternal God by reducing the human experience of the divine to a mere mental state. Instead, it will be argued that Kierkegaard, like contemporary liberationists, emphasizes orthopraxis over against orthodoxy as the basis for making the passionate leap into faith since "the justification for accepting the Christian revelation must finally be made on practical and ethical grounds."[43] Unfortunately, a reading of Kierkegaard as a fideist who defends an irrationalist conception of belief still dominates academic theology, which has contributed to the neo-orthodox and evangelical Protestant understanding of divine revelation as something above human reason and therefore not subject to critical examination by reason.

---

40. Kierkegaard, *Philosophical Fragments*, 37–48.
41. Alan Richardson and John MacQuarrie, "Fideism," in *The Westminster Dictionary of Christian Theology*, eds. Alan Richardson and John Bowden (Philadelphia: The Westminster Press, 1983), 212.
42. Ibid.
43. Emmanuel, *Kierkegaard and the Concept of Revelation*, x–xi.

1.3 FROM NEO-ORTHODOXY TO NARRATIVE THEOLOGY

Kierkegaard's critique of Kant, Hegel, and Schleiermacher illumi-
nated the development of the neo-orthodox movement post World
War I. Appropriately described as "crisis" or "dialectical" theology,
neo-orthodoxy can be viewed as a theological response to nineteenth-
century Protestant liberalism, or more accurately, a response to the
failures of Protestant liberalism in light of the cultural collapse caused
by the war. The inheritance of the German Enlightenment, with its
optimistic view of history as a progressive evolution toward greater
human freedom, new scientific discoveries, and continuous technological advancement, was radically undermined by Kaiser Wilhelm's
imperialist and expansionist policies, Germany's application of scientific and technological innovation to create and use weapons of mass
destruction (from the U-boat campaign of 1914–18 that sank almost
five thousand ships—many of them civilian freighters—to the use of
mustard gas on the Western Front in 1916), and most pertinent for
understanding the development of modern theology, the complicity of
German intellectuals, including leading theologians, in implementing
these aggressive war policies.

Germany declared war on August 1, 1914. That very day ninety-
three German intellectuals published a manifesto supporting the war
policies of Kaiser Wilhelm II and among the signatories were some of
the leading voices of nineteenth-century Protestant liberalism, including Adolf von Harnack and Wilhelm Herrmann. For Reformed pastor
and theologian Karl Barth, a former student of both Harnack and Herrmann, theological support for the war signaled "the bankruptcy of the
liberal theology he had learned. Looking back to see where theology
went astray, he [Barth] came to fix on Schleiermacher."[44] The problem
with Schleiermacher, according to Barth, is that in Schleiermacher's
theology the Christian faith had been subsumed by the dominant culture and now that the culture reached a crisis point, Protestant liberalism found itself cut off and isolated from its only distinctive source
of hope and renewal: God's revelation in Scripture. Reflecting back
on what motivated his involvement with what became known as neo-
orthodoxy, Barth summarizes his assessment of Schleiermacher's compromise with culture in this way:

44. Clifford Green, "Introduction: Karl Barth's Life and Theology," in *Karl Barth: Theologian of Freedom*, ed.
Clifford Green (Minneapolis, MN: Fortress Press, 1991), 15.

Now I must speak of the impression which the whole phenomenon made on me from the beginning and which has only increased with time: the common denominator was and is indeed Schleiermacher—not the very image of him, but certainly in a new form which accommodated itself to the "contemporary spiritual situation" or "linguistic situation" and to the contemporary (or rather one contemporary) vocabulary. Unmistakably, my old friend and enemy, Schleiermacher! Once again, the Christian exhortation relegated to that cozy nook where the contemporary society and world pretend to their authoritative claim! Once again, the symbiosis of theology and philosophy so characteristic of Schleiermacher! Once again, an anthropologizing of theology, just as obviously as in Schleiermacher, who had thereby simultaneously brought the theological learning of the eighteenth century to completion while establishing that of the nineteenth century! Once again, the tension-in-unity between subject and object which he had so masterfully described in the second of his *Speeches*! And once again, the original and ultimate unity of both which he there so triumphantly proclaimed, the glorious elimination of the "subject-object schema." Once again, the move found in *The Christian Faith* of granting supremacy to "feeling," in whose place of course one could then set "faith" in order to move somewhat closer to the Bible or the Reformation: "faith" on which was conferred sovereignty over everything which might be its ground, object, and content. So that is more or less (the list could easily be extended) how, in attentively considering its rise and development, I supposed and suppose that this most recent "modern" theology ought to be understood—as a new and vigorous Schleiermacher renaissance!"[45]

What united the various thinkers associated with the rise of neoorthodoxy, like Karl Barth, Eduard Thurneysen (1888–1974), Rudolf Bultmann (1884–1976), and even Paul Tillich (1886–1965), was their radical criticism of the nineteenth-century easy marriage of culture with Christianity first diagnosed in Søren Kierkegaard's existential critique of Hegelian Christendom.[46] Thus, while representing a broad spectrum of theological approaches, "this 'crisis' of human natural powers—of the discontinuity between the gospel and cultural life—was the dominant motif of neoorthodox thought."[47] On one hand, the

---

45. Karl Barth, "Concluding Unscientific Postscript on Schleiermacher," in *Karl Barth: Theologian of Freedom*, 77.
46. See Søren Kierkegaard, *Attack upon Christendom*, trans. Walter Lowrie (Princeton: Princeton University Press, 1968). Kiekregaard's last, posthumously published work critiques the Hegelian accommodation to culture with the simple thesis: "When all are Christians, Christianity *eo ipso* does not exist" (166).
47. Langdon Gilkey, "Neoorthodoxy," in *New and Enlarged Handbook of Christian Theology*, eds. Donald W. Musser and Joseph L. Price (Nashville, TN: Abingdon Press, 2003), 353.

neo-orthodox movement was extremely successful at reclaiming biblical language and concepts, like the transcendence of God, human sin and fallenness, and divine self-revelation as the source of Christian doctrine. On the other hand, given the movement's diversity of methodological approaches, whether Bultmann's demythologizing project, Barth's recovery of Trinitarian theology, or Tillich's method of correlation, neo-orthodoxy never coalesced into a distinct "school" so that by the 1960s the term no longer proved useful for describing contemporary theologies. Ultimately, the chief figures associated with the movement began to distance themselves from the term and from one another,[48] to the point that Tillich defined his own systematic efforts in clear opposition to Barth's brand of neo-orthodoxy:

> In so far as the liberal theology puts human development in the place of revelation, Barth's criticism also holds good for dialectic thinking. But when he deprives the human of any relation to the divine, as he does in his teaching about the God-likeness of man, about Christ, about God's word, and about the Bible, Barth's peculiar formulations are objectionable or wrong. . . . In general, Barth leaves unexplained how revelation can communicate anything to man if there is nothing in him permitting him to raise questions about it, impelling him toward it, and enabling him to understand it.[49]

Admittedly, Tillich appreciated Barth's contributions to Protestant theology, especially his earlier theology as articulated in *The Epistle to the Romans* (1922, second edition) and the Barmen Declaration (1934), claiming "what Barth did was providentially significant, for it saved Protestantism from the onslaught of the neo-collectivistic and pagan Nazism."[50] Nevertheless, Tillich rejected Barth's methodological starting point:

> Karl Barth starts from above, from the trinity, from the revelation which is given, and then proceeds to man, and in his latest period, even very deeply into man, when he speaks of the "humanity of God." Whereas, on the other hand, I start with man, not deriving the divine answer from man, but starting with the question which

---

48. Barth himself rejects the label "neo-orthodox." See Karl Barth, *Church Dogmatics*, III.3: *The Doctrine of Creation: The Creator and His Creature*, ed. by G. W. Bromiley and T. F. Torrance, trans. by G. W. Bromiley and R. J. Ehrlich (London: T. & T. Clark, 1960), xii.

49. Paul Tillich, "What Is Wrong with the 'Dialectic' Theology?" in *Paul Tillich: Theologian of the Boundaries*, ed. by Mark Kline Taylor (Minneapolis, MN: Fortress Press, 1991), 113.

50. Paul Tillich, *A History of Christian Thought: From Its Judaic and Hellenistic Origins to Existentialism*, ed. Carl E. Braaten (New York: Simon and Schuster, 1972), 536.

is present in man and to which the divine revelation comes as the answer.[51]

Furthermore, Tillich asserts a methodological commitment to the divine-human correlation over against Karl Barth's more transcendent theology, asserting that the "divine-human relation, and therefore God as well as man within this relation, changes with the stages of the history of revelation and with the stages of every personal development."[52] Barth's subordination of historical criticism in favor of a theological exegesis of Scripture,[53] while also evading the question of the "historical" Jesus, led one of his students, Dietrich Bonhoeffer (1906–1945), to accuse Barth of advocating a "positivism of revelation":

> Barth was the first theologian—to his great and lasting credit—to begin the critique of religion, but he then put in its place a positivist doctrine of revelation that says, in effect, "like it or lump it." Whether it's the virgin birth, the Trinity, or anything else, all are equally significant and necessary parts of the whole, which must be swallowed whole or not at all.[54]

Ironically, while Bonhoeffer equated Barth's doctrine of revelation with an uncritical reassertion of premodern confessional orthodoxy, evangelical theology in the United States has consistently criticized neo-orthodoxy and Barth in particular for "playing up the metaphorical character of revelational God-language."[55] Ironically, it is precisely the very point on which Barth most differs with nineteenth-century liberalism—his understanding of the historical and its role in Christian faith—that also puts Barth at odds with many evangelical theologians.

While this book looks at Barth's doctrine of revelation in greater detail in the next chapter, for the moment it is enough to note that Barth embraced Kierkegaard's critique of Schleiermacher and Hegel. While nineteenth-century Protestant dogmatics defined its task as the science of belief—its focus being the human experience of faith—*not*

51. Ibid., 538.
52. Paul Tillich, *Systematic Theology*, vol. 1 (Chicago: The University of Chicago Press, 1951), 61.
53. See Francis Watson, "The Bible," in *The Cambridge Companion to Karl Barth*, ed. John Webster (Cambridge: Cambridge University Press, 2000), 57–71.
54. Dietrich Bonhoeffer, *Letters and Papers from Prison: Dietrich Bonhoeffer Works*, vol. 8, English ed., ed. John W. de Gruchy, trans. Isabel Best, Lisa E. Dahill, Reinhard Krauss, and Nancy Lukens (Minneapolis, MN: Fortress Press, 2010), 373.
55. Gary Dorrien, *The Remaking of Evangelical Theology* (Louisville, KY: Westminster John Knox Press, 1998), 139.

the self-revealing God, Barth turns the table and makes God the "subject" of dogmatics so that the discipline is viewed as neither the objective study of God (à la Kant, we have no unmediated access to God) nor the analysis of human religious experience (he rejects Schleiermacher's emphasis on affective states) but is better understood as the science of God's self-communication as it is existentially appropriated through an act of divine agency: "It may be conceived—no, it may be asserted and described only as a miracle of the Holy Spirit (the same thing again seen from the other side) that forces us to do what we cannot do, that is to believe in God, not because we have access to God but because he, the Holy Spirit, is himself God and creates access where there is none."[56] Clear echoes of Kierkegaard's notion that revealed religion is grounded in the "new organ" of faith by an act of divine initiative. In his radical critique of liberal theology's failure to distinguish between the transcendent God and mere human conceptions of God, Barth draws on nineteenth-century intellectuals like Kierkegaard, Dostoevsky, Feuerbach, and Nietzsche to construct a theological critique of religion as the natural drive to substitute *human* in place of *divine* understanding, thereby trivializing God who is *wholly other*.[57] Nevertheless, when Barth distinguishes between ordinary or factual history (*Historie*) and what he terms "salvation" history (*Geschichte*), many evangelicals conclude Barth remains trapped within the conceptual worldview of Protestant liberalism. From Barth's perspective, Scripture is a "witness to revelation because the writers of Scripture were participants in the experience of revelation," which does not "deny that there is an objective sense in which Scripture bears the Word but only to highlight the role of the biblical writers as active participants in the revelatory task of bearing witness to the Word."[58] For many evangelical theologians, this distinction "gave further fuel to the charge that his theology completely subjectivized biblical revelation."[59] Still, some evangelicals, most notably Donald G. Bloesch (1928–2010), have championed Barth as a resource for developing a contemporary evangelical theology even while acknowledging areas of discomfort with his thought:

56. Karl Barth, *The Göttingen Dogmatics: Instruction in the Christian Religion*, vol. 1, ed. Hannelotte Reiffen, trans. Geoffrey W. Bromiley (Grand Rapids, MI: Wm. B. Eerdmans Publishing Co., 1991), 197.

57. For an analysis of Russian novelist Fyodor Dostoevsky's impact on Barth's early theology, see Elizabeth A. Blake and Rubén Rosario, "Journey to Transcendence: Dostoevsky's Theological Polyphony in Barth's Understanding of the Pauline KRISIS," *Studies in East European Thought* 59, no. 1/2, Dostoevskij's Significance for Philosophy and Theology (June 2007): 3–20.

58. Dorrien, *The Remaking of Evangelical Theology*, 148.

59. Ibid.

A cogent argument can be made that in volume 4 of his *Church Dogmatics* Barth prepared the way for narrative theology by focusing on the analysis of the text as narrative rather than on the text as the bearer of intrinsic, quasi-metaphysical meaning. But the later volumes must surely be read in the light of the earlier ones, in which Barth definitely set forth ontological truth claims.[60]

At the same time, Barth scholars have sought to distance Barth from the neo-orthodox movement, arguing for a stronger continuity between Barth's theology and his nineteenth-century liberal predecessors: "Although opinions continue to vary, the one point generally agreed upon today is that Barth's stance *vis-à-vis* the world of modern thought cannot be adequately described solely in terms of repudiation and opposition; elements of continuity can be found in the midst of discontinuity."[61]

Ultimately, neo-orthodoxy dissolved into various warring factions, in great part due to its inconsistent use of God-language: "the basic posture, and problem, of contemporary theology: it is half liberal and modern, on the one hand, and half biblical and orthodox, on the other, i.e., its world view or cosmology is modern, while its theological language is biblical and orthodox."[62] According to Langdon Gilkey (1919–2004), despite rejecting Protestant liberalism, the neo-orthodox movement articulated its understanding of divine self-revelation by employing the conceptual framework of liberalism albeit clothed in the language of an earlier orthodoxy. Gilkey's critique exposed the lack of historical contextualization in neo-orthodoxy's use of biblical narratives as a foundation for dogmatic reflection: "If in doing this we pretend that we are 'just letting the Bible speak for itself,' we are fooling no one but ourselves. Actually we are translating the biblical view into our own, at least in rejecting its concrete content of wonders and voices and so changing these categories from univocal concepts to empty analogies."[63] In the end, much like the first quest for the "historical" Jesus, the neo-orthodox attempt at understanding ancient Scriptures revealed more about contemporary understandings than "the religion and faith of the past."[64]

60. Donald G. Bloesch, *A Theology of Word and Spirit: Authority and Method in Theology* (Downers Grove, IL: InterVarsity Press, 1992), 30.
    61. Bruce L. McCormack, *Karl Barth's Critically Realistic Dialectical Theology: Its Genesis and Development 1909–1936* (Oxford: Clarendon Press, 1997), 28.
    62. Langdon B. Gilkey, "Cosmology, Ontology, and the Travail of Biblical Language," *Concordia Theological Monthly* 33, no. 3 (March 1962): 143.
    63. Ibid., 153.
    64. Ibid., 154.

1.4 NARRATIVE THEOLOGY AS PUBLIC DISCOURSE

As previously noted, Barth's later theological exegesis emphasized narrative over against ontological truth claims, focusing on the metaphorical
or analogical dimension of religious language as a means of affirming
the authority and truth of Scripture without first having to demonstrate how scriptural events are historically factual or literally true.
Whether or not Barth fully embraced this linguistic turn, a new movement arose from the ashes of neo-orthodoxy to champion the confessional language of biblical religion and the church's historical creeds in
a postmodern world: "narrative," or "postliberal," theology. Like neo-
orthodoxy before it, no single text or thinker marks the genesis of the
narrative theology movement; unlike neo-orthodoxy, which flourished
primarily within Protestant circles, narrative theology has prospered
across confessional boundaries with leading contributions made by
Roman Catholic and Protestant theologians. Still, in narrative theology's many permutations, Karl Barth's Christology in the fourth volume
of the *Church Dogmatics* stands as a clear precursor. Not surprisingly,
two names associated with the rise of narrative theology were greatly
influenced by Barth: Hans Frei (1922–1988), whose *The Eclipse of
Biblical Narrative* (1975) remains the movement's statement of intent,
and George Lindbeck, whose *The Nature of Doctrine* (1984) serves as
its most mature expression. The term "narrative theology" describes a
trend among a wide range of theological sub-disciplines to explore the
role of narrative in theological construction, from biblical studies to
homiletics, from ethics to dogmatics, but does not necessarily identify a
distinct movement or school of thought. Admittedly, during the 1970s
and 1980s a debate on theological hermeneutics arose between the
Chicago and Yale "schools," involving Paul Ricoeur (1913–2005) and
Hans Frei,[65] as well as David Tracy (1939–) and George Lindbeck,[66]
with the Chicago school advocating for greater continuity between
nineteenth-century liberal theology and contemporary constructive
theologies, and the Yale school positing a strong discontinuity with
nineteenth-century Protestant liberalism by characterizing "liberal theology as alien or fundamentally mistaken."[67] As Gary Dorrien observes:

65. See Kevin J. Vanhoozer, *Biblical Narrative in the Philosophy of Paul Ricoeur—A Study in Hermeneutics and Theology* (Cambridge: Cambridge University Press, 1990).

66. See David Tracy, "Lindbeck's New Program for Theology: A Reflection," *Thomist: A Speculative Quarterly Review* 49, no. 3 (July 1, 1985): 460–72.

67. Gary Dorrien, "The Future of Postliberal Theology," *The Christian Century* 118, no. 21 (July 18–25, 2001): 29.

"Today the advocates of Yale postliberalism and Chicago liberalism are probably outnumbered by those who, like [Kathryn] Tanner, are trying to build bridges between these approaches."[68] Consequently, it is more accurate to describe "narrative," or "postliberal," theology as a shift within academic theology away from a narrow historical criticism toward a more expansive literary approach for studying and interpreting sacred Scriptures.[69]

The emphasis on narrative discourse has impacted many disciplines, as witnessed by Alasdair MacIntyre's (1929–) landmark text in philosophical ethics, *After Virtue* (1981), in which he notes it is "because we understand our own lives in terms of the narratives that we live out that the form of narrative is appropriate for understanding the actions of others."[70] A more systematic exploration of the methodological implications of narrative across traditional disciplinary boundaries is Richard Rorty's (1931–2007) critique of modernist epistemology, *Philosophy and the Mirror of Nature* (1980), in which he contends,

> If we see knowledge as a matter of conversation and of social practice, rather than as an attempt to mirror nature, we will not be likely to envisage a metapractice which will be the critique of all possible forms of social practice. So holism produces, as Quine has argued in detail and Sellars has said in passing, a conception which has nothing to do with the quest for certainty.[71]

There is in Rorty's analysis an implied understanding of rational discourse as hermeneutics; that is, rationality as a practice that demands interdisciplinary comparisons of differing explanatory narratives and the distinctive lifestyles these different narratives produce, such that a Christian biblical narrative *and* a scientific evolutionary narrative are both considered "rational" insofar as they can both be conducive to the kind of tolerant liberal society envisioned by the project of modernity and defended by Rorty's political pragmatism.

Rorty accentuates the hermeneutical task underlying all explanatory narratives by focusing on the pragmatic dimension of rational discourse:

68. Ibid., 28.
69. See Robert Alter, *The Art of Biblical Narrative*, rev. ed. (New York: Basic Books, 2011). This text, originally published in 1981, is arguably one of the most important and influential books in contemporary biblical studies, marking a methodological shift toward reading the Bible as a human work of literary imagination by arguing that close study of how these narratives are constructed can help readers better understand their meaning.
70. Alasdair MacIntyre, *After Virtue: A Study in Moral Theory*, 2nd ed. (Notre Dame, IN: University of Notre Dame Press, 1984), 197.
71. Richard Rorty, *Philosophy and the Mirror of Nature* (Princeton, NJ: Princeton University Press, 1980), 171.

. . . an attitude interested not so much in what is out there in the world, or in what happened in history, as in what we can get out of nature and history for our own uses. In this attitude, getting the facts right (about atoms and the void, or about the history of Europe) is merely propaedeutic to finding a new more interesting way of expressing ourselves, and thus of *coping with the world*. From the educational, as opposed to the epistemological or the technological, point of view, the way things are said is more important than the possession of truths.[72]

Not surprisingly, some theologians have embraced postmodern critiques for their rejection of foundationalist epistemologies and view this emphasis on hermeneutics as an opportunity for interjecting a theological perspective into the public discourse:

In a postmodern world Christianity is intellectually relevant. It is relevant to the fundamental questions, Why does the world exist? and Why does it have its present order, rather than another? It is relevant to the discussion of the foundations of morality and society, especially on the significance of human beings. The recognition that Christianity is relevant to our society, and relevant not only to the heart but to the mind as well, is a major change in our cultural situation.[73]

All of which invites the question, is one type of explanatory narrative "better" than another? And its corollary, is theology a "private" or "public" discourse? As noted earlier, Rorty was skeptical about the place of confessional theology in civic discourse: "The main reason religion needs to be privatized is that, in political discussion with those outside the relevant religious community, it is a conversation-stopper."[74] Nevertheless, his methodological openness to a diversity of perspectives within academic discourse, even those he terms "abnormal" like religious or edifying language, help erode the stranglehold that scientific rationality has long held over the collective imagination. In its place Rorty posits a narrative of open-ended civil discourse, nay philosophy as edifying conversation: "Only if we assume that there is a value-free vocabulary which renders these sets of 'factual' statements

72. Ibid., 359.
73. Diogenes Allen, *Christian Belief in a Postmodern World: The Full Wealth of Conviction* (Louisville, KY: Westminster John Knox Press, 1989), 5–6.
74. Richard Rorty, "Religion as Conversation-stopper," in *Philosophy and Social Hope* (New York: Penguin Books, 1999), 171.

commensurable can the positivist distinction between facts and values, beliefs and attitudes, look plausible . . . [these criteria] tempt us to think of edification as having nothing to do with the rational faculties which are employed in normal discourse."[75] Recognizing that scientific descriptions are merely "no more and no less than the best idea we currently have about how to explain what is going on," epistemological criteria "are just the facts about what a given society, or profession, or other group, takes to be good ground for assertions of a certain sort"[76] For Rorty, the goal of philosophy is not epistemological certainty but rather personal edification in the context of social and cultural formation: "the point of edifying philosophy is to keep the conversation going rather than to find objective truth. Such truth, in the view I am advocating, is the normal result of normal discourse. . . . For the edifying philosopher the very idea of being presented with 'all of Truth' is absurd, because the Platonic notion of Truth itself is absurd."[77] In the end, such an approach does not seek to impose *one* normative discourse above all others but invites all rational discourses—religion included, so long as it does not seek to coerce others into accepting its views as normative for all—to contribute to the ongoing public discourse on how best to live.

According to Hans Frei, premodern/precritical readings of the Bible were "at once literal and historical, and not only doctrinal or edifying," in which "words and sentences meant what they said, and because they did so they accurately described real events and real truths."[78] In his judgment, in pre-Enlightenment Christianity, "it seemed clear that a biblical story was to be read literally" and that the events described therein "referred to and described actual historical occurrences."[79] Such stories include the creation narratives (Gen. 1:1–2:25), Jonah's three days in the belly of a great fish (Jonah 1:17–2:10), and Jesus raising Lazarus from the dead (John 11:1–44), tales that in the post-Enlightenment world are met with skepticism, outright dismissal, or explained away by an appeal to the "mythical" character of religious language. While recognizing that even the earliest Christian exegetes read the Bible allegorically as well as literally, the fact remains that much of what was taken as "historical fact" in the biblical narrative has been viewed with suspicion

---

75. Rorty, *Philosophy and the Mirror of Nature*, 364.
76. Ibid., 385.
77. Ibid., 377.
78. Hans W. Frei, *The Eclipse of Biblical Narrative: A Study in Eighteenth and Nineteenth Century Hermeneutics* (New Haven: Yale University Press, 1974), 1.
79. Ibid., 2.

since the Enlightenment, which raises the question, Does God-language make ontological claims? The question of epistemological uncertainty looms heavy over those theologies that embrace Kierkegaard's critique of Schleiermacher and Hegel, whether neo-orthodox, narrative, or postliberal. Christine Helmer suggests that Barth frames the question in terms of "how it is possible for theologians to speak about God in human words while at the same time claiming that God is the speaker of God's own word."[80] In defining theology as reflection on the Word of God, Barth makes the following threefold distinction:

> I am distinguishing the Word of God in a first address in which God himself and God alone is the speaker, in a second address in which it is the Word of a specific category of people (the prophets and apostles), and in a third address in which the number of its human agents or proclaimers is theoretically unlimited. But God's Word abides forever. It neither is nor can be different whether it has its first, its second, or its third form, and always when it is one of the three it is also in some sense the other two as well. The Word of God on which dogmatics reflects—I need only refer to the common formula to show the point at issue—is one in three and three in one: revelation, scripture, and preaching—the Word of God as revelation, the Word of God as scripture, and the Word of God as preaching, neither to be confused nor separated. One Word of God, one authority, one power, and yet not one but three addresses. Three addresses of God in revelation, scripture, and preaching, yet not three Words of God, three authorities, truths, or powers, but one. Scripture is not revelation, but from revelation. Preaching is not revelation or scripture, but from both. But the Word of God is scripture no less than it is revelation, and it is preaching no less than it is scripture. Revelation is from God alone, scripture is from revelation alone, and preaching is from revelation and scripture. Yet there is no first or last, no greater or less. The first, the second, and the third are all God's Word in the same glory, unity in trinity and trinity in unity.[81]

This central Trinitarian assumption of Christian dogmatics inevitably raises questions about the knowability of God since the very "fact of preaching, of talking about God, rests on the presupposition that God is knowable, that he is an object."[82] At the same time, like Kierkegaard, Barth does not want to conceive of God as an object of study and

80. Helmer, *Theology and the End of Doctrine*, 60.
81. Barth, *The Göttingen Dogmatics*, 14–15.
82. Ibid., 325.

analysis among other objects, choosing instead to affirm the imperfect analogy of one knowing subject encountering and getting to know another: "The difficulty in the theological question of the knowability of God is a very special one. As preachers talk about God, they declare that they know God, that they are in a position to name him, to affirm his being, his existence, to ascribe certain attributes to him."[83] Accordingly, in revelation, "God is an irremovable subject that can never be confused with an object. . . . To put it positively, his revelation consists of the fact that he himself encounters us, that we see ourselves set before God."[84] Consequently, the most apt analogy for those desiring to know God is to read the Bible as "a lover who has received a letter from his beloved—I assume that God's Word is just as precious to you as this letter is to the lover. I assume that you read and think you ought to read God's Word in the same way the lover reads this letter."[85]

The knowability of God as inherently relational is also illustrated by Søren Kierkegaard's parable of the king and the maiden, where the Christian doctrine of the incarnation is analogically compared to a fairy tale in which a powerful king falls in love and wants to wed a peasant maiden but does not want his power and status as king to be the basis of her "love" for him. How to resolve this conundrum? According to Kierkegaard, the "poet's task is to find a solution, a point of unity where there is in truth love's understanding, where the god's concern has overcome its pain, for this is the unfathomable love that is not satisfied with what the object of love might foolishly consider himself blissfully happy to have."[86] In terms of the fairy tale, "The poet has two possible strategies for removing the inequality. The king must either elevate the maiden to his own level, or else descend to her level. In both cases the king is the agent of change."[87] Kierkegaard's parable is a thinly veiled retelling of the Christian Gospel—a clumsy explanation of the miracle of the Incarnation upon which knowledge of God and eternal salvation rest—which he himself readily admits: "forgive me my curious mistaken notion of having composed it myself. It was a mistaken notion, and the poem was so different from every human poem that it was no poem at all but *the wonder*."[88] The parable, "for all its apparent simplicity, shows

83. Ibid., 326.
84. Ibid., 327.
85. Søren Kierkegaard, *For Self-Examination/Judge for Yourself!* ed. and trans. Howard V. Hong and Edna H. Hong (Princeton, NJ: Princeton University Press, 1990), 26.
86. Kierkegaard, *Philosophical Fragments*, 28–29.
87. Evans, *Passionate Reason*, 51.
88. Kierkegaard, *Philosophical Fragments*, 36.

powerfully that the Christian belief in the Incarnation is a belief that God became a man, actually *became* something which he had not been before. He was not just in the form of a man, disguised as one, but actually became one."[89] The miracle, or *wonder* as Kierkegaard calls it, is that in the Incarnation, God is fully human—indistinguishable to human perception as something other than human—yet also fully God and capable of granting us faith and eternal happiness.

Kierkegaard's argument in the *Philosophical Fragments* is that it is impossible to prove claims about the divinity of Christ through empirical verification; historical reconstruction cannot bring us to a state of contemporaneity with the man Jesus, but this should not matter since Jesus' "contemporaries were no better off than we are on the fundamental and essential matter: Is Jesus God incarnate?"[90] Not even the miracles performed by Jesus can objectively and with absolute certainty demonstrate his divinity—granted, they serve an important function bringing believers to the brink of faith by raising questions about his identity—but in the end miracles cannot establish without question that Jesus is divine. After witnessing the raising of Lazarus from the grave, many "had seen what Jesus did and believed in him," while others "went to the Pharisees and told them what he had done. . . . So from that day on they planned to put him to death" (John 11:45–46, 53). Consequently, if we were "by some means transported to Palestine in the days of Jesus, we would be essentially no better off than we are now. Nothing which Jesus did or said established that he was God."[91] What we have is testimony—eyewitness accounts—by those who heard Jesus preaching and were present for his miracles. While Christ's divinity remains a matter of faith, it is a historical fact that a certain community at a particular time and place in history made claims about the man Jesus of Nazareth. Some of their contemporaries believed them and joined this fledgling community while others disbelieved, ridiculed, and even persecuted the earliest Christians. In the end, and down through the ages, every believer must decide for him- or herself whether to believe or disregard what is claimed concerning Jesus. However, this historical testimony—the Christian community's narrative concerning the man Jesus of Nazareth—*is* the content of Christian doctrine, what George Lindbeck terms the distinctive grammar that governs the church's speech about God.[92]

89. Diogenes Allen, *Three Outsiders: Pascal, Kierkegaard, Simone Weil* (Princeton, NJ: Caroline Press, 1983), 90.
90. Ibid.
91. Ibid., 91.
92. George A. Lindbeck, *The Nature of Doctrine: Religion and Theology in a Postliberal Age*, 25th anniversary ed. (Louisville, KY: Westminster John Knox Press, 2009), 65–70.

Lindbeck's influential volume on the nature of doctrine offers a cultural-linguistic paradigm informed by Ludwig Wittgenstein and Clifford Geertz that proves useful for understanding the development and function of doctrine within the Christian community. At its core, Lindbeck's proposal embraces the Bible as a narrative discourse "that regulates intersubjective behavior and shapes intersubjective identity."[93] Accordingly, the validity of a religious truth claim "depends on how the utterance is used. Religious utterances acquire cognitive truth only insofar as they are rightly used within a correlative form of life molded by such religious activities as prayer, worship, proclamation, and service."[94] Nevertheless,

> To say that doctrines are rules is not to deny that they involve propositions. The rules formulated by the linguist or the logician, for example, express propositional convictions about how language or thought actually work. These are, however, second-order rather than first-order propositions and affirm nothing about extra-linguistic or extra-human reality. For a rule theory, in short, doctrines qua doctrines are not first-order propositions, but are to be construed as second-order ones: they make . . . *intrasystematic rather than ontological truth claims.*[95]

Despite doctrine's rule-like status in governing the church's distinctive discourse, Lindbeck cautions that even "more than the grammar in grammar books, church doctrine is an inevitably imperfect and often misleading guide to the interconnections within a religion."[96] Consequently, "truth in the sense of correspondence with reality is not an attribute religious utterances can have when considered in and of themselves."[97]

In other words, in a similar fashion to Richard Rorty's rejection of modern epistemology because of its misguided quest for a universally neutral foundation—a literal utopia, or "view from nowhere"[98]—George

93. Kevin J. Vanhoozer, *The Drama of Doctrine: A Canonical-Linguistic Approach to Christian Theology* (Louisville, KY: Westminster John Knox Press, 2005), 93.
94. George Hunsinger, "Truth as Self-Involving: Barth and Lindbeck on the Cognitive and Performative Aspects of Truth in Theological Discourse," *Journal of the American Academy of Religion* 61, no. 1 (Spring 1993): 42.
95. Lindbeck, *The Nature of Doctrine*, 66 (emphasis added).
96. Ibid., 67.
97. Hunsinger, "Truth as Self-Involving," 42.
98. See Thomas Nagel, *The View from Nowhere* (Oxford: Oxford University Press, 1986). The author argues that human beings are capable of viewing the world from a detached point of view that transcends one's own limited experiences and self-interest; at the same time, each human being stands in a particular time and place, located within a distinct culture and history, having experienced shared events but from a uniquely *individual* perspective. Nagel advocates a methodological approach that resists the objectifying impulse in modern philosophy and scientific rationalism by accommodating subjectivity and acknowledging the incompleteness of human knowing: "at a minimum it will admit the existence of things or events we don't know about now. The issue is only how far beyond our actual conception of the word we should admit that the world may extend" (108). Thus, the

Lindbeck understands theological discourse as an inherently hermeneutical task circumscribed by the "rules" of a particular faith community's religious language and praxis. Thus, the end-goal is not finding objective truth "out there in the world" but more modestly, giving voice to one among the many human ways of "making sense" of the world (Rorty). The discomfort human beings have with this hermeneutical approach is the open-ended and inconclusive quality present in all human ways of knowing: "The issues involved in this debate are even less susceptible to clear-cut decision than are comparable questions about the best overall theories in the physical sciences; and these, if T. S. Kuhn and others are to be believed, are never finally decidable."[99] Yet this existential discomfort with epistemological uncertainty is present not only within the natural sciences but also within dogmatic theology itself, which, despite Lindbeck's caveat that theological discourse does not make ontological truth claims (since dogmatic statements "affirm nothing about extra-linguistic or extra-human reality"[100]), still desires to speak to a reality beyond itself "to the externality of the linguistic referent."[101]

Lindbeck distinguishes between first-order speech directly about God and Christ (here one has to assume he refers namely to Scripture as an account by God's chosen witnesses—the prophets and apostles—concerning the divine act of revelation in human history), and second-order speech delineating what can and cannot be said about God and Christ within a particular religious community (dogmatic theology proper, what Miroslav Volf has disparagingly termed "critical talk about talk about God"[102]). Without denying that religious language "can be interpreted as possibly containing ontologically true affirmations" (even within Lindbeck's narrowly defined cultural-linguistic approach), church doctrine, as second-order discourse,

> rarely if ever succeeds in making affirmations with ontological import, but rather engages in explaining, defending, analyzing, and regulating the liturgical, kerygmatic, and ethical modes of speech and action within which such affirmations from time to time occur. Just as grammar by itself affirms nothing either true or false regarding the world in which language is used, but only about language,

---

"standpoint of morality is more objective than that of private life, but less objective than the standpoint of physics. We may think of reality as a set of concentric spheres, progressively revealed as we detach gradually from the contingencies of the self" (5).

99. Lindbeck, *The Nature of Doctrine*, 28.
100. Ibid., 66.
101. Helmer, *Theology and the End of Doctrine*, 152.
102. Volf, *Captive to the Word of God*, 57.

so theology and doctrine, to the extent that they are second-order activities, assert nothing either true or false about God and his relation to creatures, but only speak about such assertions.[103]

Lindbeck, like Schleiermacher before him, has created an oasis for Christian theology removed from the invectives of its "cultured despisers," in which the traditional language of Scripture, liturgy, and confessional creeds freely gives form to the church's own distinctive and comprehensive worldview: "In this perspective, the reasonableness of a religion is largely a function of its assimilative powers, of its ability to provide an intelligible interpretation in its own terms of the varied situations and realities adherents encounter."[104] The elegance of Lindbeck's "postliberal antifoundationalism" lies in its ability to re-describe "reality within the scriptural framework rather than translating Scripture into extrascriptural categories. It is the text, so to speak, which absorbs the world, rather than the world the text."[105] Its methodological weakness, as David Tracy has consistently pointed out, is postliberalism's tendency toward insular and sectarian discourse (most clearly evidenced in the Radical Orthodoxy movement,[106] the stepchild of narrative theology and postliberalism): "But however pressing the concern with the relationship of grammar and rhetoric for interpreting the concrete discourse of the tradition, the major problem lies elsewhere: how can theologians assess the truth-claims of Lindbeck's grammatically analyzed traditions?"[107] Thus, despite widespread support for Lindbeck's methodological proposal, even those most predisposed to embrace his narrative understanding of doctrine as the internal grammar of the believing community raise questions as to whether or not "Lindbeck's approach is able to make truth claims about anything 'outside' the intratextual story world of Scripture."[108]

Lindbeck himself recognizes the insular nature of doctrinal language and advocates for an apologetic or foundational theology within his

---

103. Lindbeck, *The Nature of Doctrine*, 54, 55.
104. Ibid., 117.
105. Ibid., 104.
106. Radical Orthodoxy is a Christian theological movement with roots in the narrative theologies of Hans Urs von Balthasar (1905–1988) and Karl Barth, characterized by its use of postmodern philosophical insights to reject the dominant paradigm of modernity as represented by epistemological foundationalism and reductive scientific rationalism that uses confessional language to critique modern secularism and reassert the role of traditional orthodox doctrines in interpreting reality. See John Milbank, Catherine Pickstock, and Graham Ward, eds., *Radical Orthodoxy: A New Theology* (London: Routledge, 1999); John Milbank, *Theology and Social Theory*, 2nd ed. (Oxford: Blackwell, 2006); and John Milbank and Simon Oliver, eds., *The Radical Orthodoxy Reader* (London: Routledge, 2009).
107. Tracy, "Lindbeck's New Program for Theology," 469.
108. Vanhoozer, *The Drama of Doctrine*, 95.

cultural-linguistic model, yet stands solidly on the side of his neo-orthodox predecessors over against any hint of accommodation to contemporary secular culture: "When or if dechristianization reduces Christians to a small minority, they will need for the sake of survival to form communities that strive without traditionalist rigidity to cultivate their native tongue and learn to act accordingly."[109] However, making oneself intelligible to those members of the culture one inhabits who do not happen to share one's core religious beliefs, ought not to be seen as "a capitulation of traditional beliefs to contemporary secular beliefs."[110] Contemplating this same seemingly inevitable compromise with secularism, ethicist Alasdair MacIntyre concludes *After Virtue* (1981) with the following enigmatic declaration: "We are waiting not for a Godot, but for another—doubtless very different—St. Benedict."[111] Perhaps MacIntyre's intention is to reinforce the importance of something like Lindbeck's cultural-linguistic understanding of religion for preserving religious identity against the forces of barbarism in much the same way Benedict, through the influence of his monastic *Rule*, helped Europe reemerge from the "dark night of history" after the fall of the Roman Empire.[112] If so, then Radical Orthodoxy, with its move toward heightened sectarianism, seems the natural heir to postliberal theology. Yet there remains within Lindbeck's work a respect for difference and theological diversity contrary to this narrow vision of the dogmatic task.

Christine Helmer, in acknowledging her debt to Lindbeck's methodological proposal, defines the task of theology as an open-ended conversation in which the "reality of God is discussed, debated, communicated, and contested in history, and in the process the limits of history as a venue for discussing, contesting, and communicating reality are tested."[113] Accordingly, Lindbeck's main contribution is to remind the discipline of theology of "theology's social constructedness all the way down" while affirming its unique theological character "because it has to do with a distinct reality that has its being and existence outside social construction."[114] Thus, rather than leading us toward a more sectarian reality, Lindbeck's constructive proposal about the nature of human religions as shared conceptual frameworks ought not to be

109. Lindbeck, *The Nature of Doctrine*, 119–20.
110. Tracy, "Lindbeck's New Program for Theology," 470.
111. MacIntyre, *After Virtue*, 263.
112. Pope Benedict XVI, "Saint Benedict of Norcia," homily delivered at a General Audience in St. Peter's Square on April 9, 2008, http://w2.vatican.va/content/benedict-xvi/en/audiences/2008/documents/hf_ben-xvi_aud_20080409.html.
113. Helmer, *Theology and the End of Doctrine*, 166.
114. Ibid., 152.

reduced merely to the notion of doctrine as the received normative formulations of a particular tradition but ought to be seen as encouraging
comparative dialogue and cooperation among religions by drawing our
attention to the first-order speech about God that gives rise to doctrinal
language in the first place: "Doctrine comprises claims to truth made
about the living God. It is the work of human hands. And the work
of doctrine includes the perennial recognition that God may decide
to surprise humans with the unexpected and unforeseen, which will
require them to correct their doctrinal formulations again and again."[115]
Thus, without settling for an easy pluralism that reduces the distinctive
truth-claims of the world's various religions to a shared "experiential
core," George Lindbeck's methodological proposal embraces religious
difference and encourages conversation among the world's religions:
"In short, while a cultural-linguistic approach does not issue a blan-
ket endorsement of the enthusiasm and warm fellow-feelings that can
be easily promoted in an experiential-expressive context, it does not
exclude the development of powerful theological rationales for sober
and practically efficacious commitment to interreligious discussion and
cooperation."[116]

1.5 RECONCILING REVELATIONAL AND
ANTHROPOLOGICAL APPROACHES

Whatever the nomenclature—Chicago versus Yale schools, liberalism
versus neo-orthodoxy, theologies of culture versus theologies of the
Word—there is a general consensus that the North American theological landscape has been dominated by two all-encompassing methodological approaches. This investigation employs the *anthropological*
typology for describing those theologies of culture employing some
variant of Paul Tillich's correlational method that see their primary task
as one of *apologetics*, that is, making Christian doctrines not only palatable but also convincing to an increasingly secularized culture. Tillich
prioritizes "the interpretation of this truth for every new generation"
while acknowledging that theology "moves back and forth between two
poles, the eternal truth of its foundation and the temporal situation
in which the eternal truth must be received."[117] Within this typology,

115. Ibid., 165.
116. Lindbeck, *The Nature of Doctrine*, 41.
117. Paul Tillich, *Systematic Theology*, vol. 1 (Chicago: The University of Chicago Press, 1951), 3.

the central question driving the theological enterprise remains, "Can the Christian message be adapted to the modern mind without losing its essential and unique character? Most theologians have believed that it is possible."[118] By contrast, the *revelational* approach most often identified with Karl Barth's critical retrieval of orthodoxy views the apologetic task of theology with suspicion, fearful that the act of translating the Christian *kērygma* for a secularized culture "will destroy the uniqueness of the message."[119] As such, the revelational typology separates itself or stands apart (*diástasis*) from culture, emphasizing divine transcendence as the only reliable foundation for human knowledge of God by defining dogmatics as "the self-examination of the Christian Church in respect of the content of its distinctive talk about God."[120]

After tracing the development of these two competing, yet surprisingly complementary, theological methodologies from the nineteenth century through to the present, both have been found wanting. First, given the multiplicity of theological movements on the contemporary theological scene, the liberal versus neo-orthodox dichotomy that dominated academic theology in the twentieth century proves inadequate for categorizing all the nascent constructive theologies of the twenty-first century. While the two typologies introduced in the introductory chapter—the revelational and anthropological approaches—adequately describe the dominant Eurocentric methodologies employed in the North American academy, they fail to account for the changing demographics of global Christianity since World War II, in which the church in Europe and North America has faced increasing secularization and decreasing cultural relevance, while the church in Africa, Asia, and Latin America continues expanding in both numbers and cultural influence. Second, since the forces of globalization have made interaction among the world's major religions an inescapable reality, dogmatic reflection also demands clarity on the relationship of Christianity to other faiths. The Pew Research Center on Religion and Public Life predicts that by the year 2050 Islam—the world's fastest growing religion—will surpass Christianity as the world's largest religion. Furthermore, over the next several decades religion will continue to assert itself in the global public square as: (1) atheists (and those who do not affiliate with any religion) will constitute a declining percentage of the total world's population,

---

118. Ibid., 7.
119. Ibid., 6.
120. Karl Barth, *Church Dogmatics*, I.1, eds. G. W. Bromiley and T. F. Torrance (Edinburgh: T. & T. Clark, 1936), 10.

(2) four out of ten Christians will live in sub-Saharan Africa, (3) Muslims will make up 10 percent of Europe's population, and (4) Islam will surpass Judaism as the largest non-Christian religion in the United States.[121] As evidenced by a growing preoccupation with the problem of other religions in the later thought of both Karl Barth and Paul Tillich, as well as George Lindbeck's postliberal challenge that we pursue interreligious dialogue and cooperation without surrendering our religious differences, the future of dogmatic thinking demands a more comparative and inclusive methodology. Finally, as suggested by Søren Kierkegaard's critique of nineteenth-century Protestant Liberalism, *orthopraxis* is a viable category for evaluating competing theological truth-claims that resonates with the theme of God's preferential option for the poor, oppressed, and powerless prevalent among the contextual theologies of Asia, Africa, and Latin America, as well as the marginalized theologies of underrepresented minorities within Europe and North America. The next chapter begins to deconstruct the dominant North American paradigm by presenting Barth's revelational and Tillich's anthropological doctrines of revelation while surveying their considerable influence on contemporary North American and European theologians. It will be argued that despite seemingly incompatible methodologies, both approaches are reactions to Enlightenment critiques of revealed religion that retain their cultural relevance by perpetuating a modernist foundationalist epistemology. Given our increasingly pluralist and globalized reality, a promising new direction for dogmatics is the reconceptualization of divine revelation as a sacramental encounter grounded in the work of the Holy Spirit that liberates doctrinal language to make ontological truth-claims while also facilitating doctrinal conversation between Christianity and other world religions.

121. Pew Research Center, April 2, 2015, "The Future of World Religions: Population Growth Projections, 2010–2050," 5–22, http://www.pewforum.org/2015/04/02/religious-projections-2010-2050/.

2

Two Sides of the Same Coin

"But [God] is known to us in clothed form—under the sign of the man Jesus Christ, in the Scriptures, and in human preaching. This knowledge of ours is true, but it is always faith."

—Karl Barth[1]

This chapter offers a closer analysis of Barth's revelational and Tillich's anthropological doctrines of revelation, delineating their methodological differences and evaluating their considerable influence on contemporary North American and European theology, while arguing that ultimately both are reacting to the post-Enlightenment crisis in Biblical hermeneutics. As such, despite diametrically opposed methodological starting points, Tillich's theology of culture and Barth's theology of the Word remain mired within the prevalent polarities of Christ and culture, revelation and reason, Scripture and tradition that have characterized academic theology since the Enlightenment.

2.1 THE POSTWAR CRISIS IN INTELLECTUAL DISCOURSE

The period after World War I was a time of deep cultural crisis in Germany, in which the dominant theological and scientific narratives no longer proved adequate: "Amidst the cultural and political chaos that followed the Great War—the *Putsches*, the War Guilt Clause and inflation—artists, authors, architects, playwrights and intellectuals of every stripe were seeking a way to reconcile humans to a more stable,

---

1. Karl Barth, *Church Dogmatics*, II.1, eds. G. W. Bromiley and T. F. Torrance, trans. T. H. L. Parker, W. B. Johnston, Harold Knight, and J. L. M. Haire (Edinburgh: T. & T. Clark, Ltd., 1957), 16.

reliable reality."[2] No better example of postwar dissolution with existing theoretical frameworks exists than Sigmund Freud's *Civilization
and Its Discontents* (1929), in which Freud weaves a complex narrative that examines the inherent tension between the individual and
civilized society in order to argue that natural primitive instincts are
sublimated into more socially acceptable activities for the sake of communal cohesion. This repression of animal instincts, however, creates a
fundamental tension between the self and the collective that can manifest as destructive antisocial behaviors, as evidenced by "the war to end
all wars." Aggressive impulses, even ethnic and cultural hatreds, can be
traced to primitive instincts of self-preservation and the fundamental
drive to procreate: "In the realm of the mind . . . what is primitive is so
commonly preserved alongside of the transformed version which has
arisen from it that it is unnecessary to give instances as evidence."[3] Nevertheless, Freud provides many such instances, which when read against
the backdrop of a nation recovering from a brutal war, only serve to
reinforce the need for stable and objective truths from which to survey
the ravaged landscape and begin to pick up the pieces: "Ethics is thus
to be regarded as a therapeutic attempt—as an endeavour to achieve,
by means of a command of the super-ego, something which has so far
not been achieved by means of any other cultural activities."[4] Though
Freud, an avowed atheist, rejects non-natural explanations for religious
beliefs, he recognizes the place of the religious impulse in human cultural evolution and affirms its civilizing effect in both *The Future of an
Illusion* (1927) and *Civilization and Its Discontents*, where he discusses
the "oceanic feeling" of wholeness that gives rise to religious cultural
practices: "From my own experience I could not convince myself of the
primary nature of such a feeling. But this gives me no right to deny that
it does in fact occur in other people."[5]

In this same historical context, the theology of crisis arose in response
to the widespread "disillusionment and loss of faith that plagued German society in the early post-War years" and marked a turning "away
from the world of theological subjectivity and the masters of its universe. In this regard, Barth's theology was part of a larger movement
in German culture that sought out a dimension of life which could

2. Amy Marga, *Karl Barth's Dialogue with Catholicism in Göttingen and Münster: Its Significance for His Doctrine of God* (Tübingen: Mohr Siebeck, 2010), 60.
3. Sigmund Freud, *Civilization and Its Discontents*, ed. and trans. James Strachey (New York: W. W. Norton & Company, 1989), 16.
4. Ibid., 108.
5. Ibid., 12.

anchor the human psyche to something objective, realistic, and cen-tered on fact—and soothe it as it suffered through widespread trauma and profound disorientation."[6] Given the later development of Barth's theology, especially his uncompromising rejection of natural theology, a driving concern for Barth is the possibility of "God's objective and concrete presence to the human knower."[7] In the opening volume of his magisterial multi-tome *Church Dogmatics* (1932–67), Barth empha-sizes the problem of God's objective presence by citing a passage from Emil Brunner published in the theological journal *Zwischen den Zeiten* ("Between the Times"), which Barth cofounded with Eduard Thurney-sen, Friedrich Gogarten, and Rudolf Bultmann:

> The problem to-day is not the nature of God but His existence, not what is revealed but whether there is such a thing as revelation, not rationalistic corruption at individual points but the questioning of the miracle of revelation as such. It is the problem of the sign and norm of all Christian theology, of the concept of revelation and not its contents. In short, it is the problem of reason and revelation.[8]

Brunner, along with Barth, Thurneysen, Gogarten, Bultmann, and even Tillich, were part of the postwar "theology of crisis," or dialectical theology, that was labeled (mostly by its critics) as neo-orthodoxy and which, despite the diversity of thought and method among its pro-ponents, concerned itself primarily with the quest for what Barth has described as the "concrete and objective presence" of God (*Gegenstän-dlichkeit*) in the wake of the cultural crisis caused by the Great War. For Barth, the act of divine revelation in human history becomes the longed-for anchor in the storm, since, "Dogmatics as an enquiry pre-supposes that the true content of Christian talk about God can be known by man," and on this premise argues that "every statement in dogmatics, as a statement of faith, must be ventured with the assurance of speaking divine and not just human truth."[9]

As argued in the first chapter, what unites the various thinkers labeled neo-orthodox is their rejection of nineteenth-century Protes-tant liberalism because it undermined the objective basis of revelation by reducing religious experience to a subjective state of mind and in the process subsumed the Christian gospel under the dominant culture.

---

6. Marga, *Karl Barth's Dialogue with Catholicism*, 59.
7. Ibid.
8. Barth, *Church Dogmatics*, I.1, 26.
9. Ibid., 12.

Even Paul Tillich, whose existential interpretations of distinctly Christian symbols for speaking about universal human concerns seem more
compatible with liberalism than Barth's hardline emphasis on a wholly
transcendent divine self-revelation, longs for something eternal upon
which to ground the human psyche in this age of profound disorientation. Thus, his response to the failure of nineteenth-century liberalism
is to develop "a new theological language that would address clearly the
urgencies of the general culture and yet remain faithful to Christian
church communities."[10] Tillich describes this new method as the marriage of a theology of culture with an ecclesial theology that still retains
its universal cultural significance:

> The church is the circle, as it were, to which is assigned—ideally
> speaking—the task of creating a specifically religious sphere and
> thus removing the element of contingency from the living religious
> elements, collecting them, concentrating them in theory and in
> practice, and in this way making them into a powerful—indeed into
> the most powerful—cultural factor, capable of supporting every-
> thing else.[11]

Consequently, during the postwar crisis facing Europe, in which the
church's persistent accommodation to secular culture did little to abate
the decline of religion as a cultural force in Germany, Barth and Tillich
stood as bulwarks for Christianity.

2.2 BARTH AND TILLICH ON THE
DOCTRINE OF REVELATION

In an age that had—to paraphrase Aleksandr Solzhenitsyn—forgotten God,[12] Barth and Tillich remained constant: two sides of the same
coin, distinct in their methodologies, yet united in their overarching
goal of resisting atheism and secularization by providing uniquely
Christian answers to Europe's postwar woes. In other words, despite
their methodological divergences, both Karl Barth and Paul Tillich
begin their theological reflections with the doctrine of revelation, and

10. Mark Kline Taylor, "Introduction: The Theological Development and Contribution of Paul Tillich," in *Paul Tillich: Theologian of the Boundaries*, ed. Mark Kline Taylor (Minneapolis, MN: Fortress Press, 1991), 17.
11. Paul Tillich, "On the Idea of a Theology of Culture," in *Paul Tillich: Theologian of the Boundaries*, 53.
12. See Aleksandr Solzhenitsyn, "Godlessness: the First Step to the Gulag," Templeton Prize Lecture, May 10, 1983 (London), http://orthodoxnet.com/blog/2011/07/men-have-forgotten-god-alexander-solzhenitsyn/.

both seem to understand revelation within the framework of a Kantian epistemological perspective.

The Greek word *apokalypsis*, translated as "revelation," literally means to uncover or disclose. In Christian theology the term has come to mean knowledge of God disclosed by an act of God, which even in this act of self-revelation remains incomprehensible mystery. Not that human beings cannot have reliable and verifiable knowledge of God, but the implication is that such knowledge is unattainable through human efforts: "The word 'revelation' ('removing the veil') has been used traditionally to mean the manifestation of something hidden which cannot be approached through ordinary ways of gaining knowledge."[13] Thus, while revelation provides some understanding of divine mystery, *full* comprehension remains beyond our human capacity: "'Mystery' should not be applied to something which ceases to be a mystery after it has been revealed. Nothing which can be discovered by a methodical cognitive approach should be called a 'mystery.'"[14] That being said, "Dogmatics as an enquiry presupposes that the true content of Christian talk about God can be known by man. It makes this assumption as in and with the Church it believes in Jesus Christ as the revealing and reconciling address of God to man."[15] Accordingly, what makes Christian theology distinctive is that its knowledge of God is thoroughly christocentric, but underlying this revelation in Christ is "the freely acting God" who "alone is the truth of revelation."[16] Thus Barth can say with all honesty, "what God can do forces theology to be humble . . . God may speak to us through Russian Communism, a flute concerto, a blossoming shrub, or a dead dog. We do well to listen to Him if He really does."[17]

All of this reinforces dialectical theology's desire for the "concrete and objective presence" of God as a way past the postwar despondency while also providing a genuine alternative to the anthropocentrism of nineteenth-century liberalism. As Gordon Kaufman argued in the late twentieth century, the dominant question of modern theology remains "whether there is some extra-human reality in relationship to which human existence gains its being and its fulfillment, some ultimate point of reference in terms of which our human life and its problems

13. Tillich, *Systematic Theology*, vol. 1, 108.
14. Ibid., 109.
15. Barth, *Church Dogmatics* I.1, 12.
16. Ibid., 15.
17. Ibid., 55.

and possibilities must be understood."[18] For both Tillich and Barth revelation overcomes the limits of Kantian epistemology by providing knowledge of the transcendent God who, from a noetic perspective, is not an object of sensory perception but lies beyond human experience. Thus, while affirming the *real* encounter with the divine *in* human history, Barth still declares "it is always faith."[19] According to Tillich, the divine always remains *noumena*, so he is quick to differentiate between empirical knowledge and revealed knowledge as "the manifestation of what concerns us ultimately."[20] In other words, the encounter between human and divine in history is not comparable to the empirical observation of objects in the world but is best conceived as an encounter with the other—an intersubjective relational encounter—albeit one between the self and the self's very ground of being, which Paul Tillich has termed our "ultimate concern":

> Revelation is the manifestation of what concerns us ultimately. The mystery which is revealed is of ultimate concern to us because it is the ground of our being. In the history of religion revelatory events always have been described as shaking, transforming, demanding, significant in an ultimate way. They derive from divine sources, from the power of that which is holy and which therefore has an unconditional claim on us. Only that mystery which is of ultimate concern for us appears in revelation.[21]

Furthermore, Tillich strongly defends the objective reality of this event despite its inherently intersubjective character: "Revelation always is a subjective and an objective event in strict interdependence. Someone is grasped by the manifestation of the mystery; this is the subjective side of the event. Something occurs through which the mystery of revelation grasps someone; this is the objective side. These two sides cannot be separated. *If nothing happens objectively, nothing is revealed.*"[22] Thus, in contradistinction to nineteenth-century liberal theology, Tillich emphasizes the objective character of divine self-revelation even while acknowledging the Kantian epistemological limits concerning the human perception of this objective divine act: "Revelation is not real without the receiving side, and it is not real without the giving side."[23]

18. Kaufman, *In Face of Mystery*, 4.
19. Barth, *Church Dogmatics*, II.1, 16.
20. Tillich, *Systematic Theology*, vol. 1, 110.
21. Ibid.
22. Ibid., 111 (emphasis added).
23. Ibid.

It is evident that Tillich's more anthropocentric theology of culture shares this emphasis on the concrete and objective presence of God in common with Barth's more ecclesiocentric and revelational approach. Furthermore, both theologians have been influenced by Søren Kierkegaard's distinction between Schleiermacher and Hegel's immanental understanding of religion, and Kierkegaard's own understanding of Christianity as a religion of transcendence grounded in an act of divine self-revelation. The revelational event is characterized by all three of these thinkers as an intersubjective encounter, originating in a concrete act by God that transcends and overcomes the epistemological limitations of human subjectivity, which is described by Kierkegaard as the "miracle," or "wonder," by Tillich as "mystery," or "miracle," and by Barth as "the mystery." In fact, Barth conceives of dogmatic theology as "rational wrestling with the mystery. But all rational wrestling with this mystery, the more serious it is, can lead only to its fresh and authentic interpretation and manifestation as a mystery."[24]

Therefore, if revelation is understood as an encounter with God, how do we understand the place of Scripture in mediating this revelation? Or how do we evaluate the propositional claims of a dogmatic theology grounded in Scripture? Within Barth's Trinitarian conception of revelation, both the written Word (Scripture) and the proclaimed Word (church doctrine) are *witnesses* to revelation—they point beyond themselves to God but they ought never be confused with the event of revelation itself. Perhaps it is anachronistic to discuss the theology of Karl Barth by employing the language of postmodernism, yet William Stacy Johnson and Graham Ward have ably demonstrated substantial affinities between Barth and nonfoundational epistemologies.[25] Even Bruce McCormack, whose work has been critical of both Johnson and Ward on this topic, grants "Barth steadfastly refused to find a foundation for theology in anything external to revelation."[26] However, having rejected a philosophical foundationalism does not mean Barth also rejects a theological foundationalism, so McCormack contends that Barth remains within a Kantian epistemology by embracing "a subjective form of foundationalism."[27] Thus, while McCormack cannot envision Karl Barth comfortable within

---

24. Barth, *Church Dogmatics* I.1, 368.
25. See Graham Ward, *Barth, Derrida and the Language of Theology* (Cambridge: Cambridge University Press, 1995); William Stacy Johnson, *The Mystery of God: Karl Barth and the Postmodern Foundations of Theology* (Louisville, KY: Westminster John Knox Press, 1997).
26. Bruce L. McCormack, *Orthodox and Modern: Studies in the Theology of Karl Barth* (Grand Rapids, MI: Baker Academic, 2008), 35.
27. Ibid.

Richard Rorty's foundationless hermeneutical approach, he is willing to grant "Barth was not a foundationalist because he refused to allow his philosophical foundations to provide an ultimate ground for his theological truth-claims," coining the term "transfoundationalism" to describe the "divine act by means of which the limitations proper to the philosophical foundations he presupposed were transcended."[28] Given the definition of postmodernity outlined in the previous section—where "modernity" is characterized by a search for rational certainty according to a single model of rationality and "postmodernity" as embracive of multiple rationalities and of the uncertainty of dissensus—it is accurate to say that one aspect of Barth's dogmatic project is the rejection of a foundationalist epistemology. It remains to be seen, however, whether or not Barth's definition of theology as "rational wrestling with the mystery" allows for a multiplicity of theological perspectives.

For Barth the only legitimate foundation for dogmatic claims is the Word of God. Theological statements are possible because God reveals God's self. More to the point, God not only reveals God's self, God is both the content of that revelation and the only means by which humans can experience and know this content. Consequently, Barth was criticized by Tillich, Bonhoeffer, and others for promulgating a "positivism of revelation" that does not allow any questioning of the content of revelation but "must be swallowed whole or not at all."[29] However, asserting that the Word of God is the foundation of theological reflection does not necessarily entail a *revelational foundationalism*. In Bonhoeffer's description of the dialectic at play in Barth's theological language a more nuanced hermeneutic is revealed than is typical of biblicism: "All of Barth's theological statements are based on the necessity of saying not-God when I speak of God—because it is *I* who speak of *God*—and not-I when I speak of the believing I."[30] God's self-revelation remains mystery because theological language is by definition human language about God and cannot limit God's freedom. Therefore, theological language is not the language of absolute certainty but that of cautious, yet faithful, acknowledgment:

> The laying of this foundation means the shaking of all and any systematic certainties that may arise. To be sure, it may in fact mean their eventual confirmation. But it can equally mean their

28. Ibid.
29. Bonhoeffer, *Letters and Papers from Prison*, 373.
30. Dietrich Bonhoeffer, *Act and Being: Transcendental Philosophy and Ontology in Systematic Theology*, ed. Wayne W. Floyd and Hans-Richard Reuter, trans. H. Martin Rumscheidt (Minneapolis, MN: Fortress Press, 1996), 85.

dissolution. And it certainly means that they are called into question . . . in dogmatics strictly speaking there are no comprehensive views, no final conclusions and results. There is only the investigation and teaching which take place in the act of dogmatic work and which, strictly speaking, must continually begin again at the beginning in every point.[31]

This conviction "to begin again at the beginning" suggests openness by Barth toward viewing theology as ongoing conversation. Still, for Barth such open-endedness does not eliminate the possibility of dogmatic certainty. Rather, instead of equating theological certainty with *epistemological* certainty, Barth locates dogmatic certainty in the obedient act of "continually listening" to the Word of God.[32] Thus, in the "face of divine mystery, theology remains a thoroughly fallible enterprise, a ceaseless activity with neither resting place nor any fixed point of unerring certainty."[33]

Paul Tillich, more so than Barth, embraces the open-endedness of dogmatic claims and also recognizes the need to constantly reevaluate the church's propositions about God, which is why Tillich embraces symbolic and mythical language as the medium for communicating revelation: "Nothing less than symbols and myths can express our ultimate concern."[34] Tillich defends the role of myth while clarifying certain misunderstandings about the term:

A myth is a whole set of symbols expressing man's relation to that which concerns him ultimately, the ground and meaning of his life. Myth is more than a primitive world-view—with which Bultmann wrongly equates it; *it is the necessary and adequate expression of revelation.* In this I agree with Barth, who for some questionable terminological reasons calls it *"Sage"* (saga). But the question is, how can we preserve the truth and the power of the myth while recognizing its mythological character, its quality of being non-historical in the empirical sense?[35]

For Tillich, myth and symbol *are* the language of faith, since they are used to describe revelation, and as noumenal reality, revelation (God)

31. Karl Barth, *Church Dogmatics*, I.2, eds. G. W. Bromiley and T. F. Torrance (Edinburgh: T. & T. Clark, 1988), 868.
32. Ibid., 777.
33. Johnson, *The Mystery of God*, 3.
34. Tillich, *Dynamics of Faith*, 53.
35. Paul Tillich, "The Present Theological Situation in Light of the Continental European Development," *Theology Today* 6, no. 3 (Oct 1949): 306 (emphasis added).

stands outside human comprehension. In other words, human language—even analogical language—fails to adequately represent our
ultimate concern and ground of all being. Just as Barth's emphasis
on God's uncompromising transcendence opened him up to criticisms of espousing a revelational positivism—which this work argues
is a misreading of Barth's conception of the discipline of dogmatics as
open-ended and continually revised—Tillich's use of myth also needs
to be differentiated from the literal use of myth typical of fundamentalist readings of Scripture: "The resistance against demythologization
expresses itself in 'literalism.' The symbols and myths are understood in
their immediate meaning. The material, taken from nature and history,
is used in its proper sense. The character of the symbol to point beyond
itself to something else is disregarded."[36]

Contra literalism, Tillich and Barth both view the task of theology
as inherently hermeneutical insofar as myths properly understood communicate the experience of revelation, but no single reading of a myth
or symbol is suitable for all times and in all places since integral to the
human understanding of revelation is a change of perspective within the
believer—what Barth calls a new understanding—that takes place during the encounter with God in revelation. So, for example, Tillich chastises both Roman Catholicism and Protestantism for their inflexible use
of tradition or Scripture, respectively, in reviving old confessional divisions rather than acknowledging and embracing the interdependence
of Scripture and tradition as sources for systematic theology: "A way
must be found which lies between the Roman Catholic practice of making ecclesiastical decisions not only a source but also the actual norm
of systematic theology and the radical Protestant practice of depriving
church history not only of its normative character but also of its function as a source."[37] Analyzing his contemporary situation, Tillich develops a descriptive typology that views the church's efforts at imposing its
confessional culture on the broader society as a damaging *heteronomy*,
a set of "alien laws and languages that violate the dynamics and structures proper to human life," and the dominant culture's imposition of
its own internal structures and values as an equally disruptive *autonomy*,
which Mark K. Taylor has characterized as "a culture's celebration of
itself."[38] Neither extreme is conducive to the kind of rebuilding and
renewal both Barth and Tillich longed for in the midst of their postwar

36. Tillich, *Dynamics of Faith*, 51.
37. Tillich, *Systematic Theology*, vol. 1, 51.
38. Taylor, "Introduction: The Theological Development and Contribution of Paul Tillich," 17.

malaise, and according to Tillich "the structures imposing 'heteronomy' and the champions of 'autonomy' were both responsible for unleashing the destructive forces that had worked the end of the European civilization and ushered in the chaos of the war's aftermath."[39] Tillich's constructive proposal is to move beyond these warring extremes toward *theonomy*, understood as a harmonious unity between culture and God (or "ultimate concern") since autonomy and heteronomy "are rooted in theonomy, and each goes astray when their theonomous unity is broken. Theonomy does not mean the acceptance of a divine law imposed on reason by a highest authority; it means autonomous reason united with its own depth."[40] By this measure, religion is best understood as the "meaning-giving substance of culture, and culture is the totality of forms in which the basic concern or religion expresses itself. In abbreviation: religion is the substance of culture, culture is the form of religion."[41] Revelation presents answers to the transcendent questions posed by culture, yet every theological formulation is itself culturally specific, and so *less than* ultimate: "Every religious act, not only in organized religion, but also in the most intimate movement of the soul, is culturally formed."[42] In other words, like Barth, Tillich acknowledges and embraces the perspectivism and contextual limits of all theological traditions while affirming a divine transcendence underlying the world as we experience it. Yet, where Tillich differs from Barth—perhaps irreconcilably—is by advocating a method of correlation that seeks to make the Christian faith meaningful to the contemporary culture by virtue of the fact that humankind is ontologically united to infinity: "A symptom of both the essential unity and the existential separation of finite man from his infinity is his ability to ask about the infinite to which he belongs: the fact that he must ask about it indicates that he is separated from it."[43] Contra Barth, Tillich claims the "divine-human encounter is a correlation," a genuine and mutual interdependence that "means something real for both sides,"[44] whereas Barth stands firmly on the side of God as the sole agent in revelation: "it is nothing more nor less than a denial of Jesus Christ and blasphemy against the Holy Spirit, resembling the act of the servant who took and hid the talent entrusted to him, if

39. Ibid.
40. Tillich, *Systematic Theology*, vol. 1, 85.
41. Paul Tillich, "Aspects of a Religious Analysis of Culture," in *Theology of Culture*, ed. Robert C. Kimball (Oxford: Oxford University Press, 1959), 42.
42. Ibid.
43. Tillich, *Systematic Theology*, vol. 1, 61.
44. Ibid.

we try to value our incapacity more highly than the capacity which God
Himself in His revelation confers upon our incapacity."[45]

Without question, where Barth and Tillich—and those revelational
and anthropological theologies influenced by each one respectively—
part ways is over the possibility of unmediated, mutual communication
between human and divine. According to Barth, all divine self-
communication is inherently asymmetrical and one-sided, always originating in divine agency to the point that the very possibility of human
receptivity is itself an act of divine omnipotence. This follows from
Karl Barth's thoroughly christocentric and Chalcedonian formulation
in which the divine-human unity is located solely in the incarnation:

> It is God who absolutely precedes and man can only follow. Even as
> sovereign acts and words of God, as His free acts of rule, judgment,
> salvation, and revelation, these events are also human actions and
> passions, works and experiences, and *vice versa*. If in their Old Testa-
> ment presentation and attestation now one side and now the other is
> given prominence, there is a general acceptance of their coexistence
> and coinherence, of their basic unity, though without any confu-
> sion or mixture of the two elements, or transformation of the one
> into the other. And if this history in its totality and interconnection
> speaks as prophetic history it does so in attestation of this living
> divine-human unity. Its word is prophecy which combines rather
> than divides, which unites rather than separates, because it comes
> from the center and proclaims the center where what is above and
> what is below, transcendent God and lowly man, are together.[46]

There is no question of a divine-human unity as a vehicle for divine
revelation, but Barth makes it clear that such communication is not only
hierarchical and asymmetrical but unidirectional from on high as well:
"Those to whom Jesus Christ in calling them gives the freedom (*exousia*)
to become the children of God, so that His call does not return empty
but reaches its goal, are not those who are born of blood, nor of the
will of the flesh, nor of the will of man, but of God (John 1:12–13)."[47]
Accordingly, divine grace "thus fully over-rules our human volition and
achievement."[48]

45. Barth, *Church Dogmatics*, II.1, 201.
46. Karl Barth, *Church Dogmatics*, IV.3.1, ed. G. W. Bromiley and T. F. Torrance, trans. G. W. Bromiley (Edinburgh: T. & T. Clark, Ltd., 1961), 63.
47. Karl Barth, *Church Dogmatics*, IV.3.2, ed. G. W. Bromiley and T. F. Torrance, trans. G. W. Bromiley (Edinburgh: T. & T. Clark, Ltd., 1962), 521.
48. Karl Barth, *Church Dogmatics*, II.2, ed. G. W. Bromiley and T. F. Torrance. (Edinburgh: T. & T. Clark, Ltd.,
1957), 19.

For Barth, epistemologically and ontologically, revelation "remains revelation and does not become a revealed state,"[49] which not only fuels his antagonism with natural theology, but also differentiates his theology from Tillich's theocentric ontology in which the "being of God is being-itself."[50] According to Tillich, the discipline of dogmatic/systematic theology ought to be cognizant of this foundational reality:

> Since God is the ground of being, he is the ground of the structure of being. He is not subject to this structure; the structure is grounded in him. He *is* this structure, and it is impossible to speak about him except in terms of this structure. God must be approached cognitively through the structural elements of being-itself. These elements make him a living God, a God who can be man's concrete concern. They enable us to use symbols which we are certain point to the ground of reality.[51]

Simply put, according to Tillich there is no estrangement between theology and philosophy, and the primary task of philosophy—to understand the structure of being—is in essence indistinguishable from the primary task of theology—to understand God, who is being-itself. Thus,

> The semantic situation makes it evident that the language of the theologian cannot be a sacred or revealed language. He cannot restrict himself to the biblical terminology or to the language of classical theology. He could not avoid philosophical concepts even if he used only biblical words; and even less could he avoid them if he used only the words of the Reformers. Therefore, he should use philosophical and scientific terms whenever he deems them helpful for his task of explaining the contents of the Christian faith.[52]

Barth's discomfort with Tillich on this matter rests on Barth's assumption that human cognition is incapable of knowing God directly without divine mediation, while for Tillich knowledge of God is possible given humankind's essential being as the unity of "finitude with the infinity in which he was created."[53] Ironically, Tillich manifests the same naive foundational trust in the communicative power of symbols ("which we are certain point to the ground of reality") he accuses Barth of exhibiting toward the Bible as the nexus of divine self-revelation. Nevertheless,

49. Barth, *Church Dogmatics*, vol. I.2, 118.
50. Tillich, *Systematic Theology*, vol. 1, 235.
51. Ibid., 238.
52. Ibid., 55.
53. Ibid., 61.

Barth and Tillich agree that (1) in revelation God is objectively present for human beings, and (2) there are limits to the claims made by theological language, which is by nature symbolic: "Revelation means the giving of signs."[54] Consequently, in revelation we never know God directly, but the self-revealing God is always experienced as mystery—a *Deus absconditus* ("hidden God"): "knowledge of God in faith is always indirect knowledge of God."[55] Methodologically, both Barth and Tillich are committed to "the shaking of all and any systematic certainties," conceptualizing dogmatic claims as contextualized and provisional statements made in faith, since "in dogmatics strictly speaking there are no comprehensive views, no final conclusions and results."[56]

Ultimately, revelation is best understood as "God manifest," whether "manifest in himself, in creation, in the history of revelation, in the final revelation, in the Bible in the words of the church and her members."[57] Both Barth and Tillich reject any usurpation of God as revealer and revealed, labeling any theology as idolatrous that attempts to displace revelation through claims of absolutism and universality, yet both affirm God's revelation in Jesus the Christ as absolute and final. They are not speaking in contradictions; rather, both accept, in faith, that the "history of revelation" (the history of all human religions, in effect) finds its ultimate expression in the incarnation. In other words, in the unique and particular life of Jesus of Nazareth, God has revealed how God overcomes human estrangement and restores the relationship between Creator and creation in human history. Yet, rather than becoming an exclusivist religious claim, Barth and Tillich view the Christ event as the universal basis for all divine-human interaction. Not that all religions are mediated through Christianity, but that Christianity is the most accessible instantiation of the divine self-manifestation that, when properly understood, can guide our understanding of divine self-revelation in all traditions. In other words, theologians ought to proceed with humility and caution, fully aware that "no activity of the church can be carried through with the certainty that it expresses the Word. No minister should claim more than his intention to speak the Word when he preaches. He never should claim that he has spoken it or that he will be able to speak it in the future, for, since he has no power over the revelatory constellation, he possesses no power to

---

54. Barth, *Church Dogmatics*, II.1, 52.
55. Ibid., 17.
56. Barth, *Church Dogmatics*, I.2, 868.
57. Tillich, *Systematic Theology*, vol. 1, 159.

preach the Word."[58] Revelation is a divine possibility; the closest corresponding human reality is to *bear witness* to divine revelation, since
even the sacred Scriptures themselves are properly categorized as bearing witness to revelation: "We thus do the Bible poor and unwelcome
honour if we equate it directly with this other, with revelation itself."[59]
Accordingly, even Scripture as the written Word becomes relativized in
relation to the living Word, Jesus Christ: "His own coming is the end
to which in its supreme consummation, in its form as God's promise,
the covenant fulfilled by Him, the reconciliation of the world with
God accomplished by Him, can only move and point as to something
beyond itself."[60] Which is why Tillich is critical of traditional confessional theologies that wield Scripture and tradition as weapons to
coerce followers into accepting rigid orthodoxies (theological totalitarianism), when in fact no theological formulation is final and absolute,
not even the canon of Scripture: "It is the Spirit which has created the
canon, and, like all things Spiritual, the canon cannot be fixed legally
in a definite way. The partial openness of the canon is a safeguard of the
Spirituality of the Christian church."[61]

2.3 WHAT IS SCRIPTURE? SOME COMPETING PERSPECTIVES

Wilfred Cantwell Smith, in his landmark comparative study of sacred
Scriptures *What Is Scripture?* (1993), cautions believers when we use
the word Scripture, "we give the impression, even to ourselves that
there is understanding of what the term means; that we all know what
Scripture is. On reflection, it turns out that this is hardly the case."[62]
To reflect on the nature of Scripture opens the door to a plethora of
unanswered critical questions: Is Scripture divine in origin? Or is it a
text written by human authors? If the latter, is the writing of Scripture inspired by God? What about the interpretation of Scripture—is
that also inspired? Is Scripture authoritative? If so, what is the role of
Scripture in organizing human societies? The history of the Christian

---

58. Ibid.
59. Barth, *Church Dogmatics* I.1, 112.
60. Karl Barth, *Church Dogmatics*, IV.1, ed. G. W. Bromiley and T. F. Torrance, trans. G. W. Bromiley (Edinburgh: T. & T. Clark, Ltd., 1956), 117.
61. Tillich, *Systematic Theology*, vol. 1, 51.
62. Wilfred Cantwell Smith, *What Is Scripture? A Comparative Approach*, 2nd ed. reprint (Minneapolis, MN:
Fortress Press, 1993), 1.

tradition contains a wealth of diverse views on the nature and role of
Scripture, from the early Christian synthesis of the literal meaning of
the text alongside typological, allegorical, and spiritual readings (in the
works of such patristic theologians as Origen and Augustine, all the way
through to the medieval exegesis of Aquinas), to the Reformation era
polemical debates on the relationship of tradition to Scripture, to challenges concerning the reliability of Scripture as historical sources posed
by historical-critical methods in the nineteenth and twentieth centuries, every generation of theologians has had to establish to what extent
Scripture is authoritative for Christian thought. Although theologians
are far from reaching a consensus on these very complex issues, in general theologians as diverse as Barth and Tillich can nonetheless agree
that the term "Scripture" applies to those texts recognized as sacred
and authoritative for the Christian community because they bear "witness to the drama of redemption in both the history of Israel and the
life, death, and resurrection of Jesus Christ."[63] This book's comparative analysis of the revelational (Barth) and anthropological (Tillich)
approaches to constructive theology, by intentionally embracing a postfoundationalist theological epistemology, argues that consensus on the
issue of Scripture's authority, and its application to the contemporary
situation, is not an attainable, or even desirable, goal of theological
work. Rather, by recognizing the localized and contextual quality of *all*
theological narratives—from the texts of Scripture to the most elaborate systematic theologies—this work honors the simple fact that "each
moment, era, and epoch raises different questions about the nature,
authority, and interpretation of Scripture, and how Scripture relates to
tradition, reason, and experience."[64] The resulting conception of systematic theology is one that views the history of Christianity as a series
of local theologies grounded in and inspired by the historical "Christ
event," each engaged in critical discourse with one another, that when
taken together form an intricate mosaic that provides a shared vision of
the Christian faith, while acknowledging that no single tradition is the
privileged interpreter of this event. Accordingly, as the human quest for
knowledge of God, theology cannot have the "last word" on God but
must propose answers to the questions of faith that are always *provisional*, with the understanding that dogmatic claims must continually
undergo self-criticism in light of the Word of God.

63. Justin S. Holcomb, "Introduction: Mapping Theologies of Scripture," in *Christian Theologies of Scripture: A Comparative Introduction*, ed. Justin S. Holcomb (New York: New York University Press, 2006), 2.
64. Ibid., 3.

Theologians, from the premodern era to the present, have recognized the biggest difficulty in speaking about God is what Søren Kierkegaard calls the "infinite qualitative difference" between Creator and creature. Language about God, in both biblical texts (Job 38:1–40:2; Phil. 4:7) and early patristic theological formulations (Justin thought it impossible to give a name to the "ineffable" God), has always emphasized God's transcendence. If God is "wholly other," the miracle of revelation is that through God's grace we can nonetheless conceive God in God's "inconceivability." Over against this Barthian conception of revelation, Tillich questions if God is so radically distinguished from God's creation, then how can believers say anything "meaningful" about God to nonbelievers, or confront beliefs about God that are contrary to the received tradition? Once revelation is conceived as event or encounter, it raises critical questions about the relationship of revelation to Scripture: Are sacred Scriptures revelation, or merely a witness to revelation? Following both Barth and Tillich, this investigation affirms that the Bible is not revelation itself but a witness to revelation. Furthermore, this work also asserts that it is through an act of God's grace by the Holy Spirit that the Bible becomes a revelational event for the reader. By emphasizing these points, the hope is to move beyond the impasse between these two dominant schools of thought—the revelational and anthropological— toward an alternative constructive proposal that embraces theology's need to address the broader public beyond the church, affirms the need for speaking from within one's own particular theological tradition, yet takes seriously God's concrete and objective presence in human history.

John Calvin, arguably Karl Barth's theological precursor, provides a pneumatological entryway into this transgenerational conversation by describing the role of grace in facilitating the reading and comprehension of Scripture: "Those whom the Holy Spirit has inwardly taught truly rest upon Scripture, and the Scripture indeed is self-authenticated; hence, it is not right to subject it to proof and reasoning. And the certainty it deserves with us, it attains by the testimony of the Spirit."[65] Much like Kierkegaard's concerns about the irrelevance contemporaneity to the historical event of revelation has in the process of coming to faith (see previous chapter), Calvin understands that coming to accept Jesus' words as truthful and authoritative rests primarily with God. During his lifetime many people heard Jesus speak and witnessed his miraculous acts, yet not all who witnessed these events walked away

---

65. Calvin, *Institutes of the Christian Religion*, 1.7.5.

convinced Jesus was the Messiah, the Son of God, and God in the flesh. The notion of the internal, secret witness of the Spirit underlying the authority of Scripture is one of Calvin's major contributions to Western Christian thought. For Calvin, "the Word and Spirit belong inseparably together," though this "inner witness/testimony does not *prove* that the Bible is the Word of God; nor does it *establish* the authority of the Word."[66] Rather, "by the internal witness of the Spirit the authority of Scripture is *confirmed* and *authenticated* for the believer."[67] In terms that bring to mind Kierkegaard's argument about the failure of historical-critical method, Hesselink summarizes Calvin's position on the inward witness of the Holy Spirit: "no amount of argumentation will convince anyone that the Bible is the very Word of God."[68] Calvin's doctrine of the Word of God prioritizes Scripture above church and tradition, identifying Scripture as the primary means of God's self-revelation and the sole means of avoiding doctrinal error:

> Just as old or bleary-eyed men and those with weak vision, if you thrust before them a most beautiful volume, even if they recognize it to be some sort of writing, yet can scarcely construe two words, but with the aid of spectacles will begin to read distinctly; so Scripture, gathering up the otherwise confused knowledge of God in our minds, having dispersed our dullness, clearly shows us the true God. This, therefore, is a special gift, where God, to instruct the church, not merely uses mute teachers but also opens his own most hallowed lips.[69]

While neither Barth nor Tillich place the same level of trust in our capacity to read and interpret Scripture without error as does Calvin, they both agree with Calvin that the "proof of Scripture" rests with the secret testimony of the Spirit:

> [T]he testimony of the Spirit is more excellent than all reason. For as God alone is a fit witness of himself in his Word, so also the Word will not find acceptance in men's hearts before it is sealed by the inward testimony of the Spirit. The same Spirit, therefore, who has spoken through the mouths of the prophets must penetrate into our hearts to persuade us that they faithfully proclaimed what has been divinely commanded.[70]

66. I. John Hesselink, "Calvin, Theologian of the Holy Spirit," in *Calvin's First Catechism: A Commentary* (Louisville, KY: Westminster John Knox Press, 1997), 180.
67. Ibid., 181.
68. Ibid.
69. Calvin, *Institutes of the Christian Religion*, 1.6.1.
70. Ibid., 1.7.4.

For Barth, "the work of the Holy Spirit in revelation is a work which can be ascribed only to God and which is thus expressly ascribed to God."[71] In other words, it is "only by the continual bestowal of grace that God is knowable at all."[72]

Admittedly, on the surface this appears a circular argument, insofar as the Bible is accepted as Word of God by an act of the Spirit, yet belief that the Spirit acts in this way is itself grounded in the witness of Scripture (John 16:12–13; Acts 1:6–8). Nevertheless, despite this circularity, the claim made by Calvin, Kierkegaard, Barth, and others is not that we are then left with a rationally indefensible fideistic statement. Rather, if we are to talk rationally about the act of divine self-revelation, we need to accept that on some level the content and authority of revelation rests with the revealer by whose grace it is accepted in faith by human beings. And here, as demonstrated above, Barth and Tillich stand on similar ground. This does not make the content of revelation mere subjective opinion, but it does limit the means by which theology can defend and justify claims grounded in revelation. Ultimately, theology is burdened with the task of making truth claims about God and God's will for humankind intelligible to believers and unbelievers alike, yet it is limited as to the kind of evidence it can offer on behalf of these truth claims to those outside the faith. There is a wide range of views on Scripture, its authority, and how it is interpreted within the Christian tradition, but as argued throughout this work, the tendency within academic theology, in both seminaries and universities, is to classify theological methodologies under one of two categories—either the more church-centered revelational approach or the more anthropocentric theologies of culture.

Karl Barth stands as the most influential advocate of the revelational approach, who not only influenced postliberal narrative theologies, but also informs the contemporary Radical Orthodoxy movement. According to Bruce McCormack, "Barth's view is that human language in itself has no capacity for bearing adequate witness to God."[73] Consequently, Scripture is understood as *Deus dixit*—God has spoken—in such a way that the gracious and sovereign God elevates human language in order to enable it to bear witness to the divine self-revelation: "God unveils Himself by veiling Himself in human language. In truth, the

---

71. Barth, *Church Dogmatics* I.1, 467.
72. George Hunsinger, *How to Read Karl Barth: The Shape of His Theology* (Oxford: Oxford University Press, 1991), 67.
73. McCormack, *Karl Barth's Critically Realistic Dialectical Theology*, 17.

Realdialektik of veiling and unveiling is the motor which drives Barth's doctrine of analogy and makes it possible."[74] Thus, in reading and interpreting Scripture, Barth employs both a dialectical method "which calls for every theological statement to be placed over against a counter-statement, without allowing the dialectical tension between the two to be resolved in a higher synthesis,"[75] and the *analogia fidei,* or "analogy of faith," which "refers most fundamentally to a relation of correspondence between an act of God and an act of a human subject; the act of divine self-revelation and the human act of faith in which that revelation is acknowledged."[76] Technically, Barth does not view the *analogia fidei* as a theological method, but as the only possible human way of describing, or witnessing the *Deus dixit.* Given that revelation not only begins with God, but that our very capacity to understand the analogy is itself a gift from God, epistemologically knowledge of God is simply an act of obedience: "human knowledge is made by grace to conform to its divine object."[77] Thus, for Barth the whole of the canon, both Old and New Testaments, is read christologically, thereby preserving a unified narrative with Jesus the Christ at its center despite objections from biblical scholars, many of whom view the Bible as a collection of disparate sources. While Barth finds some value in the contributions of historical-critical methods, ultimately he sees the whole of Scripture as a history or narrative account of God's work of reconciliation in and through Christ such that "all the concepts and ideas used in this report (God, man, world, eternity, time, even salvation, grace, transgression, atonement and any others) can derive their significance only from the bearer of this name and from His history, and not the reverse. . . . They can serve only to describe this name—the name of Jesus Christ."[78] As far as Barth is concerned, rather than allowing the issues of the day to guide our exegesis or conforming our interpretations to fit secular modes of thought, there is only one definitive direction of interpretation: Scripture interprets the world (to paraphrase Lindbeck). Not that Barth is unconcerned with the concrete realities in which we live, since he clearly practiced a socially and culturally engaged Christianity ("Take your Bible and take your newspaper, and read both. But interpret newspapers from your Bible."[79]), but such exegesis "should

---

74. Ibid., 18.
75. Ibid., 11.
76. Ibid., 16–77.
77. Ibid., 17.
78. Barth, *Church Dogmatics,* IV.1, 16–17.
79. Karl Barth, from an interview in *Time* magazine (Friday, May 31, 1963).

and must be carried out in serene confidence that it will in fact do this; but it must be left to Holy Scripture to decide how far it does so."[80] In other words, we must always resist the temptation to impose our own interpretation onto Scripture and instead develop the art of listening to Scripture since, while the Bible is itself not revelation, it is still our most reliable witness to divine self-revelation: "In this very specific sense, then, the Bible is the first mediation and norm, the standard or principle of all communication, the historical basis of all experience, the salutary caveat that must be set over against all experience."[81]

In contrast with Barth, Paul Tillich stands as the staunchest advocate of the anthropological approach, since in "advocating the method of correlation, Tillich charts a course which Barth refuses."[82] The goal of this correlational method is to make the Christian faith meaningful to the contemporary culture, and this is possible because the use of correlation,

> qualifies the divine-human relationship within religious experience. The third use of correlative thinking in theology has evoked the protest of theologians such as Karl Barth, who are afraid that any kind of divine-human correlation makes God partly dependent on man. But although God in his abysmal nature is in no way dependent on man, God in his self-manifestation to man is dependent on the way man receives his manifestation.[83]

Though like Barth he grants that knowledge of God originates in a divine act, and that the Scriptures serve as a reliable witness to this divine revelation, unlike Barth, Tillich affirms a mutuality between human and divine that makes correlation possible: "it makes an analysis of the human situation out of which the existential questions arise, and it demonstrates that the symbols used in the Christian message are the answers to these questions."[84] Despite Barth's misapprehensions, Tillich actually cites Calvin's opening sentences of the *Institutes of the Christian Religion* (1549) in defense of this method of correlation: "Nearly all the wisdom we possess, that is to say, true and sound wisdom, consists of two parts: the knowledge of God and of ourselves. But, while joined by many bonds, which one precedes and brings forth the other is not easy

---

80. Barth, *Church Dogmatics*, I.2, 738.
81. Karl Barth, *The Göttingen Dogmatics*, vol. 1, trans. G. W. Bromiley, ed. Hannelotte Reiffen (Grand Rapids, MI: Wm. B. Eerdmans Publishing Co., 1991), 216.
82. Paul L. Allen, *Theological Method: A Guide for the Perplexed* (London: T. & T.Clark, 2012), 183.
83. Tillich, *Systematic Theology*, vol. 1, 61.
84. Ibid., 62.

to discern."[85] While the Bible remains a source of theological reflection, Tillich asserts that the proper object of theology is not God but "the symbols given by the original revelatory experiences and by the traditions based on them."[86] By extension, the whole of the Bible is a collection of texts rich in symbolic power, so the task of theology is not to demythologize religious language but to analyze and interpret these symbols as symbols, since the most appropriate way of speaking about our "ultimate concern" is through metaphorical language:

> Anthropomorphic symbols are adequate for speaking of God religiously. Only in this way can he be the living God for man. But even in the most primitive intuition of the divine a feeling should be, and usually is, present that there is a mystery about divine names which makes them improper, self-transcending, symbolic. Religious instruction should deepen this feeling without depriving the divine names of their reality and power. One of the most surprising qualities of the prophetic utterances in the Old Testament is that, on the one hand, they always appear concrete and anthropomorphic and that, on the other hand, they preserve the mystery of the divine ground. . . . Nothing is more inadequate and disgusting than the attempt to translate the concrete symbols of the Bible into less concrete and less powerful symbols.[87]

So, for example, rather than simply viewing the New Testament as a historical record of the life of Jesus of Nazareth, or even as a confessional statement by the followers of Jesus, Tillich explores the meaning of the symbol "the Christ" in order to establish a christological "rule" by which to interpret the life of "Jesus who is the Christ":

> Jesus as the Christ is both a historical fact and a subject of believing reception. One cannot speak the truth about the event on which Christianity is based without asserting both sides. . . . If theology ignores the fact to which the name Jesus of Nazareth points, it ignores the basic Christian assertion that Essential God-Manhood has appeared within existence and subjected itself to the conditions of existence without being conquered by them.[88]

Despite their differences, there are multiple overlaps between Barth's theology of crisis and Tillich's correlational theology, in great part due

85. Calvin, *Institutes of the Christian Religion*, 1.1.1.
86. Tillich, *Systematic Theology*, vol. 3, 201.
87. Tillich, *Systematic Theology*, vol. 1, 242.
88. Tillich, *Systematic Theology*, vol. 2, 97.

to the influence that Kierkegaard's understanding of Christianity as a religion of transcendence had on both their thought.

Yet Tillich moves beyond Barth in emphasizing the role of the Spirit in articulating "a broader view of revelation."[89] Critiquing those sixteenth-century Reformers who rejected experience as a source of revelation, Tillich embraces those traditions descended from "Evangelical enthusiasm" (like the global Pentecostal movement) that "derived new revelations from the presence of the Spirit."[90] This unmediated experience of the Spirit does not transcend "the Christian message," as critics of the spiritual enthusiasts often contend, but is, in fact, the ultimate ground of revelation: "The experience of the man who has the Spirit is the source of religious truth and therefore of systematic theology. The letter of the Bible and the doctrines of the church remain letter and law if the Spirit does not interpret them in the individual Christian. Experience as the inspiring presence of the Spirit is the ultimate source of theology."[91]

Undoubtedly, Tillich distances himself from Barth by defining the task of constructive theology more broadly than Barth's christocentric focus allows:

> The encounter with great non-Christian religions, the evolutionary scheme of thought, the openness for the new which characterizes the pragmatic method, have had the consequence that experience has become not only the main source of systematic theology but an inexhaustible source out of which new truths can be taken continually. Being open for new experiences which might even pass beyond the confines of Christian experience is now the proper attitude of the theologian.[92]

Still, though methodologically committed to a thoroughly christocentric (while still Trinitarian) doctrine of revelation, Barth stands with Calvin in recognizing and affirming the work of the Holy Spirit *wherever* it is located:

> Whenever we come upon these matters in secular writers, let that admirable light of truth shining in them teach us that the mind of man, though fallen and perverted from its wholeness, is nevertheless clothed and ornamented with God's excellent gifts. If we regard the Spirit of God as the sole fountain of truth, we shall neither reject the

89. Tillich, *Systematic Theology*, vol. 1, 127.
90. Ibid., 45.
91. Ibid.
92. Ibid.

truth itself, nor despise it *wherever it shall appear*, unless we wish to dishonor the Spirit of God.[93]

Thus, it would be a mistake to conclude that Barth's christological exclusivism prevents him from recognizing and affirming legitimate truth-claims in non-Christian sources: Barth is not a fundamentalist—not even a biblicist. At worst, he can be charged with cultural paternalism for affirming the universality of divine revelation *exclusively* through the Christ event:

> Jesus Christ is the hope of all men, and therefore also of non-Christians, of the heathen, of the theoretically or practically ungodly. . . . He is the hope of these others too. And supposing more importance is attached to those who are not yet Christians? . . . Supposing His light shines brighter here, and His Word is more living and active? Supposing the unconverted are sometimes dearer to Him than the converted? Supposing the knowledge of Jesus Christ which divides Christians from non-Christians, when imparted to the latter in fulfillment of the promise seriously given to the heathen too, brings forth among them more rich and varied and useful fruits than among those who already know Him, so that the last are first and the first last? Supposing the Christian is deceived when he adjudges his fellow a non-Christian, because the knowledge of Jesus Christ has already found a lodging in him in a form which the Christian and perhaps the man himself does not recognize? Supposing, finally, the Christian is deceived as to his own Christianity, being more of a non-Christian than a Christian, and basically perhaps not really being a Christian at all? In face of these by no means irrelevant questions the Christian should be glad that he lives under the lordship of Jesus Christ who is the hope even of those who are not for Him as He is for them, and under the promise, and in the power of the promise, which is also given to non-Christians of every kind."[94]

One finds a similarly paternalistic view of religious pluralism in his Roman Catholic contemporary Karl Rahner's notion of the Anonymous Christian:

> Anonymous Christianity means that a person lives in the grace of God and attains salvation outside of explicitly constituted Christianity—Let us say, a Buddhist monk—who, because he follows his

---

93. Calvin, *Institutes of the Christian Religion*, 2.2.15 (emphasis added).
94. Karl Barth, *Church Dogmatics*, IV.3.1, ed. G. W. Bromiley and T. F. Torrance (Edinburgh: T. & T. Clark, Ltd., 1961), 364–65.

conscience, attains salvation and lives in the grace of God; of him I must say that he is an anonymous Christian; if not, I would have to presuppose that there is a genuine path to salvation that really attains that goal, but that simply has nothing to do with Jesus Christ. But I cannot do that. And so, if I hold if everyone depends upon Jesus Christ for salvation, and if at the same time I hold that many live in the world who have not expressly recognized Jesus Christ, then there remains in my opinion nothing else but to take up this postulate of an anonymous Christianity.[95]

The previously cited extended passage from the *Church Dogmatics* is particularly relevant for understanding Barth's conception of theological truth, since it affirms the Spirit's role as a potential avenue for interfaith dialogue and cooperation insofar as the possibility exists for the non-Christian—*as a non-Christian*—to receive divine revelation given that the phrase "than among those who already know Him" implies those receiving the fruits of the Spirit do not yet know Christ. Both Barth and Tillich became more interested in the question of other religions late in their lives, and there is in their works a framework for not only articulating a theology of religions, as in Barth's language of "secular parables of the kingdom,"[96] but also perhaps a means for engaging in explicitly comparative theology. This, at least, is the direction suggested by Paul Tillich's last public lecture, given at the divinity school at the University of Chicago in 1965, in which he, like Barth, attempts to speak to the universality of divine revelation in all religions while still speaking from a distinctly Christian location: "The universality of a religious statement does not lie in an all-embracing abstraction which would destroy religion as such but in the depths of every concrete religion. Above all, it lies in the openness to spiritual freedom both from one's own foundation and for one's own foundation."[97] As has been argued throughout this chapter, both Barth and Tillich share a common understanding of God's self-revelation as a transcendent yet objectively real encounter with humanity that, despite methodological divergences, views all theological traditions as witnesses to revelation without equating any single tradition with revelation itself. Consequently, theological truth-claims are made cautiously and with great

95. Karl Rahner, with Paul Imhof and Hubert Biallowons, *Karl Rahner in Dialogue: Conversations and Interviews, 1965–1982*, ed. Paul Imhof, Hubert Biallowons, and Harvey D. Egan (New York: Crossroad Publishing, 1986), 207.
96. See Barth, *Church Dogmatics*, IV.3.1, §69.2; also see Hunsinger, *How to Read Karl Barth*, 234–80.
97. Paul Tillich, "The Significance of the History of Religions for the Systematic Theologian," in *Paul Tillich: Theologian of the Boundaries*, ed. by Mark Kline Taylor (Minneapolis, MN: Fortress Press, 1991), 323.

humility in recognition of the fact that all too often church doctrines reveal more about the community in which they originate (Lindbeck) than they reveal about the God to whom they purportedly witness.

2.4 PAST THE IMPASSE: A PNEUMATOLOGICAL PROPOSAL

Reformed theologian Jürgen Moltmann, though heavily influenced by the theology of Karl Barth, has drawn inspiration from the ecumenical dialogue with Orthodox churches and the growing influence of the global Pentecostal movement to reclaim a pneumatological perspective for theological construction that corrects the tendency within "established" churches to fear religious "free thinking," whether in the "patristic pneumatology of the Orthodox church," the "Pentecostal experiences of the young churches," or even the "rationalism and pietism of the Enlightenment [that] was every bit as Enthusiastic as Pentecostal Christianity today."[98] Moltmann describes Barth's revelational approach as "an alternative which today is proving unfruitful," suggesting that by so strongly emphasizing the asymmetry of the divine-human relationship to the point that "there is no continuity between Creator and what he has created," Barth undermines the very possibility of divine self-communication.[99] Thus, despite a strong pneumatological aspect to Barth's Trinitarian doctrine of revelation, by imposing an artificial "antithesis between revelation and experience," Barth—and those revelational theologies informed by his thought—end up "with revelations that cannot be experienced, and experiences without revelation."[100] On this issue Moltmann is closer to Tillich, who identifies the work of the Spirit with the believer's experience despite hesitations that to "begin with experience may sound subjective, arbitrary and fortuitous," arguing that the believer's experience of the Spirit implies "an awareness of God in, with and beneath the experience of life, which gives us assurance of God's fellowship, friendship and love."[101]

This work has consistently argued that despite their methodological differences, Barth and Tillich stand on similar ground, both conceiving divine revelation as an encounter with the divine mediated by the Holy Spirit such that rather than conveying an objective cognitive

98. Jürgen Moltmann, *The Spirit of Life: A Universal Affirmation*, trans. Margaret Kohl (Minneapolis, MN: Fortress Press, 1992), 2.
99. Ibid., 5, 6.
100. Ibid., 7.
101. Ibid., 17.

content (i.e., predicate statements about God), revelation is best understood as an interpersonal encounter. Revelation is not a *what* but *who*.
Accordingly, it becomes necessary to move past the stalemate created by
dominant theologies that continue to view this divine-human encounter in terms of irreconcilable polarities—divine-human, Christ-culture,
revelation-experience—in order to articulate a theology of the Holy
Spirit that validates the experience of God without which there is no
knowledge of God: "There are no words of God without human experiences of God's Spirit. So the words of proclamation spoken by the
Bible and the church must also be related to the experiences of people
today, so they are not—as Karl Rahner said—merely 'hearers of the
Word,' but become spokesmen of the Word too."[102]

Not only does this recovery of religious experience and the work
of the Spirit allow for greater ecumenical cooperation as Mark Heim,
Raimundo Panikkar, and Gavin D'Costa have argued, retrieving the
Christian doctrine of the Trinity is crucial for "interpreting the theological significance of religious diversity."[103] According to Heim, the
doctrine of the Trinity cultivates a methodological humility among
theologians by reminding them that the "fullness of God's mystery is
never grasped by us. It is hidden in the Father and source, overflows in
Christ beyond the measure of our means to receive it, and is continually active in all of creation through the Spirit."[104] Trinitarian thought,
by emphasizing the role of the Holy Spirit in God's act of self-revelation
in Christ, opens the Christian faith to the possibility of encountering
the Spirit in other religions: "The wind blows where it chooses, and
you hear the sound of it, but you do not know where it comes from or
where it goes. So it is with everyone who is born of the Spirit" (John
3:8). Consequently, if "Christians confess the coeternality of the Spirit
and stand equally under the Spirit's judgment, then the conviction that
the Spirit works in other faiths makes relations with those faiths vital
and not incidental for Christians."[105]

This pneumatological starting point makes comparative theology a
viable option, even in Karl Barth's christologically exclusivist approach,
since he recognizes that "Jesus is the light of life" while also acknowledging

---

102. Ibid., 3.
103. S. Mark Heim, *Salvations: Truth and Difference in Religion* (Maryknoll, NY: Orbis Books, 1995), 166. See
Gavin D'Costa, *Theology and Religious Pluralism* (Oxford: Oxford University Press, 1986), and "Christ, the Trinity,
and Religious Plurality," in *Christian Uniqueness Reconsidered: Myth of Pluralistic Theology of Religions*, ed. by Gavin
D'Costa (Maryknoll, NY: Orbis Books, 1990), 16–29; Raimundo Panikkar, *The Trinity and the Religious Experience
of Man* (Maryknoll, NY: Orbis Books, 1973).
104. Ibid., 167.
105. Ibid.

"other" lights exist.[106] For Barth, Jesus Christ is the unique revelation of God, which "means that there is no other light of life outside or along his,"[107] yet he consistently affirms that divine revelation "is not restricted to his working on and in prophets and apostles. . . . His capacity transcends the limits of this sphere."[108] In other words, it remains possible to proclaim the uniqueness of Jesus Christ as the one Word of God while also affirming the possibility of other avenues of divine revelation. Furthermore, since "the Trinity also discloses loving relationship as the fundamental mode of being, love of neighbor is an imperative for Christians. If Christ is understood in trinitarian terms, then the self-giving love of Jesus is normative for believers, requiring dialogue and justice-making."[109] The role of the Spirit in allowing the one Word of God to be heard in various religious contexts is most obvious in the early church's interaction with the traditional religion of Israel as the church sought to affirm the radical monotheism at the heart of biblical Judaism (Deut. 6:4–5) while making sense of the incarnation of God in Jesus Christ (John 1:9–14). Thus, Heim concludes: "The Trinity *is* Christianity's 'pluralistic theology.' Its basis was set by the disciples' conviction that their encounter with Jesus could be correlated with the encounter with Israel's one God and with the new life they experienced within and among themselves as a result of Jesus."[110]

Christian theology does not speak about God abstractly but speaks in concrete terms because the sacred Scriptures of the Christian faith—the Hebrew Bible, called the Old Testament in the Christian tradition, and the New Testament, together comprising a *single* history of God's relationship with humanity that encompasses both the people of Israel and the Church—present a consistent witness. Answering the questions, "Who is God?" and "What is God like?" Christian theology is confronted by the mystery of a God who remains hidden even in the process of revealing God's self. This inherent incommunicability of the divine nature is attested by the doctrine of the Trinity, in which the church has attempted to put into words the mystery of God's grace as revealed in the Christ who is present by the power of the Holy Spirit. As with all theological

106. Barth, *Church Dogmatics* IV.3.1, 86.
107. Ibid.
108. Ibid., 118.
109. Heim, *Salvations*, 167.
110. S. Mark Heim, *The Depth of the Riches: A Trinitarian Theology of Religious Ends* (Grand Rapids, MI: Wm. B. Eerdmans Publishing Co., 2001), 133 (emphasis added). For a constructive theological proposal advocating the Trinity as a framework for religious tolerance and cooperation from an Evangelical perspective, see Gerald R. McDermott and Harold A. Netland, *A Trinitarian Theology of Religions: An Evangelical Proposal* (Oxford: Oxford University Press, 2014).

constructions, Trinitarian doctrine proves inadequate at communicating the fullness of divine reality yet has become an integral part of the ecumenical creeds of the church because it has been deemed an appropriate—if ultimately wanting—conceptualization of God as revealed and encountered in the New Testament. In other words, the concrete and distinctly "Christian" way of speaking about the one true God by referencing God the Father, Creator and sovereign over all creation; Jesus the Son, the Christ of God through whom sinful humanity is redeemed before God; and the Holy Spirit, by whose efforts God's revelation is received and the true God known (Mark 1:10; Matt. 3:16–17; 28:19; 1 John 5:7), lends itself to the discursive model of theology as an open-ended, continually revised human undertaking, which implies that "the experiences of God must not be restricted to controlled religious forms."[111]

111. Moltmann, *The Spirit of Life*, 267.

3

Postmodern Babylon

"We are always already in the presence of an absolute mystery. . . . But for the Christian, that revelation (as self-manifestation of God) has in fact occurred in the free and decisive event called Jesus Christ—a position explicated in systematic theology."

—David Tracy[1]

The discipline of systematic (or constructive) theology needs to adapt to the increasing diversity within Christian religious thought while simultaneously contending with the realities of religious pluralism in global context and the prevailing secularism within the academy. This chapter examines the parameters upon which new, post-Enlightenment, twenty-first-century dogmatics ought to embark. Acknowledging that both Tillich and Barth became concerned with the problem of other religions in their later work, and recognizing the need for a theological accounting of the realities of religious pluralism, this book argues for a Christian systematic theology that is both comparative and inclusive, and recommends the doctrine of the Holy Spirit (pneumatology) as a natural starting point for such a project. While the dominant theological traditions of Europe and North America have, until recently, played a normative role in the doctrine and practice of world Christianity, the contextual theologies of Asia, Africa, and Latin America—along with marginalized theologies within Europe and North America—stand as guideposts for overcoming the stalemate between secular and theological modes of reasoning. By rejecting the notion of a singular Christian tradition within the global church, third-world theologies are articulating an alternative to the modernist epistemologies dominating the

---

1. David Tracy, *The Analogical Imagination: Christian Theology and the Culture of Pluralism* (New York: Crossroad, 1981), 162.

academy, offering in its stead God's preferential option for the poor, oppressed, and powerless.[2]

3.1 BEYOND THE THEOLOGIES OF WORD AND CULTURE

David Tracy's theology is characterized by its hermeneutical approach; its driving concerns appear to be the same challenges of modernity and secularism motivating Karl Barth and Paul Tillich's earlier efforts: "In a culture of pluralism must each religious tradition finally either dissolve into some lowest common denominator or accept a marginal existence as one interesting but purely private opinion?"[3] On the surface, Tracy seems to favor Tillich's anthropocentric method so his theology can be described as a theology of culture. Yet his description of the task of the theologian as interpreter of "the religious classic" manages to preserve the "concrete and objective presence" (*Gegenständlichkeit*) of God, affirming the transcendent and divine source of revelation: "Any act of interpretation involves at least three realities: some phenomenon to be interpreted, someone interpreting that phenomenon, and some interaction between these first two realities."[4] Tracy describes this revelational "phenomenon" by employing the language of interpersonal encounter:

> Authentic religious experience, on the testimony of those all consider clearly religious, seems to be some experience of the whole that is sensed as the self-manifestation of an undeniable power not one's own and is articulated not in the language of certainty and clarity but of scandal and mystery. The religious person does not claim a new control upon reality but speaks of losing former controls and experiencing, not merely affirming, a liberation into a realm of ultimate incomprehensibility and real, fascinating and frightening mystery. When religious persons speak the language of revelation, they

---

2. See Rubén Rosario Rodríguez, "Liberating Epistemology: Wikipedia and the Social Construction of Knowledge," *Journal of Religion and Theology* 26, no. 2 (2007): 173–201. In this article I argue that the work of human liberation is better served by liberating epistemology from the more authoritarian aspects of the Enlightenment scientific tradition—especially popular positivist conceptions of rationality. A similar approach is explored and developed by Pope Francis I in his apostolic exhortation, *Evangelii Gaudium* ("Joy of the Gospel"), in which Francis links the *sensus fidei* ("sense of the faith") with the lives and experience of the poor: "Each individual Christian and every community is called to be an instrument of God for the liberation and promotion of the poor, and for enabling them to be fully a part of society. This demands that we be docile and attentive to the cry of the poor and to come to their aid" (paragraph 187), http://w2.vatican.va/content/francesco/en/apost_exhortations /documents/papa-francesco_esortazione-ap_20131124_evangelii-gaudium.html.

3. Tracy, *The Analogical Imagination*, ix.

4. David Tracy, *Plurality and Ambiguity: Hermeneutics, Religion, Hope*, reprint (Chicago: The University of Chicago Press, 1994), 10.

mean that something has happened to them that they cannot count as their own achievement.[5]

Despite affirming the transcendent yet concrete and objective encounter communicated by the religious classic, in employing this literary category Tracy remains stuck at the impasse separating the revelational theologies of the Word (Barth and his methodological kin) and the anthropological theologies of culture (Tillich and his methodological kin), insofar as for Tracy human understanding always and only "occurs in linguistic form."[6] Furthermore, by emphasizing the inadequacy of language to capture these foundational limit experiences, Tracy paints a picture of the theologian as an almost impotent player within the broader pluralist conversation: "Theologians can never claim certainty but, at best, highly tentative relative adequacy."[7]

Therefore, while theologians have a "responsibility for authentically public discourse" and "should be held accountable for the plausibility or implausibility of their advice,"[8] this involves a high level of personal risk—and potential ridicule—since, unlike the scholar of religion, "every theologian is engaged in making claims to meaning and truth."[9] Granted, while contemporary scholarship recognizes that all scholars of religion make normative claims, the modernist assumption prevalent in academia asserts "theology" is distinguished from "religious studies" by the latter's methodological commitment to scholarly "objectivity" over against the former's "confessional" commitments.[10] In this hostile environment, Tracy lays out a herculean task for the theologian that incorporates philosophy, apologetics, and dogmatics:

> Hermeneutically, I am clearly not bound to either accept or reject any religious claims prior to the conversation itself. But if I would understand that claim, I am bound to struggle critically with the fact that its claim to truth is part of its meaning. To understand the religious classic at all, I cannot ultimately avoid its provocations to my present notions of what constitutes truth. The religious classic may be simply using another language to speak a truth I already know. If so, I should know how this is the case. The religious classic may be manifesting some reality different and other—even terrifyingly different and alienatingly

5. Tracy, *The Analogical Imagination*, 173.
6. Ibid., 101.
7. Tracy, *Plurality and Ambiguity*, 84–85.
8. Tracy, *The Analogical Imagination*, 29.
9. Ibid., 19.
10. See Thomas A. Lewis, *Why Philosophy Matters for the Study of Religion—and Vice Versa* (Oxford: Oxford University Press, 2015), 43–61.

other—from what I usually believe. If so, I should make clear how I understand this otherness and difference in this manifestation. . . .[11]

Despite Tracy's best efforts to locate theology within the mainstream of academic and public discourse, rather than creating a space where genuine conversation can take place between religious and nonreligious perspectives, the postmodern relativizing of all interpretive traditions more often strengthens the hold of modernist and positivist assumptions within the academy and the public square. Consequently, some liberation theologians—notably Justo L. González and Roberto S. Goizueta—have approached postmodernism with reservation and suspicion: "Is it mere coincidence that, just when U.S. Hispanics, African Americans, and Native Americans—so long excluded from the world of rational discourse—are engaging in a rational, *critical* way the dominant culture and its intellectual elites, those same elites throw up their hands and declare all intellectual arguments to be irrational?"[12]The radical pluralism characterizing the postmodern moment claims that all perspectives have equal validity insofar as they are "true," but only for those persons who share a particular perspective or social location. In practice, however, the views of the privileged, dominant groups in any given society are elevated and absolutized while those groups excluded from the centers of power remain marginalized; as González has noted, "There is a sense, however, in which talk about postmodernity remains captive to the same parochial self-deception. Jean-François Lyotard acknowledges as much when he declares, at the very opening of his now-famous *The Postmodern Condition*, that he is concerned only with the status of knowledge in the most developed societies."[13] Not surprisingly, Goizueta works toward a common moral discourse amid postmodernity's celebration of multiculturalism and diversity because pluralism as defined by the dominant discourse threatens to further marginalize minority perspectives. In a conscious effort to embrace Alastair MacIntyre's critical retrieval of tradition, yet move beyond him, Goizueta raises a more fundamental set of questions: "*Whose* pluralism? *Whose* multiculturalism? *Whose* rationality? *Whose* truth?"[14]

David Tracy outlines a model for theological interpretation in a postmodern context by employing certain axioms first articulated by

---

11. Tracy, *Plurality and Ambiguity*, 98.
12. Roberto S. Goizueta, *Caminemos con Jesús: Toward a Hispanic/Latino Theology of Accompaniment* (Maryknoll NY: Orbis Books, 1999), 147 (emphasis in the original).
13. Justo L. González, "Metamodern Aliens in Postmodern Jerusalem," in *Hispanic/Latino Theology: Challenge and Promise*, ed. Ada María Isasi-Díaz and Fernando F. Segovia (Minneapolis, MN: Fortress Press, 1996), 343–44.
14. Goizueta *Caminemos con Jesús*, 172.

Bernard Lonergan: "Be attentive, be intelligent, be responsible, be loving, and, if necessary, change."[15] Accordingly, the interpretation of texts and traditions is viewed as a dialogical undertaking in a context of radical pluralism, involving multiple voices within and without a particular religious tradition:

> Conversation is a game with some hard rules: say only what you mean; say it as accurately as you can; listen to and respect what the other says, however different or other; be willing to correct or defend your opinions if challenged by the conversation partner; be willing to argue if necessary, to confront if demanded, to endure necessary conflict, to change your mind if the evidence suggests it.[16]

According to Tracy, this diversity of competing perspectives is integral to the Christian religion:

> Any observer of contemporary Christian theology cannot avoid noticing how pluralistic, how diverse, even how conflicting are the theological interpretations of Christianity in our period. Nor is that cause for either surprise or despair. If the systematic theologian must correlate an interpretation of Christianity with an interpretation of the situation, the interpretations, as personal responses, are likely to prove as conflicting as the situation itself, *and as diverse as the Christian tradition.*[17]

Furthermore, Tracy recognizes it "makes little sense to claim that only a scholarly elite can interpret the religious classics,"[18] so scholars of religion and theology bear the responsibility of engaging contemporary theologies outside the narrow publics of the academy and the church by conversing with grassroots and populist groups that have developed their own practical hermeneutics in resistance to the elitism of academic interpretations:

> These options range widely: "street theologies" that narrate the lives of different Christian groups; the resurgence of social-justice concerns in many evangelical theologies; the radical mystical-political turn of many monastic communities; the liberation theologies of the base communities of the Third World; the calls for communal solidarity among the embattled Christian communities of Eastern

---

15. Bernard Lonergan, *Method In Theology* (New York: Seabury, 1972), 231.
16. Tracy, *Plurality and Ambiguity*, 19.
17. Tracy, *The Analogical Imagination*, 372 (emphasis added).
18. Tracy, *Plurality and Ambiguity*, 102.

and Central Europe. All these practical theologies have considerable import for all academic theologians and, by extension, all interpreters of religion.[19]

Inevitably, as evident in this last comment, theological reflection in a radically pluralist situation demands dialogue and cooperation with other religions, so it is no surprise that David Tracy is on the vanguard of comparative theology. "Comparative theology," a growing subdiscipline within Christian theology, is distinguished by a methodological commitment to the thoughtful consideration of and engagement with other religious traditions. Comparative theology engages in theological reflection on God as Ultimate Reality from an explicitly pluralistic perspective, affirming a plurality of theological approaches even while granting primacy to one particular understanding of God. Tracy recognizes that many belief systems are not—strictly speaking—theistic but continues to employ the term comparative theology because this term is widely accepted within the academy as descriptive of "any explicitly intellectual interpretation of a religious tradition that affords a central place to the fact of religious pluralism in the tradition's self-interpretation."[20] That being said, however, as a *Christian* theologian Tracy first outlines a typology of Christian theological responses to the Christian religious classic (comprised of the Hebrew Bible and the Greek New Testament) before articulating a more explicitly comparative methodology.[21]

According to Tracy, "individual and communal Christian theological responses" to the Christ event take one of three paradigmatic forms: manifestation, proclamation, or liberation.[22] A critical reading of Tracy's typology potentially opens a door past the impasse—beyond the theologies of word and culture—that embraces the concrete and objective action of God in the event of revelation while still taking the contemporary situation seriously. An overview of Tracy's three paradigmatic Christian responses to the Christian religious classic follows via an analysis of the work of three contemporary theologians (Sallie McFague, John Milbank, and Miguel De La Torre), each one

19. Ibid.

20. David Tracy, "Comparative Theology," in *The Encyclopedia of Religion*, vol. 14, ed. Mircea Eliade (New York: MacMillan Publishing Co., 1987), 447.

21. See David Tracy, *Dialogue with the Other: The Inter-Religious Dialogue* (Louvain: Peeters Press, 1990), for Tracy's foray into comparative theology, in which he brings diverse traditions (Judaism, Christianity, and Buddhism) into conversation with one another as well as such varied figures as Sigmund Freud, Jacques Lacan, William James, and Meister Eckhart.

22. Tracy, *The Analogical Imagination*, 371–404.

representing one of the three types, which will set the stage for a constructive pneumatological proposal that builds on Tracy's typology in order to articulate an understanding of revelation that is not bound by culture yet speaks to the particularities of culture.

3.2 SALLIE MCFAGUE'S METAPHORICAL THEOLOGY

Sallie McFague's metaphorical theology, by attempting to construct new, culturally relevant models of God, stands as a clear example of what Tracy means by a theology of manifestation: "Much *deconstruction* of the traditional imagery has taken place, but little *construction*. If, however, metaphor and concept are, as I believe, inextricably and symbiotically related in theology, there is no way to do theology for our time with outmoded or oppressive metaphors and models."[23] David Tracy defines the theological engagement with the Christian religious classic—the very task of systematic theology—as "a response in the present to the event and person of Jesus Christ."[24] Within this framework, the human act of theological construction is a creative engagement with the divine act of self-revelation, which the Christian tradition defines as "grace," and the believer experiences "through some personal sense of the uncanny."[25] This grace, "the grace of Jesus Christ—is mediated through the ecclesial and cultural traditions" in three distinct forms, manifestation, proclamation, and historical action (liberation), yet despite its culturally specific mediation, always retains its character as an intersubjective encounter with a transcendent other: "experienced in the present uncanny situation by Christians as uncanny gift and command, a power not one's own."[26] Clearly influenced by Mircea Eliade's phenomenological approach to the study of religion,[27] Tracy's first descriptive typology is the route of *manifestation*, understood as the "sheer eruption of the powers of the cosmos."[28] Admittedly, this trajectory is greatly muted in the contemporary era, even for Christians "whose religious experience is likely to move in the direction of vision, image, ritual, reflection, meditation," yet there remains within

23. Sallie McFague, *Models of God: Theology for an Ecological, Nuclear Age* (Philadelphia: Fortress Press, 1987), xi.
24. Tracy, *The Analogical Imagination*, 371.
25. Ibid.
26. Ibid.
27. See Mircea Eliade, *The Sacred and the Profane: The Nature of Religion* (San Diego, CA: Harcourt Brace Jovanovich, 1987).
28. Tracy, *The Analogical Imagination*, 376.

contemporary Christianity a strand of theological reflection grounded
in the "sheer immediacy of the power of manifestation."[29]

Influenced by Paul Tillich's anthropological approach, theologians
like Gordon D. Kaufman and Sallie McFague fit Tracy's category of
manifestation because they equate the constructive work of the contemporary theologian with the preaching of the biblical prophets and
apostles. In other words, Kaufman and McFague contend the proper
object of theology is not the transcendent God but human talk about
God: "the symbols given by the original revelatory experiences" and
"the traditions based on them."[30] Like Tillich, both also affirm the
mythical dimension of religious language as the medium through
which revelation is known and experienced: "Nothing less than symbols and myths can express our ultimate concern."[31] For Kaufman,
theology is a work of human "imaginative construction" in which the
concept of God—while informed by biblical language—is ultimately
assessed through essentially humanistic categories: "what role has [the
Bible] actually played in the emergence of human self-definition and
self-understanding and self-transformation in the process we have
been calling 'humanization'?"[32] For McFague, all theological language
is metaphorical and as such does not describe God's being but rather
articulates the human experience of God. Consequently, a metaphorical theology "will emphasize personal, relational categories in its language about God, but not necessarily as the tradition has interpreted
these categories."[33] The problem with many contemporary theologies
of culture is that they continue to resemble nineteenth-century liberal
Protestantism insofar as they are methodologically unable to differentiate prescriptive theological claims from prevailing cultural trends. Thus,
while one of "the most important features of the notion of theology as
imaginative construction is that it demands that we clearly distinguish
our ideas—especially when we speak of God—from the mysteries to
which we intend them to refer,"[34] the theologies of culture more often
than not remain trapped within a Kantian epistemology that cannot
speak about noumenal reality: "No one model is adequate and indeed,
all models together are not adequate to express our experiences of

29. Ibid., 377.
30. Tillich, *Systematic Theology,* vol. 3, 201.
31. Tillich, *Dynamics of Faith,* 53.
32. Gordon D. Kaufman, *In Face of Mystery: A Constructive Theology* (Cambridge, MA: Harvard University Press, 1993), 353.
33. McFague, *Metaphorical Theology,* 21.
34. Kaufman, *In Face of Mystery,* 353.

relating to God."[35] In the end, "The last word as well as the first word in theology is surrounded by silence. We know with Simone Weil that when we try to speak of God there is nothing which resembles what we can conceive when we say that word."[36]

While post-Enlightenment thinking has undermined the naiveté of religions to experience the divine in "sheer immediacy," Tracy argues that the route of mediation allows for a second naiveté (Ricoeur) insofar as the task of interpretation initiated by the religious classic—experienced as ambiguity that yields a multiplicity of interpretations—creates new opportunities for divine-human encounter. In other words, what makes a particular sacred text, event, ritual, space, or person a "religious classic" is its ability to "bear an excess of permanence of meaning, yet always resist definitive interpretation."[37] According to Tracy, in our contemporary context this power of manifestation "is rarely sensed as erupting from nature itself, as of old," but is now located primarily in the religious classic, "disclosed through the critical mediations of reason reflecting upon the ultimate reality of God as well as an attendant trust in all reality as graced."[38] The paradigm for this conflation of nature and grace, reason and revelation, immanence and transcendence is Jesuit theologian Karl Rahner's transcendental method,[39] informed by philosophy of religion and fundamental theology, in which "Rahner formulates the reality of a transcendental revelation whereby we recognize ourselves as always already in the presence not of an object but of a horizon of absolute mystery."[40] Tracy acknowledges this trajectory of theological responses also crosses confessional lines by locating Paul Tillich, Langdon Gilkey, and John Cobb under the category of manifestation and observing how,

> despite their many obvious and crucial differences, the theological responses of many Catholic and Liberal Protestant theologians tend to be analogous in structure and in spirit: their similar trust in the mediating powers of critical and/or speculative reason, their openness to metaphysical inquiry, their love for the logos tradition of Christology, their openness, however guarded, to mystical experience.[41]

35. McFague, *Metaphorical Theology*, 190.
36. Ibid., 194.
37. Tracy, *Plurality and Ambiguity*, 12.
38. Tracy, *The Analogical Imagination*, 379.
39. See Karl Rahner, *Foundations of Christian Faith: An Introduction to the Idea of Christianity*, trans. William V. Dych (New York: Crossroad, 1999), 44–90.
40. Tracy, *The Analogical Imagination*, 378.
41. Ibid., 379.

Sallie McFague (1933–) is a feminist Christian theologian unabash-
edly committed to a methodological approach that engages the most
pressing issues of the day, as evidenced by her focus on the nuclear
and environmental crises of the late twentieth- and early twenty-first
centuries. As a constructive theologian, McFague explicitly embraces
her commitment to feminism in a first-world context yet recognizes
that the problems of environmental degradation are organically and
complexly interconnected with other social issues such as gender dis-
crimination, racism, and economic injustice. Not surprisingly, her end-
point in the book *Models of God* (1987), in which she asserts, "We
meet God in the body of the world,"[42] becomes the starting point for
The Body of God (1993), in which she "attempts to look at everything
through one lens, the model of the universe or world as God's body."[43]
In doing so, McFague hopes to overcome the obstacles of God's immanence and transcendence by affirming that human beings only and
always encounter God's transcendence immanently: "The world is our
meeting place with God, and this means that God's immanence will be
'universal' and God's transcendence will be 'worldly.'"[44]

Despite giving methodological preference to the contemporary situation, Sallie McFague acknowledges that *Christian* constructive theology must remain accountable to the normative vision of the Christian
tradition. Without valuing Scripture over tradition—while always
grounding her theological reflections on human experience—McFague
identifies Scripture as the *earliest* layer of tradition but argues that
the form, not the content, of Scripture is normative for theological
method. She thus approaches Scripture and tradition as a "Christian
classic": "For what we have in the New Testament are confessions of
faith by people who, on the basis of their experience of the way lives
were changed by Jesus' Gospel and by Jesus, *gave* authority to him and
to the writings about him. The New Testament writings are foundational; they are classics; they are a beginning."[45]

Building upon Paul Ricoeur's theory of metaphor,[46] McFague lays
the groundwork for her later metaphorical theology in her second
book, *Speaking in Parables* (1975), in which she argues that it "will be

42. McFague, *Models of God*, 184.
43. Sallie McFague, *The Body of God: An Ecological Theology* (Minneapolis, MN: Fortress Press, 1993), vii.
44. McFague, *Models of God*, 185.
45. McFague, *Metaphorical Theology*, 19.
46. Sallie McFague, *Speaking in Parables: A Study in Metaphor and Theology* (Philadelphia: Fortress Press, 1975),
40. In a footnote McFague states that "Ricoeur's understanding of symbol is practically identical with my view of
metaphor—in both cases there is no way *around* the image" (40). See Paul Ricoeur, *The Symbolism of Evil*, trans.
Emerson Buchanan (New York: Beacon Press, 1967), 161–74.

through the search for new metaphors—poems, stories, even lives—which will 'image' to us, in our total existential unity, the compassion of the father."[47] Thus, when interpreting a biblical text "we only get at the meaning through the metaphor,"[48] since "parables make ontological as well as existential 'assertions'—they tell us something about God as well as something about our life—but the assertions about God are made lightly, indirectly, and cannot be extricated finally and completely from the story that expresses or, better, 'images' them."[49]

More fundamental for the discipline of theology is McFague's contention that beyond modeling theological discourse on Jesus' preaching and his use of parables, theologians ought to view "Jesus himself as a parable of God."[50] According to McFague, parables produce meaning by intentionally *jarring* the listener or reader, so rather than drawing upon a presumed similarity (analogy), they exploit the difference between the referent and its analogue (metaphor). Given that all language for the divine is metaphorical, images for God do not work on the basis of similarity between the divine and human but are grounded in some resemblance discovered when the image is shifted from its original context to an unexpected one. While metaphors manipulate emotional connections, they are also highly cognitive and are employed when communicating meaning. However, the use of metaphor in theological construction "is a highly risky, uncertain, and open-ended enterprise,"[51] in great part because metaphorical language is inherently ambiguous. Comparing religious language to that of the empirical sciences, McFague suggests this ambiguity and open-endedness is part of what makes metaphorical theology an attractive proposition, insofar as it underscores the ambiguity inherent in divine self-communication: "Conceptual language tends toward univocity, toward clear and concise meanings for ambiguous, multileveled, imagistic language. In this process something is lost and something is gained: richness and multivalency are sacrificed for precision and consistency."[52] Although theology strives for greater conceptual clarity (like the natural sciences), it also recognizes the metaphorical character of religious language (as "ambiguous, multileveled, imagistic") while affirming that metaphors work in great part because of the dissimilarity revealed in the process

47. McFague, *Speaking in Parables*, 23.
48. Ibid., 16.
49. Ibid., 17.
50. McFague, *Metaphorical Theology*, 19.
51. McFague, *Speaking in Parables*, 44.
52. McFague, *Metaphorical Theology*, 26.

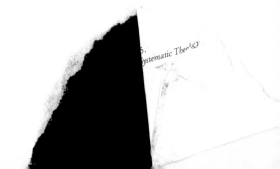

of comparison: "Thinking metaphorically means spotting a thread of similarity between two dissimilar objects, events or whatever, one of which is better known than the other, and using the better-known one as a way of speaking about the lesser known."[53]

Given this drive for conceptual clarity, metaphors for God eventually (and perhaps inevitably) become models of God—extended metaphors that, because of their explanatory power, have become *paradigmatic* within Christianity. These models provide a coherent framework for fleshing out theological concepts that ultimately inform creedal statements and doctrinal traditions. The problem with models of God is that over time they become ossified, lose their metaphorical character, and start being taken literally by believers. According to McFague, when theological language loses its hermeneutical ambiguity, traditional models become both idolatrous and irrelevant. For McFague, this tendency toward ossification in religious language is most evident in the paternal-monarchical model that has dominated Christian theology and practice for much of Christianity's history:

> The issues of idolatry and irrelevance come together in the image of God as father, for more than any other dominant model in Christianity, this one has been absolutized by some and, in recent times, found meaningless by others. The feminist critique of God as father centers on the *dominance* of this one model to the exclusion of others, and on the *failure* of this model to deal with the anomaly presented by those whose experience is not included by this model.[54]

In other words, feminist theology argues that Christianity needs to develop other, more inclusive models because the patriarchal model has become idolatrous by exerting what under Tillich's schema would be termed a "theological totalitarianism"[55] and culturally irrelevant by ignoring the historical emancipation of women, ethnic minorities, and other marginalized groups. The model of "God the Father" lost its metaphorical character because over time it began to be taken literally, and thus as exclusively normative for Christian belief and praxis, despite a longstanding tradition within Christian theology of a methodological humility that asserts no human discourse can fully and adequately describe God. Making masculinity normative for Christian belief, the paternal-monarchical model has also become increasingly irrelevant

53. Ibid., 15
54. Ibid., 14
55. Tillich, ̲   ̲ ̲ vol. 1, 90–91, 96–97.

because, by marginalizing the experiences of women, it fails to reflect the broad spectrum of human experience.

Granted, Sallie McFague recognizes that the metaphor of God as father has survived and become widely accepted as a normative model precisely because of its high explanatory value: "the central role of models in theology is to provide grids or screens for interpreting this relationship between the divine and the human."[56] Historically, "the dominant model through which the church has interpreted the root-metaphor of life in relationship to God is a personal one, and specifically, a paternal one."[57] Unfortunately, despite the inadequacy of all metaphorical models, necessitating a methodological commitment to *multiple* models for God, the paternal model has gained such widespread cultural dominance it has been mistaken for the "root-metaphor" of Christian theology; one that overwhelms and blocks out all other competing interpretive models. McFague warns that all models run the risk of losing their metaphorical character, especially when one model is allowed to dominate (as with the paternal-monarchical model), thus McFague advocates developing a *plurality* of models for God: "A truly metaphorical theology will encourage a variety of interpretive models in order to be in continuity with its relational, tensive parabolic base. Life according to the rule of God is too complex, rich, and varied to be captured in any one model and any model so elevated is bound to become idolatrous."[58] McFague concludes *Metaphorical Theology* (1982) by proposing a "thought experiment" she brings to fruition in *Models of God*: What if Christianity were to think within *different* models for God? Is it possible to articulate a model of "God as friend" in place of "God as king" or "God as father" that is nevertheless adequately grounded in the Christian "religious classic" (the Bible)?

The methodological foundation of metaphorical theology is human experience. Sallie McFague argues that successful theological models must speak to human experience at its deepest level; however, rather than conflating the divine to the human, she argues that metaphorical theology draws attention to the gap between the human and divine, which is why she emphasizes the *tentativeness* of all theological language. *Models of God* presents three fully articulated alternative models for God—God as mother, lover, and friend. The image of "God as mother" serves to overcome the dominance of patriarchal models

56. McFague, *Metaphorical Theology*, 125.
57. Ibid., 128.
58. Ibid.

because, "in spite of Western and Christian uneasiness over female imagery for God, since the *imago dei* is twofold, female as well as male, both kinds of metaphors ought to be used."[59] The "God as lover" model intentionally destabilizes and sexualizes our language for God since just "as female sexuality had to be squarely faced with the proposal of God as mother, so eroticism must be considered with the model of God as lover."[60] McFague's methodological commitment to the breadth of human experience necessitates that we consider this most personal and intimate of human relationships, that of the lover to the beloved, in our faithful discourse about God just as we have considered the love of parents to children, or risk "cutting off a central dimension of human experience as outside the concern of the Christian gospel."[61] Ultimately, all three of McFague's constructive proposals seek to provide alternatives to the dominant patriarchal model in order to articulate a distinct Christian ethic that promotes mutual caring and interdependence while expressing "the saving presence of God," not just within human relationships but also within humankind's relationship to nature.[62] Therefore, McFague's third and final model, "God as friend," stresses the relationality and interdependence of all life. Friendship is here defined as mutual commitment to a common project; this concept originates in the covenant between YHWH and Israel, but friendship is also found in Jesus' fellowship with "outcasts," resulting in an ethic of solidarity and mutual commitment to a common project. By emphasizing solidarity—understood as companionship and accompaniment—McFague overcomes objections that friendship so construed ignores the inherent inequality within the divine-human relationship because it is ultimately grounded in God's loving act of creation:

> If God is the friend of the world, the one committed to it, who can be trusted never to betray it, who not only likes the word but has a vision for its well-being, then we as the special part of the body—the *imago dei*—are invited as friends of the Friend of the world to join in that vision and world for its fulfillment. God as lover of the world gave us the vision God finds the world valuable and desires its wounds healed and its creatures free; God as friend asks us, as adults, to become associates in that work. The right name for those

59. McFague, *Models of God*, 98.
60. Ibid., 125.
61. Ibid., 126.
62. Ibid., 78.

involved in this ongoing, sustaining, trustworthy, committed work for the world is neither parents nor lovers but friends.[63]

According to this model, the work of salvation is viewed as healing, and the divine-human relationship is imaginatively constructed as a mutually beneficial friendship committed to responsible stewardship of God's creation: "In an ecological, nuclear era, salvation must mean this; hence, the friendship is not between two—God and individual human beings—but between all those who are united by love for the world."[64]

In *The Body of God*, McFague develops an ecological theology and accompanying ethic grounded in the models of God as mother, lover, and friend that seeks to overcome humanity's alienation toward the creation by exploring our most fundamental experience as incarnate and embodied beings in order to think of God as incarnate and embodied as well. Naturally, the Christian doctrine of the Incarnation makes Christianity "the religion of the incarnation *par excellence*. Its earliest and most persistent doctrines focus on embodiment: from the incarnation (the Word made flesh) and Christology (Christ was fully human) to the eucharist (this is my body, this is my blood), the resurrection of the body, and the church (the body of Christ who is its head), Christianity has been a religion of the body."[65] However, McFague's conception of God's embodiment resembles a form of panentheism, the belief that the divine pervades and interpenetrates every part of the universe, which is likely to meet with objections from more Christocentric theological perspectives: "everything that is is the sacrament of God (the universe as God's body), but here and there we find that presence erupting in special ways."[66] In other words, McFague acknowledges that the manifestation of God in Jesus of Nazareth is *paradigmatic* for understanding the divine-human relationship *without* asserting this Christic paradigm is absolute and exclusive: "The question, however, for those of us who choose to remain Christian is, What does, can, the Christian faith contribute to an embodied theology, to an ecological sensibility? . . . What does Christian faith, and especially the story of Jesus, have to offer in terms of a distinctive perspective on embodiment?"[67] The unique insight of the Christian understanding of the Incarnation is its potential for emancipation and inclusivity, summed up in McFague's simple

63. Ibid., 165.
64. Ibid., 175.
65. McFague, *The Body of God*, 14.
66. Ibid., 162.
67. Ibid., 163.

proposal: "*The story of Jesus suggests that the shape of God's body includes all, especially the needy and outcast.*"[68]

Perhaps McFague's biggest contribution in this latest volume is to build bridges between theology and the natural sciences, as her engagement of Thomas Kuhn's philosophy of science (specifically his analysis of "paradigm shifts" in science)[69] explores the possibility that science and theology share some conceptual models in common. McFague not only argues that theological models ought to cohere with scientific explanatory models, but suggests that scientific models actually enrich the theological imagination insofar as "both positions are ideologies, both are readings"[70] yet certain scientific models can actually help us articulate a notion of God's embodiment "as composed of multitudes of embodied beings who presently inhabit a planet that has evolved over billions of years through a process of dynamic change marked by law and novelty into an intricate, diverse, complex, multileveled reality, all radically interrelated and interdependent."[71] Ultimately, McFague presents a compelling creative reimaging of traditional Christian doctrines informed by feminist and ecological concerns:

> Hence, as a revisioning of traditional Trinitarian thinking, I would suggest that rather than "the Father, Son, and Holy Spirit," which does not preserve either the radical transcendence or radical immanence of God, we consider the following: the mystery of God (the invisible face or first person), the physicality of God (the visible body or second person), and the mediation of the invisible and the visible (the spirit or third person).[72]

Still, McFague's project of theological reconstruction exposes certain limits inherent in David Tracy's way of manifestation, in which Christian symbols serve not as ontological realities but as guiding paradigms. Ultimately, by relativizing the claims of distinctly Christian dogmas like the incarnation, McFague leaves us at the foot of Babel's tower still mired in the confusion of human languages, our only response a passionate assertion that our point of view seems most adequate, at least for the moment: "I have not found it possible as a contemporary Christian to support an incarnational Christology or a canonical

---

68. Ibid., 164 (emphasis in the original).
69. See Thomas S. Kuhn, *The Structure of Scientific Revolutions*, 50th anniversary ed. (Chicago: The University of Chicago Press, 2012), 43–51.
70. McFague, *The Body of God*, 92.
71. Ibid., 96–97.
72. Ibid., 193.

Scripture; nevertheless, I have found it possible to support a 'parabolic' Christology and Scripture as the Christian 'classic.'"[73] To which Tracy responds, "Really to live life, we must live it as if only the paradigmatic *is* the real."[74]

These words, not written about McFague's use of sexual love as a model for God yet entirely apropos, celebrate the power of mythical language and symbol for mediating divine self-revelation:

> In some lives today the experience of sexual love is the last out-post of the power of manifestation in the extraordinary. From those experiences to some sense, however feeble, of the extraordinary in the classic events, persons, rituals, images and myths scattered as paradigmatic signs of releasement throughout our culture, the shock of recognition in and by the power of a paradigmatic manifestation still reverberates in the culture and in the Christian tradition. That sense lies even in a world that has tried to conquer nature, deny the body, trivialize sexuality, and empty the mythic unconscious of all its healing powers.[75]

This sacralization of the ordinary—or discovery of the extraordinary in the ordinary—is a chief component of the theologies of manifestation, embracing both cataphatic and apophatic theologies in order to affirm "the sense of God's radical transcendence" alongside "a yet more intensi-fied affirmation of God's radical nearness."[76] As suggested earlier, this understanding of divine manifestation can lead to a form of panentheism:

> This transcendent God is available to other human beings princi-pally through the work of the spirit of Christ, that is, by means of the sacraments and the reading of Scripture. The rest of creation is more or less neglected in this view linking divine transcendence and immanence. We will suggest a different picture, one that agrees with the tradition that transcendence is available to us only immanently, only through the mundane, the physical, the bodily—but a body that is not limited to Jesus of Nazareth.[77]

Yet if all is grace (which David Tracy suggests is a key component of the theologies of manifestation), if all experience becomes sacramentalized, in what sense is divine revelation distinct from human experience or

73. McFague, *Metaphorical Theology*, viii.
74. Tracy, *The Analogical Imagination*, 384 (emphasis in the original).
75. Ibid.
76. Ibid., 386.
77. McFague, *The Body of God*, 161.

the natural order? Feuerbach's claim that all theology is in fact anthropology looms large.

McFague's focus on the religious imagination (the leap from primary religious language to increasingly abstract conceptual language) exposes certain limits of metaphorical theology: (1) It fails to adequately relate the creative act of the theologian to the traditional belief and praxis of living communities of faith; (2) it precludes the possibility of making ontological claims about God and God's actions in the world; and (3) it cannot differentiate the Bible from other "classic" texts, thereby undermining the power of divine manifestation as concretely experienced in Jesus the Christ. According to Tracy, what unites the various theologians of manifestation is "the power of the event of manifestation in Jesus Christ" as an affirmation of "some pervasive yes at the heart of the universe, some radical mystery sensed as power, as an abiding love that undoes all our more usual senses of the futility and absurdity of existence."[78] However, even though Christ stands as the chief paradigm underlying McFague's model of the whole of creation as the "body" of God, this Christic paradigm does not refer exclusively to Jesus, but to a cluster of meaningful theological "events" that include (but are not limited to) the life of Christ. This "wider view of Christ" is best understood as a new way of ordering social relationships (and humanity's relationship to nature) "inaugurated" in God's incarnation in Christ but continuing into the present, with Christ's self-sacrifice serving not as sacrificial scapegoat but as a paradigm for both, the divine-human relationship, and the ordering of our lives in relation to God, one another, and the cosmos. And always guided by the methodological principle that "God transcends all our models, but in so doing allows us to imagine the backside in all sorts of ways."[79]

While metaphorical theology avoids the idolatry and literalism that has historically plagued religious language, and also provides a way to make religious discourse more relevant to people excluded by traditional doctrinal formulations, when theology is defined narrowly as "imaginative construction," Paul Tillich's claim to "final answers" for our existential questions in the disruptive act of divine manifestation is quietly replaced by the more modest claim that foundational Christian paradigms are *still* relevant to modern culture. Lost in translation is the underlying divine act—the *mysterium tremendum et fascinans*

78. Tracy, *The Analogical Imagination*, 386.
79. McFague, *The Body of God*, 193–94.

("a mystery that is at once terrifying and fascinating")—still in need of mediation that Tracy describes as "its real concreteness, or the re-presentative mediation of the extraordinary, the paradigmatic and the sacramental."[80]

3.3 JOHN MILBANK'S TRANSCENDENTAL ONTOLOGY

As argued in the first chapter of this book, the theology of crisis that arose between the two world wars (and came to be known by its critics as neo-orthodoxy) exerted its influence on European and North American theology well into the 1960s. Furthermore, despite a multiplicity of critical voices proclaiming the death of neo-orthodoxy, from liberation to feminist to "death-of-God" theologies, its impact continues to this day in the postliberal theologies associated with the work of Hans Frei and George Lindbeck. According to David Tracy's typology, the strength of both neo-orthodoxy and postliberalism stems from its methodological decision to shift "away from all experiences of manifestation into the empowering experience of God's decisive word of address in Jesus Christ."[81] This trajectory of response to divine self-revelation that Tracy terms the "route of proclamation" (and the current work has identified as theologies of the Word) recoils from the subjective religious experience emphasized in nineteenth-century liberal Protestantism—and celebrated in the theologies of manifestation discussed above—in order to bring the believer face-to-face with the divine source of revelation: "No depth experience, no quest for the ultimate, no mysticism, they urged, can save us in this situation. Only if God comes as an eschatological event, as unexpected and decisive Word addressing each and all; only if God comes to disclose our true godforsakenness and our possible liberation can we be healed."[82] Today it is Radical Orthodoxy (RO), a movement most commonly associated with a series of monographs published under the editorial direction of John Milbank, Catherine Pickstock, and Graham Ward that most clearly represents what Tracy means by a trajectory of proclamation.[83]

---

80. Tracy, *The Analogical Imagination*, 384–85.
81. Ibid., 386.
82. Ibid.
83. See *Radical Orthodoxy: A New Theology*, ed. John Milbank, Catherine Pickstock and Graham Ward (London: Routledge, 1999); D. Stephen Long, *Divine Economy: Theology and the Market* (London: Routledge, 2000); Graham Ward, *Cities of God* (London: Routledge, 2001); John Milbank and Catherine Pickstock, *Truth in Aquinas* (London: Routledge, 2000); and Daniel M. Bell Jr., *Liberation Theology After the End of History: The Refusal to Cease Suffering* (London: Routledge, 2001).

Though its proponents repudiate the claim that Radical Orthodoxy constitutes a distinct theological school or movement, claiming, "RO has no program, it has no headquarters, it has none of the definitiveness of, say, the Yale School," the fact remains there is a shared set of values and methodological commitments uniting its various practitioners.[84] One of those shared commitments is a genealogical, or at least methodological relationship, to postliberal theology as evidenced by Stanley Hauerwas's impact on Radical Orthodoxy, himself one of Karl Barth's many intellectual progeny currently dominating the North American theological landscape. Still, it is John Milbank's movement-defining masterpiece, *Theology and Social Theory* (1990), that starkly distinguishes Radical Orthodoxy as a genuine alternative to both modern theology and modern secularism by boldly proclaiming: "It is theology itself that will have to provide its own account of the final causes at work in human history, on the basis of its own particular, and historically specific faith."[85] Simply put, Milbank does not view theology as one among several competing voices within the contemporary public discourse but argues instead for an understanding of theology as its own distinct ontology providing an alternative metanarrative to the modernist secular politics of statecraft, which according to Milbank, also includes most so-called political theologies: "The task of such a theology is not apologetic, nor even argument. Rather it is to tell again the Christian *mythos*, pronounce again the Christian *logos*, and call again for Christian *praxis* in a manner that restores their freshness and originality. It must articulate Christian difference in such a fashion as to make it strange."[86] Into this mix Milbank brings not only the radical transcendence of Barth via Hauerwas, tempered by the latter's Anabaptist anti-Constantinian sectarianism, but also a rigorous Thomism mediated by Alasdair MacIntyre's reclaiming of the Aristotelian-Thomistic tradition. Whereas both neo-orthodoxy and postliberalism were movements led primarily by Protestant thinkers, Milbank's brand of Radical Orthodoxy engages key French and German Thomists, Catholic philosopher Jean-Luc Marion, and most surprisingly, the *nouvelle théologie* that influenced the Second Vatican Council (1962–65) of the Roman Catholic Church.[87] In fact, Milbank's project fits easily under the category of *ressourcement*—the critical retrieval of

84. Graham Ward, "In the Economy of the Divine: A Response to James K. A. Smith," *PNEUMA: The Journal of the Society for Pentecostal Studies* 25, no. 1 (Spring 2003): 117.
85. John Milbank, *Theology and Social Theory: Beyond Secular Reason* (Oxford: Blackwell Publishers, Ltd., 1993), 380.
86. Ibid., 381 (emphasis in the original).
87. See Milbank, *Theology and Social Theory*, 206–55.

patristic and medieval resources most often associated with the work of
Henri de Lubac and Hans Urs von Balthasar—in the process of articulating a theological ontology that genuinely differs from the prevailing
modernist worldview by pressing "de Lubac and von Balthasar's perspectives in the direction of a social and political theology."[88]

The politically radical potential of *ressourcement* and the *nouvelle
théologie* stems from its rejection of what amounts to a "fundamentally
humanist-Marxist" political ideology dominating political discourse,
rechristened with theological language, yet failing to overcome the gap
between the individual and the communal at the core of the modernist
conception of politics *as* conflict:

> The social realm is thought to possess its own immanent ethical
> principles, which are those of an emergent 'humanity' and which
> cannot be qualified by theology. All that theology can do is give these
> principles of liberation another name: 'salvation'. Theology is able to
> declare that natural, human ethics is approved by God. It is able to
> do this because natural, human ethics has the goal of liberation—
> the setting free of the human capacity for transcendence, which is
> precisely the supposed source and foundation for our knowledge of
> God's existence. All revolves within this futile circle.[89]

Given modern political theology's inability to articulate a distinctly
Christian political vision, Milbank chastises Barth, neo-orthodoxy, and
postliberalism by arguing that "Henri de Lubac was a greater theological revolutionary than Karl Barth, because in questioning a hierarchical duality of grace and nature as discrete stages, he transcended,
unlike Barth, the shared background assumption of all modern theology. In this way one could say, anachronistically, that he inaugurated a
postmodern theology."[90] Thus, Barth's asymmetrical emphasis on the
role of divine agency as the only source and means of attaining knowledge of God, instead of preventing the encroachment of secularism or
the mediation of grace by the theologies of culture, reinforces Less-
ing's metaphorical "ugly ditch" that claims God (revelation) cannot be
known in history insofar as a religion founded on a historical event (the
incarnation) cannot match the epistemological certainty of the necessary truths of reason. As Milbank notes,

88. Milbank, *Theology and Social Theory*, 234.
89. Ibid., 233.
90. John Milbank, "The Programme of Radical Orthodoxy," in *Radical Orthodoxy? A Catholic Inquiry*, ed.
Laurence Paul Hemming (Burlington, VT: Ashgate Publishing, 2000), 35.

In the case of Karl Barth, a broad acceptance of a post-Kantian
understanding of philosophy is turned to neo-orthodox advantage,
in that he can insist that natural reason discloses nothing of God
and yet that this opens the way to a renewed and, indeed, now more
radical recognition that only God discloses God in the contingency
of events as acknowledged not by reason but by faith.[91]

In Milbank's estimation, Karl Barth uncritically embraces a Kantian
epistemology that in the end, "by allowing legitimacy to a methodologically atheist philosophy," leaves the believer isolated from both
the secular culture and the noumenal God: "The danger here is, as is
well exemplified in Barth, that if we fail to redefine being and knowledge theologically, theological difference, the radical otherness of God,
will never be *expressible* in any way without idolatrously reducing it to
our finite human categories."[92] In other words, by perpetuating the
nature-grace bipolarity of nineteenth century neo-scholasticism, or
Kierkegaard's "absolute qualitative difference" between the Creator and
the Creation, theologies of the Word risk silencing any and all human
expressions of divinely revealed truth. According to D. Stephen Long,
Milbank "denies an account of grace that de-naturalizes it and so thoroughly separates it from human history that it remains extrinsic, inef-
fably mysterious, and secure from critique in some noumenal realm."[93]

The counternarrative of Radical Orthodoxy suggests that modernism has developed a secular reductionist descriptive framework within
which all human experiences are subsumed after having been distilled
to their universally "common" core. Consequently, particular faith traditions are not analyzed and described in their particularity, but only
in comparison to what they share with other "religions." The conse-
quence of locating theological explanatory narratives within and under
the descriptive categories of a secular, and supposedly value-neutral scientific method, is obvious:

> The division for political and liberation theology is therefore clear:
> insofar as salvation is 'religious', it is formal, transcendental and pri-
> vate; insofar as it is 'social', it is secular. What is occluded is the real
> practical and linguistic context for salvation, namely the *particular
> society* that is the Church. . . . Therefore, they realize that to uphold

91. John Milbank, "KNOWLEDGE: The theological critique of philosophy in Hamann and Jacobi," in *Radical Orthodoxy: A New Theology*, ed. John Milbank, Catherine Pickstock, and Graham Ward (London: Routledge, 1999), 21.
92. Ibid., 22.
93. Long, *Divine Economy*, 248.

ecclesial (rather than political or private) practice as the site of salvation involves subscribing to a particular theological interpretation of history and society (an enterprise which they take to be rendered impossible by the Enlightenment and its aftermath). . . . If one takes one's salvation from the Church, if one identifies oneself primarily as a member of the body of Christ, then inevitably one offers the most 'ultimate' explanations of socio-historical processes in terms of embracing or refusal of the specifically Christian virtues. . . . Thus if the Enlightenment makes this sort of thing impossible, it also rules out salvation through the Church as traditionally understood.[94]

Contrary to the "methodological atheism" that dominates post-Enlightenment discourse, Christian theology "purports to give an ultimate narrative, to provide some ultimate depth of description, because the situation of oneself within such a continuing narrative is what it means to belong to the Church, to be a Christian. However, the claim is made by faith, not a reason which seeks foundations."[95] Accordingly, Milbank does not seek to overcome the arguments of "secular reason" by means of instrumental reason (Lévinas), but argues that modernism "is only a *mythos* and therefore cannot be refuted, but only out-narrated, if we can persuade people—for reasons of 'literary taste'—that Christianity offers a much better story."[96]

Radical Orthodoxy's counternarrative—its overt attempt at seduction by means of Theopoetics—begins by "unmasking the theological and metaphysical sources of current mythologies and revealing the distortions and perversions of their current secularized forms."[97] In other words, by deconstructing the narrative of Enlightenment modernism with its promises to emancipate humanity from oppressive authorities like the church or monarchic rule, RO exposes the incessant conflict at the heart of this secular myth (Thomas Hobbes's *bellum omnium contra omnes*—"the war of all against all"),[98] revealing the absolute usurpation of power by the modern secular state in which society is "conceived of as a collection of individuals presided over by a sovereign state that maintains the peace between these individuals by securing rights through a monopoly on the use of violence."[99]

94. Milbank, *Theology and Social Theory*, 245–46.
95. Ibid., 249.
96. Ibid., 330 (emphasis in the original).
97. Graham Ward, *Politics of Discipleship* (Grand Rapids, MI: Baker Academic, 2009), 165.
98. Thomas Hobbes, *Leviathan*, rev. student ed., ed. Richard Tuck (Cambridge: Cambridge University Press, 1996), 88.
99. Daniel M. Bell Jr., "Postliberalism and Radical Orthodoxy," in *The Cambridge Companion to Christian Political Theology*, ed. Craig Hovey and Elizabeth Phillips (Cambridge: Cambridge University Press, 2015), 118.

The secularized state then depoliticizes the church, a rival political player, by positing a neutral discursive arena in which all values and perspectives are welcomed, but only insofar as participants play by the rules of secular modernity—appeals to faith and tradition must be couched in the value-neutral rational methodology of "science"— and participants who refuse to abandon the language of religious sectarianism find themselves marginalized from the public discourse and relegated to the ghetto of the private/personal sphere. Yet, as RO contends, this scientific objectivity is merely illusion, a convoluted metanarrative that "provides the metaphysical foundations for modern secular politics by establishing a dualism of nature and grace, which underwrites the separation of religion and politics and forges the bars of the iron cage or merely human politics."[100] Milbank repudiates this myth, offering in its stead the Christian myth, suggesting that modern Christian political theologies have embraced their own depoliticization by uncritically employing the atheist methodology of modernity and inadvertently relegating salvation to a private transcendence.[101] Given that the Enlightenment metanarrative "always implies the displacing of the Christian metanarrative, essential for the constitution of the faith, by new modern stories, which arose partially as an attempt to situate and confine faith itself,"[102] the way forward for Christian theology is to assert its place as a distinctly Christian "counter-ontology": "For this reason George Lindbeck and Hans Frei have been quite right to call us back to narrative as being that alone which can 'identify' God for us."[103]

D. Stephen Long argues that, "John Milbank, like James Cone, regards capitalism as a Christian heresy. But, unlike Cone, Milbank is willing to insist on a normative Christian orthodoxy against which capitalism fails."[104] Here, in a nutshell, is both the promise and the failure of Radical Orthodoxy insofar as, despite its grand goal of establishing a Christian counter-ontology, RO leaves us at the same impasse where neo-orthodoxy and postliberalism had previously led. Yes, the Christian worldview is proclaimed loudly and distinctly, and these "theologians remain as rocks upon which crash all later attempts to forge a merely cultural Christianity,"[105] but instead of Christianity as a

---

100. Ibid., 119.
101. Milbank, *Theology and Social Theory*, 234–40.
102. Ibid., 245.
103. Ibid., 385.
104. Long, *Divine Economy*, 242.
105. Tracy, *The Analogical Imagination*, 389.

political power player on the world stage, we are handed the "Benedict Option." Ethicist Alasdair MacIntyre, in his landmark book *After Virtue* (1981), described our current era "as a new dark ages," and political discourse today as "civil war carried on by other means."[106] While *After Virtue* offers some hope for the possibility of common moral discourse, the author pessimistically concludes that the only hope for peaceful coexistence lies with a retreat into small intentional communities of shared belief "within which the moral life could be sustained so that both morality and civility and the intellectual moral life can be sustained."[107] The tome ends with this muted hope: "We are waiting not for a Godot, but for another—doubtless very different—St. Benedict."[108] Today MacIntyre's critical insight has been coopted by Christian evangelicalism, specifically Rod Dreher's impassioned plea for Christians to embrace the "Benedict Option," in which believers ought to follow the example of sixth-century monk Benedict of Nursia who established cloistered religious communities removed from the world while the Roman Empire collapsed all around them.[109] As David Brooks has recently opined in *The New York Times*, "The right response to the moment is not the Benedict Option, it is Orthodox Pluralism. It is to surrender to some orthodoxy that will overthrow the superficial obsessions of the self and put one's life in contact with a transcendent ideal."[110]

The failure of Dreher's sectarian purism is the failure of any movement that seeks to trap God in a box: "that can't tolerate difference because it can't humbly accept the mystery of truth."[111] The question remains, however, whether Radical Orthodoxy can provide just such a counter-ontology; whether the distinctly Christian metanarrative defended by Radical Orthodoxy can stand on its own as a genuine alternative to secular modernism; or whether it will collapse into narrow sectarianism à la Dreher. According to David Tracy, only a generous orthodoxy (Frei) can accommodate the vast mosaic that is contemporary Christianity while tolerating the ambiguity and uncertainty that comes from encountering transcendence in the midst of our profane everyday existence. Such theologies

106. Alasdair MacIntyre, *After Virtue: A Study in Moral Theory*, 2nd ed. (Notre Dame, IN: University of Notre Dame Press, 1984), 253.
107. Ibid, 263.
108. Ibid.
109. See Rod Dreher, *The Benedict Option: A Strategy for Christians in a Post-Christian Nation* (New York: Penguin, 2017).
110. David Brooks, "The Benedict Option," in *The New York Times* (March 14, 2017): A23.
111. Ibid.

. . . live on the resources of the explosive power of the Word first
released in the prophetic and eschatological strains of both Testaments, paradigmatically expressed in the parables of Jesus and the
Pauline theology of the cross, retrieved in the word event which was
the Reformation and recalled for and in our word-impoverished,
wordy culture by those early twentieth-century classic exponents of
the power of the Christian proclaimed word as that proclamation
disclosed anew in the event of Jesus Christ.[112]

To that end, Milbank builds upon George Lindbeck's articulation of a
"metanarrative realism" to present the Christian story as an alternative
to the insidious and ubiquitous Enlightenment metanarrative: "These
stories are not situated within the world: instead, for the Christian, the
world is situated in these stories. They define for us what reality is, and
they function as a 'metanarrative', not in the sense of a story based on,
or unfolding foundational reason (Lyotard's sense) but in the sense of a
story privileged by faith, and seen as the key to the interpretation and
regulation of all other stories."[113]

For Milbank, conversion—not apologetics—marks the way forward
for Christian theology. Seduction, not coercion, is its methodology.
However, by "conversion" something very specific is meant: hearing
the message of the "kingdom of God" in such a way that it drastically
transforms our lives accordingly, with all the attendant risks and dan-
gers implied. Genuine conversion implies risk (waiting on the Holy
Spirit, as scary as that is), which from a human perspective includes
the possibility of failure because "coercion" is not an option for the
Christian faith. In the end, the church cannot *force* the "reigning of
God," it can only witness to it.[114] Sadly, too many Christians view this
acceptance of God's lordship as political *impotence* then refashion the
Word in their own image—some going so far as to employ coercion as
the church's main missional tool. By contrast, evangelism understood
as seduction also means something very specific: theology conceived as
theological aesthetics (here Milbank is greatly indebted to the work of

---

112. Tracy, *The Analogical Imagination*, 389.
113. Milbank, *Theology and Social Theory*, 385–86.
114. See Rubén Rosario Rodríguez, *Christian Martyrdom and Political Violence: A Comparative Theology
with Judaism and Islam* (Cambridge: Cambridge University Press, 2017), 221–68. In this comparative study of
martyrdom as nonviolent political resistance in the three Abrahamic religions, I argue "for the place of divine
action in human history as an alternative to political expediency and instrumentality" (260). Accordingly, "the
Christian alternative to instrumental political action is not another program for social transformation—not even
one built on an ethic of self-sacrifice—but an apocalyptic vision—a glimpse of the eschatological future that we
are expected to incarnate as much as humanly possible while recognizing that all such efforts will inevitably fall
short of the mark" (264).

Hans Urs von Balthasar)[115] contends that "theology contains an intrinsic beauty that commands attention, and this shape, although the basis for and thus prior to, is also consonant with worldly beauty."[116] God's self-revelation is encountered on its own terms even while incarnate "in the beauty of the world," but rather than drawing upon a particular cultural aesthetic norm, *God* determines the specific content of the beautiful in "Christ's atoning life, death and resurrection."[117] Furthermore, this divine revelation in Jesus Christ is inherently compelling as demonstrated by the historical human desire to "gaze upon Jesus, and all those saints whose lives embody the beauty of Christ."[118] This leads Milbank to characterize revelation as a "poetic encounter with God" in which human creativity and moral action are assumed into divinity (by the incarnation):

> The transcendental possibility of revelation is the decision of God to create the poetic being humankind, and with this realization one can, at once, overcome a liberal, merely 'ethical,' reading of religion, and also an (equally modern and deviant) positivistic notion of revelation as something in history 'other' to the normal processes of historicity. The event of revelation itself may be defined as the intersection of the divine and the human creations.[119]

Unfortunately, Milbank's Christology, perhaps because of his desire to avoid the instrumental reason employed by many modern (secularized) theologies, loses much of the concreteness desired by neo-orthodoxy, postliberalism, and other theologies of the Word that manifest Tracy's "route of proclamation."

According to Milbank, in the proclamation of the church, "Jesus cannot be given any particular content: for the founder of a new practice cannot be described in terms of that practice, unless that practice is already in existence, which is contradictory."[120] In other words, the christological narrative is not chiefly about *how* God brings about salvation but ought to be viewed as an extension of the incarnation, in which humanity is assumed into the (mystical) body of Christ and participates *in* the work of salvation as "the (re)foundation of a new

115. See Hans Urs von Balthasar, *The Glory of the Lord: A Theological Aesthetics*, vol. 1, *Seeing the Form*, ed. John Riches, trans. Erasmo Leiva-Merikakis (Edinburgh: T. & T. Clark, 1982); and *Love Alone: The Way of Revelation* (London: Sheed & Ward, 1977).
116. Long, *Divine Economy*, 250.
117. Balthasar, *The Glory of the Lord*, vol. 1, 80, 180.
118. Long, *Divine Economy*, 251.
119. John Milbank, *The Word Made Strange: Theology, Language, Culture* (Oxford: Wiley-Blackwell, 1997), 130.
120. Ibid., 152

community."[121] In other words, in making sense of the traditional doctrines of incarnation and atonement, ecclesiology takes primacy in Milbank's thought: "What Jesus institutes is a new community to promulgate this teaching [the Ten Commandments, the Sermon on the Mount], and his own vision and presence, to sustain it. We then participate in it through our own poetic activity."[122]

How is this Christian "counter-ontology" known? And what types of praxis does it engender? D. Stephen Long has noted that Milbank differentiates himself from liberationists like James Cone by acknowledging humankind has access to a "normative Christian orthodoxy." Despite this reliance on a tangible orthodoxy, however, it is evident that Milbank is cautious about making absolutist claims on matters of belief and praxis because doing so perpetuates the teleological rationality of secular modernism, and "this means that the church has less definite ideas about the roles and characters it seeks to produce than does the *polis*."[123] For Milbank, there is no return to "a past epoch of Christian dominance," neither as a reestablishment of theocracy nor as a construct of contemporary Christian political theologies, which as Milbank has argued, are caught within the "cycle of the ceaseless exhaustion and return of violence" that distinguishes secular politics.[124] In fact, Milbank is particularly critical of European political theologies, Latin American liberation theologies, and perhaps most stringently, eco-theologies for manifesting a form of crypto-fascism:

> Eco-theology may not entirely escape the danger of under-girding this crypto-fascism, because, instead of finding in Biblical tradition ample support for recognition of animal subjectivity, the careful tending of nature, and divine glory and sublimity as disclosed therein, it insists (after little historical reflection) on jettisoning orthodoxy, and constructing a more purely immanent, embodied, developing, limited Godhead.[125]

Clear echoes of Sallie McFague's project to conceptualize the natural world as the embodiment of God (see above) can be heard in this criticism, and the thrust of Milbank's criticism is that eco-theologies, like most modern political theologies, employ the "atheist methodology" of secular modernism in order to promote a singular vision of Christian

121. Ibid., 150–52.
122. Long, *Divine Economy*, 254.
123. Ibid.
124. Milbank, *Theology and Social Theory*, 432, 433.
125. Milbank, *The Word Made Strange*, 262.

ethics that quickly dissolves into an intolerant theological totalitarianism. Whatever else RO's vision of a Christian "counter-ontology" might look like, for Milbank this latter option—surrendering to the modernist politics of coercion—seems a fundamental betrayal of the divinity revealed in Jesus Christ:

> as we are situated on the far side of the cross—the event of the judgment of God . . . the absolute Christian vision of ontological peace now provides the only alternative to a nihilistic outlook. Even today, in the midst of the self-torturing circle of secular reason, there can open to view again a series with which it is in no continuity: the emanation of harmonious difference, the exodus of new generations, the path of peaceful flight . . .[126]

Milbank responds to this critique of his work—that despite emphasizing ecclesiology in the interpretation of atonement and incarnation his proposal is blatantly lacking a concrete ecclesiology—with a simple assertion: "It was not the purpose of *Theology and Social Theory* to imagine the Church as Utopia."[127] In other words, Milbank refuses to identify "some single ideal exemplar" of church because by definition the new community inaugurated and sustained by Christ does not exist "as a peace we must slowly construct, piecemeal, imbibing our hard-learned lessons"—that is the project of modern political science—"but as a peace already given, superabundantly, in the breaking of the bread by the risen Lord, which assembles the harmony of peoples then and at every subsequent Eucharist."[128] Accordingly, the only appropriate response is not one of programmatic exactness but one of faithful witness (Rev. 1:5) to the unfolding work of God in the world since Christ "refused the temptation of present power, and his post-ascended availability by no means reverses that refusal. To be governed by this Lord, to internalize his rule, can only mean to come under his sign of the reversal of all worldly norms of knowledge and authority."[129] Without endorsing the "Benedict Option," Milbank nonetheless envisions the church as a haven from the tragic cycle of political conflict that marks human history by acknowledging that "we *all* dwell in enclaves. . . . The enclave is henceforwards our hospital and asylum. Here—nowhere

---

126. Milbank, *Theology and Social Theory*, 433–34.
127. John Milbank, "Enclaves, Or Where Is the Church?" in *The Future of Love: Essays in Political Theology* (Eugene, OR: Cascade Books, 2009), 133.
128. Ibid.
129. Ibid., 136.

yet—is the Church. Everywhere."[130] Elsewhere Milbank describes this poetic vision of church as "the gradual *end* of human self-government, a kind of ordered anarchy,"[131] which is why in *Theology and Social Theory* he refused to provide a defense of any one particular ecclesiology, since the church is "not primarily an institution at all, but a dissemination of love which is the repetition of the occurrence of complete love in the world, a bearing of evil and death within humanity to the point of exposure of their predatory unreality by the divine *Logos* itself."[132] Nevertheless, Milbank privileges the eucharistic community as the locale where humanity most directly encounters divine self-revelation, which has prompted harsh criticism from Jewish theologian Daniel Boyarin: "what of those 'within' the body excluded from it?"[133] Without question, the biggest challenge to Radical Orthodoxy's vision of a postsecular political theology is its unapologetic use of exclusively Christian dogmatic language to articulate a "politics ordered toward the common good,"[134] which finds its most extreme presentation in Milbank's response to Boyarin's legitimate query about the place of other religions in Milbank's vision of the Christian eucharistic political order: "Pluralism is better guaranteed by Christianity than by the Enlightenment."[135]

Given the troubled history of Christian-Jewish-Muslim interaction, Milbank and other proponents of RO are demanding an unwarranted level of trust from their interlocutors in a religiously pluralistic setting; this becomes particularly problematic if conversion to the Christian ontology rests on its inherent beauty. History matters—whether interpreted from a secular modernist perspective or from a distinctly Christian theopoetics—and a critical reading of Christian history cannot give Christianity a pass simply by concluding that "horror and intolerance follow [only] when the Church ceases to be the Church."[136] This is a convenient act of hermeneutical prestidigitation. Milbank's theological edifice, while awe-inspiring in scope and aspiration, will benefit from a more thorough engagement of critical voices—especially those liberative perspectives dismissed by Milbank after only a cursory and shallow analysis. Like Radical Orthodoxy, liberation theology (LT) also seeks to liberate Christianity

---

130. Ibid., 144 (emphasis in the original).
131. John Milbank, "On Theological Transgression," in *The Future of Love: Essays in Political Theology* (Eugene, OR: Cascade Books, 2009), 167 (emphasis in the original).
132. Ibid., 166.
133. Ibid., 170. See Daniel Boyarin, "A Broken Olive Branch," in *Symposium on John Milbank's Theology and Social Theory*, special issue, *Arachne* 2, no. 1 (1995): 124–30.
134. Bell, "Postliberalism and Radical Orthodoxy," 128.
135. Milbank, "On Theological Transgression," 170.
136. Ibid., 169.

from its captivity to power and empire. Like RO, LT also seeks to ground theology in a distinctly Christian metanarrative. However, unlike RO, LT does not shy from concrete articulations of ecclesial practice, opting to name as "church" those practices that maximize human liberation while also recognizing that these workings of the Spirit might be located *extra muros ecclesiae* ("beyond the walls of the church").

3.4 MIGUEL DE LA TORRE AND THE POLITICS OF *JESÚS*

Radical social instability characterized the decade of the 1960s, especially the interaction between Christian churches and socialist revolutionary movements in various third-world contexts, demanding a Christian response to the breakdown of European colonialism after the Second World War. Liberation theology (LT) sprang up almost simultaneously across many parts of the world in reaction to the realities of endemic poverty caused by economic globalization and the accompanying erosion of democratic freedoms once held sacrosanct by modern political liberalism. Often linked to post-Vatican II theologies as first articulated in Latin America (at the 1968 Conference of Latin American Bishops in Medellín, Colombia), similar movements of liberation also arose in first-world contexts, such as African American and feminist liberation theologies, manifest in Catholic, Protestant, and post-Christian forms. While the magisterial theologies emerging from the Second Vatican Council (1962–65) challenged the church to integrate doctrine with pastoral practice in order to bring its mission to bear on the harsh realities facing much of the world, liberation theologies have their genesis in the pastoral practice and theological reflection of local Christian communities that predated Vatican II, often in a context of ecumenical cooperation, which only later coalesced into a global movement. While LT is arguably the most influential *Christian* theological movement of the last fifty years, liberating theologies are being articulated across the religious spectrum, demonstrating the appeal of a religious narrative that takes a prophetic stance against repression and exploitation. As Miguel De La Torre suggests, "any spiritual movements (not necessarily Christian) that seek to dismantle the global social structures responsible for causing so much poverty and oppression can be called *liberative*."[137]

---

137. Miguel A. De La Torre, "Liberation Theology," in *The Cambridge Companion to Christian Political Theology*, ed. Craig Hovey and Elizabeth Phillips (Cambridge: Cambridge University Press, 2015), 23–24.

Like Radical Orthodoxy, LT has a troubled critical relationship with modernism, especially capitalism and its political defenders: "Neoliberalism, and the oppressive political structures designed to economically privilege the few, seems to have won."[138] Yet, while RO has refrained from articulating an explicit political program, LT has argued for concrete resistance to the forces of unchecked predatory capitalism and anti-democratic economic deregulation: "We are left asking if capitalism and Christianity are compatible or irreconcilable."[139] In David Tracy's organizing typology, the route of history and praxis has risen to prominence because "the classic routes of manifestation and proclamation are not sufficient for the distinctively Christian journey," suggesting that "we are primarily neither hearers of the word nor seers of a manifestation" but "doers of the word in history."[140] In other words, for political and liberation theologians, this emphasis on praxis disallows "the temptation in all expressions of Christianity, whether manifestation or proclamation, to unduly interiorize, spiritualize, individualize the content of God's eschatological promises."[141] Citing Brazilian educator Paulo Freire and his concept of *conscientização* ("consciousness raising" or "critical consciousness"), De La Torre defends LT's "move away from Christendom's complicity with political and economic oppressive structures that contribute to the people's false-consciousness" by emphasizing praxis understood as *political* action, as the means by which the "oppressed move from being objects toward subjects of their own destiny."[142]

Gustavo Gutiérrez, one of the earliest proponents of liberation theology, argues for political and cultural revolution on theological grounds because "only a radical break from the status quo, that is, a profound transformation of the private property system, access to power of the exploited class, and a social revolution that would break this dependence would allow for the change to a new society."[143] According to Gutiérrez, the Bible "presents the work of Christ as a liberation" and identifies the root of oppression as sin, with sin defined as "a selfish turning in upon oneself. To sin is to refuse to love one's neighbors and, therefore, the Lord himself. Sin—a breach of friendship with God and others—is

138. Miguel A. De La Torre, *The Politics of Jesús: A Hispanic Political Theology* (Lanham, MD: Rowman & Littlefield, 2015), 3.
139. Ibid., 5.
140. Tracy, *The Analogical Imagination*, 390.
141. Ibid.
142. De La Torre, "Liberation Theology," 26.
143. Gustavo Gutiérrez, *A Theology of Liberation: History, Politics and Salvation*, rev., ed. and trans. by Sister Caridad Inda and John Eagleson (Maryknoll, NY: Orbis Books, 1988), 17.

according to the Bible the ultimate cause of poverty, injustice, and the oppression in which persons live."[144] This perspective from the underside of history (Bonhoeffer) leads to the *preferential option for the poor*, which means that it is "to the oppressed that the Church should address itself and not so much to the oppressors; furthermore, this action will give true meaning to the Church's witness to poverty."[145] Granted, by embracing a view of history as class conflict then choosing to side with the oppressed over against the oppressor, early proponents of liberation theology opened themselves up to the judgment that they had uncritically embraced Marxist ideology. For example, in the Vatican's first official statement on the theology of liberation (authored by Cardinal Joseph Ratzinger, later Pope Benedict XVI), the argument is made that liberation theologians have borrowed the theoretical framework of Marxist political and economic thought to such a degree it has become "damaging to the faith and to Christian living."[146] Stanley Hauerwas, an ethicist and theologian sympathetic to Radical Orthodoxy, chides the move within North American theology toward a praxis-oriented, justice-focused approach by saying that, "The current emphasis on justice and rights as the primary norms guiding the social witness of Christians is in fact a mistake."[147] Even Milbank, who despite praising liberation theologians for being "aware, as de Lubac, Congar and von Balthasar are not, that ecclesial history is not insulated from political and social history,"[148] ultimately dismisses liberation theology for submitting to "methodological atheism," instead arguing that "Theology as 'metanarrative realism' will replace theology mediated by social science, just as supernatural pragmatism replaces foundational practice."[149] Regardless, the trajectory of liberative praxis as one of the leading Christian responses to the contemporary situation thrives, and with it a thorough critique of theological approaches that emphasize theory and belief over distinctly Christian practice. Therefore, Gutiérrez writes, "Faith in God does not consist in asserting God's existence, but rather in acting on [God's] behalf."[150] Even one of Christianity's harshest critics, Friedrich

144. Ibid., 23–24.
145. Ibid., 70.
146. Cardinal Joseph Ratzinger, Congregation for the Doctrine of the Faith, "Instruction on Certain Aspects of the 'Theology of Liberation' (Aug. 6, 1984)," in *Liberation Theology: A Documentary History*, ed. Alfred T. Hennelly (Maryknoll, NY: Orbis Books, 1990), 394.
147. Stanley Hauerwas, *After Christendom? How the Church Is to Behave If Freedom, Justice, and a Christian Nation Are Bad Ideas* (Nashville, TN: Abingdon Press, 1991), 45.
148. Milbank, *Theology and Social Theory*, 246.
149. Ibid., 251–52.
150. Gustavo Gutiérrez and Richard Shaull, *Liberation and Change* (Richmond, VA: John Knox Press, 1977), 89.

Nietzsche, recognized the need to critique *orthodoxy* via the lens of *orthopraxy*: "To reduce being a Christian, Christianism, to a matter of considering something true, to a mere phenomenon of consciousness, is to negate Christianism."[151] Nietzsche strongly condemns Christianity's mistaken emphasis on doctrine rather than praxis: "It is false to the point of nonsense to find the mark of the Christian in a 'faith,' for instance, in the faith in redemption through Christ: only Christian *practice*, a life such as he *lived* who died on the cross, is Christian."[152] Thus Gutiérrez concludes that a Christian response to the contemporary situation, contra Milbank, entails a "definite practice," involving criticism of both society and the church, "worked out in the light of the Word accepted in faith and inspired by a practical purpose—and therefore indissolubly linked to historical praxis."[153]

In *Latina/o Social Ethics: Moving Beyond Eurocentric Moral Thinking* (2010), ethicist Miguel A. De La Torre suggests a new direction for Christian liberative praxis: an ethic *para joder*. Employing the Spanish verb *joder*, a not-too-polite colloquialism that translates as "to f*ck with," De La Torre encourages the disenfranchised to mess with the powers that be as a way of destabilizing unjust power structures and exposing institutionalized white, male, Eurocentric privilege. An ethic that prioritizes undermining the status quo through satirical social commentary—in which a "trickster" figure like Juan Bobo in Puerto Rican folktales exposes societal hypocrisy through his childish innocence—is a desirable component of nonviolent political resistance.[154] De La Torre finds inspiration in biblical "tricksters" like Abraham or Jacob who employ deception as a means of self-preservation, arguing that even Jesus employs an ethic *para joder*, insofar as Jesus' preaching destabilized the status quo through his use of parables, placing him and his followers into direct conflict with the reigning religious and political powers.[155]

Christian ethics from a Latino/a perspective begins with an intentional act of political activism on behalf of the marginalized and oppressed; such activism is grounded in the lived experience of Latino/a

151. Friedrich Nietzsche, *The Antichrist*, in *The Portable Nietzsche*, ed. and trans. by Walter Kaufmann (New York: The Viking Press, 1968), 613.
152. Ibid., 612.
153. Gutiérrez, *A Theology of Liberation*, 9.
154. Miguel A. De La Torre, *Latina/o Social Ethics: Moving Beyond Eurocentric Moral Thinking* (Waco, TX: Baylor University Press, 2010), 111.
155. De La Torre's subversive praxis shares common ground with Walter Wink's *Jesus and Nonviolence: A Third Way* (Minneapolis, MN: Fortress Press, 2003), in which Jesus calls us to transcend both passivity and violence by finding a third way, one that offers resistance to injustice yet is nonviolent. This third way is demonstrated in Wink's creative reinterpretation of Jesus turning the other cheek as an act of cultural defiance against oppressive masters.

communities through the academic theologian's active involvement in the community of faith: "This keeps ethical analysis real and practical, because it focuses on the struggle against the dehumanization and disenfranchisement of Latina/os."[156] De La Torre recognizes that "we all create Jesus in our own image," so he advocates for a hermeneutics of suspicion to counteract how "Jesus has been constructed throughout history by those wielding political power" in order to redeem Jesus from this ideological captivity: "How can the symbolic justifier of so much global oppression ever be redemptive? Can Jesus be saved from Jesus?"[157] Like RO, this liberative hermeneutic questions the neutrality and methodological objectivity of secular Modernism, but rather than arguing for a "counter-ontology" to challenge the myth of modernity, LT adopts a countercultural political mode of resistance to undermine and expose the normative status of this Enlightenment myth: "There is no one true Jesus that can be objectively known; there only exists subjective interpretations of Jesus. The social, cultural, political, and global economic power of Euroamericans allows them to impose their subjective interpretation of Jesus as the objective Truth (with a capital *T*) for everyone else."[158] Consequently, rather than employing a historical-critical method, liberative hermeneutics intentionally appropriates a subjective interpretive perspective that recognizes the dishonesty of claiming a neutral "view from nowhere":

> I propose that we engage in creating a Jesus that resonates with our particular marginalized community (for me, it would obviously be a Latina/o community). But rather than focusing on some essentialized characteristics of what it means to be Hispanic, I will argue for a preferential option in the creation of Jesús. . . . While every interpretation of Jesus or Jesús reflects the life of the author, our task is to remain as faithful as possible to the biblical narrative while exploring aspects of the text that might indicate how Jesús would understand and sympathize with the plight of today's Latino/as. . . . Reading the text with our own Hispanic eyes has the potential of freeing the text from the institutionalized Eurocentric church by reinterpreting the text through a more liberative lens.[159]

Without completely dismissing the Jesus of the dominant culture (De La Torre acknowledges a debt to Howard Yoder's nonviolent Jesus), LT

156. De La Torre, *Latino/a Social Ethics*, 77.
157. De La Torre, *The Politics of Jesús*, 1, 2.
158. Ibid., 7 (emphasis in the original).
159. Ibid., 8.

embraces a critical reconstruction of Jesús over the Jesus of contemporary biblical criticism because "the Euroamerican Jesus has historically been used (or muted) to divinely justify societal actions that have silently contributed to or loudly maintained the marginalization" of Latino/as and other groups marginalized because of race, ethnicity, gender, or class.[160]

In much the same way that James H. Cone has argued for a black Jesus,[161] in *The Politics of Jesús* (2015) De La Torre contends that Hispanics embrace a Latino/a Jesús not because of "some psychological need existing among Latina/os to see a Divine through their own cultural signs. Jesús is Hispanic because the biblical witness of God is of one who takes sides with the least among us against those who oppress them."[162] In other words, like Gutiérrez—but in contrast to Milbank's Radical Orthodoxy—De La Torre asserts that God speaks clearly and concretely in order to ground ecclesiology in definite practices. Recognizing the human tendency to "create" Jesus in our own image does not mean all Christological claims are equally valid. LT argues that some reconstructions of the life of Jesus are closer to the biblical witness than others by highlighting certain texts that provide a hermeneutical framework for understanding his earthly ministry: "In the famous biblical parable of the sheep and the goats (Matt. 25:31–46), Jesús divides those destined for glory (the sheep) from those destined for damnation (the goats). The salvation of those with power and privilege is contingent upon how they treated those who were starving, thirsty, aliens, unclothed, ill, and imprisoned."[163] In other words, by understanding the biblical Jesus through the experiential lens of the marginalized and despised of *his* era, LT emphasizes the political dimension of the Gospel and argues against any spiritualization or depoliticization of the Christian Gospel that ignores the preferential option for the poor present in the Bible, from the Mosaic covenant to the prophetic texts, and from the Magnificat of Mary to the parables of Jesus. Yet the liberating Jesús of Latino/a theology is not a savior for Hispanics alone, since by critiquing and unmasking the false idol that is the Eurocentric Jesus, the Latino/a Jesús provides "guidance as to what praxis can be implemented to realistically bring about a more just society, not solely for Hispanics, but for all," by providing concrete "ethical precepts concerning God and God's call for love, mercy, and justice."[164]

160. Ibid., 14.
161. See James H. Cone, *God of the Oppressed* (Maryknoll, NY: Orbis Books, 1975), 99–126.
162. De La Torre, *The Politics of Jesús*, 15.
163. Ibid., 17.
164. Ibid., 19.

Preserving the basic human dignity (*dignidad*) of all persons as creatures made in the image of God (*imago Dei*) leads liberation theology to criticize the dominant socioeconomic structures. While supporters of neoliberalism (economic and social policies that emphasize free trade and relatively open markets) argue that globalization has improved wages and working conditions for workers in underdeveloped nations, detractors contend that the exploitation of weaker nations by the first world has led to a widened economic gap between developed and underdeveloped nations, contributed to environmental degradation, and when factoring for inflation, has actually resulted in reduced workers' wages. Trade liberalization has also triggered the commodification of human labor through the mass exportation of migrant laborers. While a Latino/a ethical response to globalization is not necessarily adverse to capitalism, an ethic that espouses universal human liberation cannot allow corporate profits to supersede preserving basic human dignity. LT's preferential option for the poor remains relevant in today's world because, in spite of the economic gains of neoliberal policies, the dehumanizing and lethal effects of global poverty remain. A Christian political theology born from the margins of Latino/a experience in the United States attacks the root causes of economic injustice; the unchecked consequences of neoliberal economic policies work against the liberative goals of the self-revealing God of the Bible. By looking closely at the everyday reality of Latino/as in the United States, De La Torre challenges Christians to engage in ethics *en conjunto* ("done together"), seeing economic realities through the eyes of the marginalized, nurturing political solidarity with the disenfranchised, while articulating a biblically informed concrete social praxis that can transform oppressive situations.

Not all proponents of Radical Orthodoxy have dismissed the liberationist theological response to the contemporary situation. Daniel M. Bell Jr., in *Liberation Theology After the End of History* (2001), argues that "the body of Christ that is the Church of the poor" offers the best hope for liberating culture from "the clutches of capitalism."[165] Unfortunately, like Milbank and Hauerwas, Bell believes that LT has taken a wrong turn by emphasizing social justice and individual rights for in doing so LT remains "embedded in the modern narrative that divorces religion from the social-political-economic dimensions of life."[166]

---

165. Bell, *Liberation Theology After the End of History*, 35.
166. Ibid., 3.

Consequently, Bell rejects the liberationists' call for political resistance to capitalism—and its accompanying "technologies of desire"—while praising their "refusal to cease suffering" through an act of forgiveness toward their oppressors, even when that act of forgiveness might lead to their own martyrdom: "I begin by arguing that forgiveness avoids both the theological and practical deficiencies that undercut the liberationists' account of justice."[167] Here Bell criticizes the futility of much of the political resistance offered by the Latin American Church of the poor toward oppressive political regimes and predatory capitalist systems in order to advocate for forgiveness as a distinctly Christian form of resistance to capitalism:

> Central to this account of forgiveness are those whom Jon Sobrino and Ignacio Ellacuría call "the crucified people." In spite of their own commitment to justice as the guardian of rights, the liberationists acknowledge that many of the crucified people who constitute the Church of the poor are facing their oppressors and extending the gift of forgiveness, not demanding what is due in accord with their "rights." More importantly, the crucified people are extending forgiveness precisely as a form of resistance to capitalism.[168]

As with Milbank, Bell's shortcoming is that his ecclesial praxis remains unsatisfactorily vague in the face of real human suffering on a grand scale. Admittedly, RO's concerns that liberationists have succumbed to the secular reasoning of the Enlightenment, further facilitating "the Church's retreat to the apolitical space" in which "the state assumes control of the temporal realm"[169] are corroborated by the growing impotence of the church as a political player in places like Nicaragua where the church actively participated in statecraft under the Sandinista government.[170] Nevertheless, given the humanitarian crisis confronting the church of the poor in Latin America, especially in places like El Salvador where, under the shadow of the Salvadoran Civil War (1980–92), narco-trafficking regimes have undermined the rule of law and given way to unprecedented levels of violence,[171] Bell's "therapeutic" ecclesiology places an unfair burden on the victimized.

167. Ibid., 5.
168. Ibid.
169. Ibid., 65.
170. See Emelio Betances, *The Catholic Church and Power Politics in Latin America: The Dominican Case in Comparative Perspective* (Lanham, UK: Rowman & Littlefield, 2007), 49–98.
171. Tim Padgett, "El Salvador's New President Faces Gangs, Poverty and Instability," National Public Radio (March 19, 2014), http://www.npr.org/sections/parallels/2014/03/19/291428131/el-salvadors-new-president-faces-gangs-poverty-and-instability (accessed June 3, 2017).

Those who have endured economic exploitation, political repression, and cultural marginalization are being asked to once again take on the yoke of suffering, only this time for the spiritual well-being of their oppressors: "The redemptive power of the therapy of forgiveness resides not in the suffering itself but in the gracious generosity and vulnerability to the one who is/was the enemy. Redemption is found in the embrace that breaks down the walls of hostility and reconciles crucified and crucifier."[172]

Bell, citing Jon Sobrino's work on Latin American martyrology, acknowledges the very real possibility that the victim's offer of forgiveness might be rejected thereby causing the sinner to then turn "on the one offering forgiveness with even greater fury."[173] In other words, for proponents of Radical Orthodoxy an ethic of forgiveness implies great risk—what Bell characterizes as "a wager on God"—because it rejects direct political action as idolatrous. RO's callousness toward human suffering is shrouded in the language of devotion and self-sacrifice: "When history's losers, the crucified people, follow in the steps of Jesus and forgive their enemies, they are wagering on God. They are wagering that God is who the Gospel proclaims God to be, the one who defeats sin and wipes away every tear, not with the sword of justice that upholds rights but with the gift of forgiveness in Christ."[174]

Its various proponents, from Milbank to Hauerwas to Long, all make similar arguments about the inadequacy of LT's theorization of the political sphere as an uncritical acceptance of Enlightenment instrumental reason: "Thus, I fear, the politics of Jesus that Gutiérrez discovers does not challenge the dominant tradition's view of 'politics,' but assumes it."[175] Yet none of RO's proponents recognize a fundamental premise of liberationist thought: the biblical witness provides multiple examples of Jesus' political praxis beyond just passive acceptance of innocent suffering by turning the other cheek. At least Long acknowledges, without elaborating, that the "redemption Jesus brings certainly contains positive political implications in Gutiérrez's theology, particularly Jesus' victory over sin."[176]

Miguel De La Torre, in his latest book titled *Embracing Hopelessness* (2017), takes on the reality addressed by Bell—this "refusal to cease suffering" by history's losers, the ever-present reality of human

172. Bell, *Liberation Theology After the End of History*, 193.
173. Ibid., 175.
174. Ibid., 195.
175. Long, *Divine Economy*, 134.
176. Ibid., 133.

suffering caused by economic and social injustice—*without* under-mining the political agency of the oppressed. Drawing inspiration from Job, De La Torre embraces this political reality: "The faithful of the world, especially those relegated to the underside of white and class privilege, have little hope of resolution to the hopeless situation in which they find themselves. The piles of innocent corpses litter-ing history testifies to the bankruptcy of any type of dialectical or salvation history ushering some utopia."[177] Recognizing the hope-lessness (from a strictly "political" point of view) experienced by the world's oppressed peoples, De La Torre nevertheless insists it is not enough to rest on divine promises of a future-oriented eschatologi-cal resolution, and like Gutiérrez turns to a liberative Christology to articulate a concrete ecclesial praxis grounded in the biblical witness that does not limit itself to just forgiving the enemy. Without wield-ing the power of the sword (i.e., coercion by the state), De La Torre envisions a model of nonviolent liberative political resistance aim-ing to disrupt the regimes of power, both political and economic, that perpetuate this hopelessness. In other words, LT is able to envi-sion an alternative model of political resistance that is grounded in ecclesial praxis *without* employing the tactics of modern statecraft, one which views the church as a radical counterculture embodied in acts of solidarity and nonviolent resistance capable of preserving the dignity and moral agency of the victimized without divorcing justice from mercy. Expounding on the concept of an ethic *para joder* intro-duced in *Latina/o Social Ethics*, De La Torre clarifies that to "*joder* is not a praxis where disenfranchised groups engage out of a desire for vengeance."[178] On the contrary, to *joder* "is an act of love toward oppressors designed to force them to live up to their rhetoric in the hopes of confronting their complicity with oppressive structures so as to lead them toward their own salvation."[179] Consequently, there is much that can be done in the political sphere, be it through leg-islation, political organizing, investigative reporting, etc., that can accomplish the desired destabilization of the status quo without reducing Christian political action to the politics of coercion: "To *joder* is thus far a nonviolent survival strategy based on love designed to liberate the abused from death-dealing social structures denying

177. Miguel A. De La Torre, *Embracing Hopelessness* (Minneapolis, MN: Fortress Press, 2017), xiv.
178. Ibid., 153–54.
179. Ibid., 154.

them of their humanity, and the abuser whose own humanity is lost through their complicity with these same structures."[180]

Radical Orthodoxy rejects any model of "political liberation through regime change" as capable of producing genuine forgiveness and reconciliation by overcoming the vicious cycle of reciprocal violence. According to the "counter-ontology" of RO, overcoming the human desire for retribution is a work of grace that lies beyond any Christian political or ecclesial praxis. Liberation theology agrees with RO that Christ on the cross, forgiving his torturers and executioners, offers a way forward that appears to break the cycle of violence, but the inherent danger in readily offering forgiveness to the oppressor is to risk making "a mockery of the millions who have suffered at the hands of the violent—battered women, exploited and dehumanized slaves, tortured dissidents, persecuted minorities."[181] Miroslav Volf suggests that despite the tendency of liberation narratives to perpetuate reciprocal violence by characterizing historical injustices as oppositional struggles, it is necessary to strongly condemn injustice: "Suspend justice and truth, and you cannot redeem the world; you must leave it as it is," abandoning the world "to the darkness of hell; the world will remain forever awry, the blood of the innocent will eternally cry out to heaven. There can be no redemption unless the truth about the world is told and justice is done."[182] Unlike Radical Orthodoxy, which seems to speak from a position of cultural power and economic privilege (even while disdaining the politics of statecraft), and is therefore oblivious to the inherent political impotence that gives rise to hopelessness, De La Torre has articulated a theology of liberation that refuses complicity in perpetuating oppression while affirming the role of *active* nonviolent resistance:

Yes, we should do everything in our power to avoid decimation and destruction, martyrdom is not something to be sought; but at times death cannot be avoided, for it provides meaning and purpose to life. Justice probably will not determine the future of humanity; nevertheless, its pursuit is what makes life worth living in the present—and maybe, just maybe, this is what it means to hope against all hope.[183]

180. Ibid.
181. Miroslav Volf, *Exclusion and Embrace: A Theological Exploration of Identity, Otherness, and Reconciliation* (Nashville, TN: Abingdon Press, 1996), 103.
182. Ibid., 294.
183. De La Torre, *Embracing Hopelessness*, 155–56.

3.5 EMBRACING AN EXILIC THEOLOGY

This chapter's analysis of the contemporary situation in Christian theology, described as a postmodern Babylon in which distinctly Christian perspectives find themselves culturally exiled from the dominant secular culture, employed David Tracy's three distinct types of Christian theological responses—manifestation, proclamation, and liberation—in order to highlight the strengths (while exposing deficiencies) of each approach in addressing the current crisis. During the Babylonian captivity (597–538 BCE), the people of Israel experienced a political impotence that permeated every facet of their lives—from their public cultic worship to their most private devotion—and this experience of exile left them mired in hopelessness:

> By the rivers of Babylon—
>> there we sat down and there we wept
>> when we remembered Zion.
> On the willows there
>> we hung up our harps.
> For there our captors
>> asked us for songs,
> and our tormentors asked for mirth, saying,
>> 'Sing us one of the songs of Zion!'
>
> How could we sing the Lord's song
>> in a foreign land?
>>   *(Ps 137:1–4)*

In the current age, religious perspectives are marginalized and silenced within academic and political discourse, so that theologians seeking to embody a public theology that embraces civic responsibility and works for the common good also find themselves attempting to sing the Lord's song in a foreign land. Yet unlike the Israelites, who would return to Jerusalem to rebuild the temple (even if only temporarily), the analysis of both Radical Orthodoxy and liberation theology make it clear there is no return from this exile—no nostalgic rebirth of a politically dominant Christendom or a politically viable Utopian future built by an activist church. Accordingly, the visions of church offered by these two movements *embrace* the marginalized location of theological perspectives in the public discourse and seek to transform the world from the margins—whether as a sectarian counterculture to the dominant metanarrative (Milbank) or as a politically subversive culture of nonviolent resistance (De La Torre).

Not only are Christian theological perspectives marginalized within public discourse, as evidenced by how little impact theological discourse receptive to and engaging of the natural sciences (McFague) has had outside theology, Christian theological perspectives are also competing with other religions in an increasingly globalized pluralistic society. If the way forward is not a return to Christian cultural dominance, and if the religious "other" is no longer considered an infidel but is viewed more as a fellow pilgrim on the journey of spiritual enlightenment, then the discipline of theology cannot continue operating as it has. As we have learned from Sallie McFague's metaphorical theology, one of the criteria for a contemporary constructive theology is that it embraces a multiplicity of perspectives by not allowing any one metaphor to dominate God-talk but instead nurtures a theological method that intentionally cultivates many and varied metaphors for God. At the same time, religious perspectives are particular and concrete, oftentimes making exclusivist claims about their distinctive God-talk. Consequently, what is learned from John Milbank's Radical Orthodoxy is the need to let theological discourses operate on their own terms without succumbing to the dominant cultural trends. Unfortunately, exclusivist religious claims are likely to create conflict between competing religions, especially as the forces of globalization bring us into closer proximity with our neighbors throughout the world. Accordingly, liberation theology confronts the challenge of religious pluralism with the belief that God requires liberation for the oppressed, justice for the victims, and most demanding of all, love for the political enemy. For De La Torre, the religious other need not be a rival but can become a fellow worker in solidarity guided by a grander vision than any one of our cultural or political projects can capture: "Working for justice, liberation, and salvation, as already mentioned, is not conducted because the hope of success exists. The disenfranchised undertakes this work because no other alternative exists. Even in the absence of any assurance of future success, the work toward justice continues for its own sake."[184]

Given this methodological commitment to pursuing an understanding of divine revelation in comparative dialogue with other religions, this work embraces the need for theology to address a broader public beyond the church yet also affirms the need for speaking from within

184. Ibid., 155.

one's own theological tradition by avoiding untenable universal claims about religiosity and allowing each tradition to enter the comparative conversation from within its own internal reasoning. Therefore, while offering a constructive proposal for a comparative doctrine of revelation in conversation with Judaism and Islam, embracing religious pluralism and interfaith cooperation also necessitates further comparative engagement with non-Abrahamic and non-theistic religions. For the moment it is possible to proceed on the normative assumption that theology is inherently hermeneutical and that a primary task of theologians is to interpret the truth-claims of one's own religious tradition for a particular time and place. It follows that comparative theology is a constructive enterprise grounded in a particular confessional faith perspective yet engaged in thorough comparative analysis with another religious tradition, which leads to the critical reconstruction of one's own doctrines as a direct result of this comparative encounter.

4

Dogmatic Claims in Pluralistic Context

> "When I was a boy . . . all the people of all the nations which had
> fought in the First World War were silent during the eleventh minute of
> the eleventh hour of Armistice Day, which was the eleventh day of the
> eleventh month.
>
> It was during that minute in 1918, that millions upon millions of
> human beings stopped butchering one another. I have talked to old men
> who were on battlefields during that minute. They have told me in one
> way or another that the sudden silence was the Voice of God. So we still
> have among us some men who can remember when God spoke clearly
> to mankind."
>
> —Kurt Vonnegut[1]

The postmodern moment has "made room" for theology in the public and
academic discourse by relativizing all rational discourses and undermining modernity's reliance on scientific rationalism. However, this celebration of multiple rationalities—at least within academic discourse—still
tends to privilege secular modes of reasoning. Like neo-orthodoxy in
the twentieth century, Radical Orthodoxy in the twenty-first century
has attempted to make an impact on the broader culture without com-
promising its distinctively theological content. Yet, aside from the occa-
sional public intellectual (Cornel West, Stanley Hauerwas, or Miroslav
Volf), theology remains a largely marginalized discourse that endures
essentially unheard. Liberation theology also articulates its own critique
of Enlightenment modernism's secularizing tendencies but does so by
embracing the inherently political dimension of the Gospel in order to
critique—and hopefully transform—the dominant culture. This chapter
argues that the marginalization of theological perspectives in the public
discourse continues in part because the discipline of theology facilitates
its own depoliticization by playing the game according to the rules of
the European and North American academies. Affirming the reality that
theological modes of reasoning have a broad social and cultural impact
throughout the rest of the world, it is time for Christian academic theology to embrace its global social location and learn to make concrete

1. Kurt Vonnegut, *Breakfast of Champions*, reprint (New York: Delacorte Press, 1973), 6.

dogmatic claims in a pluralistic context *without* resorting to some form
of theological totalitarianism.

Given that Christianity and Islam are the largest and fastest growing religions in the world, together encompassing over half the world's
population, the strategy here advocated is a Christian comparative
theology that begins by engaging the three Abrahamic religions at the
doctrinal level through an analysis of their respective doctrines of revelation, with special emphasis given to the notion of divine hiddenness
in God's self-revelation. Ultimately, this comparative discourse between
the Abrahamic religions—with their shared scriptural and cultural histories—will model dialogue and cooperation between *all* the world's
religions. However, in order to situate theology within the contemporary cultural conversation, it is important to first reflect on the relationship of explicitly theological discourse with secular modes of reasoning
before speaking to the realities of religious pluralism.

4.1 DOGMATIC THEOLOGY IN
INTERDISCIPLINARY CONTEXT

Scholars of religion have long sought to reconcile the premodern,
culturally specific, and exclusive claims of particular religions over
against the equally exclusive claims of competing worldviews, even
while granting religion's universality as a phenomenal reality present in all human cultures throughout history. In order to navigate
the Babel of competing truth-claims marking our current global
reality, the discipline of theology needs tools for navigating various
"publics"—Christian ecumenism, modern secularism, religious pluralism—so despite neo-orthodoxy and postliberalism's methodological
commitment to speak the church's distinct "grammar," this "does not
exclude the development of powerful theological rationales for sober
and practically efficacious commitment to interreligious discussion
and cooperation."[2] Building on Clifford Geertz's definition of culture
as "an historically transmitted pattern of meanings embodied in symbols, a system of inherited conceptions expressed in symbolic forms
by means of which men communicate, perpetuate, and develop their
knowledge about and attitudes toward life," this book views religion as
the subset of human cultural creations that render certain transcendent

---

2. George A. Lindbeck, *The Nature of Doctrine: Religion and Theology in a Postliberal Age,* 25th anniversary ed.
(Louisville, KY: Westminster John Knox Press, 2009), 41.

truths intellectually defensible as part of the process of articulating a theoretical framework that enables believers to interpret and describe "the actual state of affairs."[3] Recognizing that the subjective dimension of religious belief (Kierkegaard) does not lend itself to the same level of empirical verification as the natural sciences, or even the social sciences, Geertz suggests that religious beliefs are grounded in certain core "sentiments" that religionists invoke as "experiential evidence for their truth."[4] This does not mean that religious truth claims cannot be subjected to rational scrutiny or external verification, but merely circumscribes the limits of theological language when entering the interdisciplinary conversation.

The modernist habit of describing certain phenomena as distinctly "religious"—an idea derived from Immanuel Kant's transcendental critique of knowledge—is no longer tenable in the postmodern age, especially in light of criticisms from the natural sciences as evidenced, for example, by the proliferation of studies examining religious belief from an evolutionary perspective.[5] According to Kant, human experience and knowledge are mere appearance (*phenomena*), while how things are in-themselves (*noumena*) remains epistemologically unknowable, in effect reducing all knowledge to the contents of human subjectivity. By postulating certain universal human beliefs as reasonable, despite the fact that from an empirical perspective they appear contradictory and unresolved (such *antinomies* include belief in human freedom or belief in God), Kant attempts to provide a practical yet no less rational basis for religion. Against the background of Kantian epistemology, Friedrich Schleiermacher explores the possibility of understanding that which is by definition beyond all human experience: the transcendent God. In *On Religion: Speeches to Its Cultured Despisers* (1799), Schleiermacher argues that religion is not a form of knowing and therefore not in conflict with science. Theology, as developed in *The Christian Faith* (1830), consists of reflection upon the contents of religious self-consciousness, specifically consciousness of "our feeling of absolute dependence" and "being in relation with God."[6] Thus, while distancing himself from

3. Clifford Geertz, *The Interpretation of Cultures* (New York: Basic Books, 1973), 89.

4. Ibid., 90.

5. See Robert Wright, *The Evolution of God* (New York: Little, Brown, 2009); Dominic D. P. Johnson, Hillary L. Lenfesty, and Jeffrey P. Schloss, "The Elephant in the Room: Do Evolutionary Accounts of Religion Entail the Falsity of Religious Belief?" *Philosophy, Theology and the Sciences* 1, no. 2 (2014): 200–231; *The Biology of Religious Behavior: The Evolutionary Origins of Faith and Religion*, ed. Jay R. Feierman (Santa Barbara, CA: Praeger, 2009); and *The Believing Primate: Scientific, Philosophical, and Theological Reflections on the Origins of Religion*, ed. Jeffrey Schloss and Michael J. Murray (Oxford: Oxford University Press, 2010).

6. Friedrich Schleiermacher, *The Christian Faith*, vol. 1, ed. and trans. Terrence N. Tice, Catherine L. Kelsey, and Edwina Lawler (Louisville, KY: Westminster John Knox Press, 2016), 18–27.

Enlightenment efforts to establish knowledge of God by reason alone, Schleiermacher nonetheless embraces the modern turn to the subject by centering theological reflection on the believer's religious experience.

Admittedly, Schleiermacher's language can steer theology toward emotivism, pietism and fideism, but his use of the language of "religious experience" is not intended to safeguard traditional doctrines from rational criticism; it is simply an affirmation that some people interpret experiences as having religious significance while others interpret the very same experiences in nonreligious ways. Delwin Brown (1935–2009) advocates for interdisciplinarity in theological discourse, even granting theology the status of a "public" discipline with a rightful place in the university curriculum so long as "it is an open, fallible, developing, correctable, disciplined pursuit of clarity about, intelligibility in, and understanding of our commerce with our shared worlds."[7] Yet here the term "public" is simply descriptive of the plurality of disciplines and perspectives vying for legitimacy, not a guarantee that theology is deserving of an *equal* place within academic discourse. Consequently, Brown is critical of theologies that appeal to distinctly "religious" experience, do not provide reasons for preferring a religious interpretation in favor of a scientific explanation, and fail to articulate criteria for resolving conflicts between competing traditions.

Certain implications stemming from Brown's project—namely, that our religious traditions extend beyond their own borders and are interwoven with other perspectives thus allowing for interdisciplinary discourse[8]—lead him to grant that experiences someone might explain with "ordinary" language someone else can explain using "religious" language. Ironically, Brown's choice of terms, "ordinary" versus "religious" experience, seems to betray a modernist bias against religious interpretations given Brown's questioning *why* anyone would interpret an otherwise "ordinary" experience as *also* having "religious" significance.[9] In fact, by differentiating between "ordinary" and "religious" explanatory narratives Brown commits the same categorical mistake Richard Rorty criticizes in modernist epistemologies. To borrow an analogy from woodworking, Brown's discomfort arises from the fact that certain interpretive models and corresponding interpreted experiences fit together like a finely crafted piece of furniture with nearly

---

7. Delwin Brown, "Public Theology, Academic Theology: Wentzel van Huyssteen and the Nature of Theological Rationality," *American Journal of Theology and Philosophy* 22, no. 1 (January 2001): 2.

8. See Delwin Brown, *Boundaries of Our Habituations: Tradition and Theological Construction* (Albany, NY: SUNY Press, 1994), 146.

9. Brown, "Public Theology, Academic Theology," 93.

imperceptible joints (scientific rationality), while other explanatory narratives hold together like a roughly hewn log cabin with clearly discernible gaps between its timbers (one has to assume Brown would here include "religious" rationality). It cannot be denied that scientific interpretive models yield quantifiable and repeatable descriptions that offer a high degree of accuracy and predictability concerning the material universe while the symbolic language of religion lends itself to multiple, often contradictory, interpretations. Nevertheless, foundational religious narratives allow human beings to "make sense" of the world, even while remaining rough conceptual frameworks, because they have withstood the test of time by providing answers for existentially meaningful questions despite lacking scientific exactness. Consequently, Brown treads dangerously close to endorsing a form of foundationalist positivism by privileging scientific rationality as the norm for interpreting so-called ordinary experience. While scientific interpretive models are highly successful at describing certain types of phenomena, its methods are not universally applicable.

The natural sciences and theology are disparate academic disciplines, each with its own methodology, areas of study, and investigational goals. Still, despite a popular perception—somewhat warranted—that the interactions between science and theology are primarily conflictual, recent efforts by both scientists and theologians have fostered an interdisciplinary space in which the possibility of methodological overlap can lead to mutually beneficial conversation. Dissatisfied with approaches that posit an absolute disjunction between theology and science, such as the "new atheism" of Richard Dawkins, Sam Harris, and Daniel Dennett,[10] and convinced that Stephen Jay Gould's conception of "non-overlapping magisteria" undermines genuine multidisciplinary engagement by relegating theological perspectives to an epistemological ghetto,[11] a more consistently cooperative discursive model for the discipline of theology is needed that does not gloss over methodological conflicts with the natural sciences yet avoids taking "refuge in pre-Darwinian understandings."[12] The goal is to establish

10. See Richard Dawkins, *The God Delusion* (Boston: Houghton Mifflin Company, 2006); Sam Harris, *The End of Faith: Religion, Terror, and the Future of Reason* (New York: W. W. Norton & Company, 2005); and Daniel C. Dennett, *Breaking the Spell: Religion as a Natural Phenomenon* (New York: Penguin, 2006). For an explicitly Christian theological appraisal and critique of the "new atheism," see John F. Haught, *God and the New Atheism: A Critical Response to Dawkins, Harris, and Hitchens* (Louisville, KY: Westminster John Knox Press, 2008); also Joshua M. Moritz, *Science and Religion: Beyond Warfare and Toward Understanding* (Winona, MN: Anselm Academic, 2016).

11. See Stephen Jay Gould, "Nonoverlapping Magisteria," *Natural History* 106 (1997):16–22.

12. John F. Haught, *Making Sense of Evolution: Darwin, God, and the Drama of Life* (Louisville, KY: Westminster John Knox Press, 2010), xvii.

some basis for multidisciplinary cooperation on fundamental philosophical questions concerning the human condition. Recognizing that
no methodological approach—whether in theology or science—can
provide absolute certainty on life's big questions, the door is opened for
creating a conversational space within which reason and rationality are
redefined so as to allow for cooperation and cross-fertilization of ideas
between theology and science.

To that end, this book employs a postfoundationalist model of
rationality as a constructive alternative to positivist models of scientific
rationality that once dominated academic discourse and still shape popular opinion concerning the relationship of science to religion (as evidenced by the "new atheism").[13] The strength of postfoundationalism
is its ability to acknowledge the contextuality and embeddedness of all
knowledge without undermining the universal scope of certain truth-
claims. Here the empirical and inductive method of Aristotle proves
instructive: "fire burns both in Greece and in Persia; but conceptions of
justice shift and change."[14] In other words, while scientific rationality
is appropriate for describing and predicting certain material processes,
its methods and criteria are not adequate in all areas of human experience. There are different but complementary ways of describing and
interpreting the same phenomenon, and because all rationalities are
always embedded within traditions of interpretation, every discipline
ought to be evaluated by means of a multidisciplinary, cross-contextual
process of inquiry. Calvin Schrag's understanding of transversality[15]—
the space in which critical conversation is possible because multiple
patterns of interpretation, while distinct and discipline-specific, also
overlap one another—provides a methodological alternative to Gould's
"non-overlapping magisteria." The resulting model of public discourse
is one in which multiple explanations of a complex reality—say, human
consciousness—are possible, with competing explanations viewed as
mutually corrective rather than mutually exclusive: "a coherence where
dissensus and a variety of opinion provide for creative enhancement,
rather than impoverishment of our intellectual culture."[16] Accordingly,

---

13. For a critique of the "new atheism" as "scientism" from an atheist perspective, see Curtis White, *The Science Delusion: Asking the Big Questions in a Culture of Easy Answers* (Brooklyn, NY: Melville House, 2013).

14 Aristotle, *The Ethics of Aristotle: The Nicomachean Ethics*, trans. James Alexander Kerr Thomson (New York: Penguin Books, 1976), 1134b18.

15. See Calvin O. Schrag, *The Resources of Rationality: A Response to the Postmodern Challenge* (Bloomington: Indiana University Press, 1992), 148–79; also see J. Wentzel van Huyssteen, *The Shaping of Rationality: Toward Interdisciplinarity in Theology and Science* (Grand Rapids, MI: Wm. B. Eerdmans Publishing Co., 1999), 17–60.

16. J. Wentzel van Huyssteen, "Pluralism and Interdisciplinarity: In Search of Theology's Public Voice," *American Journal of Theology and Philosophy* 22, no. 1 (January 2001): 85.

rationality is better understood as the innate human ability to "make sense" of the world manifest in multiple reasoning strategies that develop discipline-specific explanations without granting precedence to any one strategy or discipline. However, overcoming the cultural power of scientific rationalism as a universal and objective "language" will not come easy.

Historian Yuval Noah Harari, in his widely acclaimed book *Sapiens: A Brief History of Humankind* (2015), offers an engaging and extremely layered narrative about the human species' rise "to the top rung in the food chain" on its way to becoming "the deadliest species in the annals of planet Earth."[17] A unique work that synthesizes a wide array of disciplinary contributions to our general understanding of what it means to be human, from evolutionary biology to anthropology to neuroscience, the book inevitably suffers from a "thin" presentation of some very "thick" issues that sometimes leads the author into making sweeping generalizations that ultimately cannot withstand thorough analysis. Take the author's claim that the agricultural revolution, once believed to mark "a great leap forward for humanity," ought to be dismissed as "history's biggest fraud" on the premise that the "average farmer worked harder than the average forager, and got a worse diet in return."[18] This conclusion ignores the wider impact this moment in human history had on the creation and evolution of human cultures through the creation of greater leisure time, even if only for a small ruling elite. From the more esoteric pleasures of a Mozart symphony, to the tangible advances in medical science (my son's life was saved as a direct result of the great progress made in treating childhood cancers over the last forty years), human cultural evolution has vastly improved the overall quality of life for a greater number of people than ever before, even while burdening us with a great many stresses completely unknown to the earliest *Homo sapiens* eking out an existence on the African savannah.

Despite Harari's argument to the contrary, contemporary humans are happy with the fruits of progress and would not seek a return to the "simpler" life of the primitive hunter-gatherer, even if our cultural advances have created such high expectations they cause greater disappointment when left unmet: "Suppose science comes up with cures for all diseases, effective anti-ageing therapies and regenerative treatments that keep people indefinitely young. In all likelihood, the immediate

17. Yuval Noah Harari, *Sapiens: A Brief History of Humankind* (New York: HarperCollins, 2015), 64.
18. Ibid., 78–79.

result will be an unprecedented epidemic of anger and anxiety."[19] Provocative? Sure. But also an unwarranted generalization based on a rather shallow, one-dimensional understanding of what it means to be human, and more to the point, of what genuine happiness entails. The major fault with Harari, as with most popular notions of science and progress, is that he has placed scientific rationality and the scientific method on a pedestal so far above all other ways of knowing that the only way he can preserve some notion of human happiness is by arguing that what has allowed the human species to survive, despite our irrational drive for self-destruction, is our almost pandemic capacity for self-deception. Consequently, his analysis is filled with reductionist descriptions of universal human experiences that not only reveal a positivist bias, but also fail to satisfy our deep fundamental questions about the human condition:

> So our medieval ancestors were happy because they found meaning to life in collective delusions about the afterlife? Yes. As long as nobody punctured their fantasies, why shouldn't they? As far as we can tell, from a purely scientific viewpoint, human life has absolutely no meaning. Humans are the outcome of blind evolutionary processes that operate without goal or purpose. Our actions are not part of some divine cosmic plan, and if planet Earth were to blow up tomorrow morning, the universe would probably keep going about its business as usual. As far as we can tell at this point, human subjectivity would not be missed.[20]

There is so much wrong with these statements—and the assumptions on which they rest—that a fuller critique of Harari's "history" will entail a completely different and separate work. For the moment, suffice it to say that where he gets it right is in arguing that what gives life meaning, purpose, and direction are the stories we construct about this human life.

Sadly, instead of embracing the vital role of narratives as a positive development in human cultural evolution, perhaps by viewing the species *Homo sapiens* as *Homo narrativus*, Harari dismisses most explanatory narratives (save those of "science") as useful "fictions" or "imagined realities."[21] In other words, Harari rejects that possibility that imaginative poetic explanations for complex realities that defy explanation

19. Ibid., 384.
20. Ibid., 391.
21. Ibid., 25–32.

via the reductive language and methods of scientific rationalism can in any way contribute to our understanding of the "real" world. The Christian theological tradition has elevated and valued narratives for their ability to provide a comprehensive foundational orientation for interpreting and making sense of reality *despite* lacking the precision of scientific language. As *Homo narrativus*, the human species makes sense of the world by creating meaningful narratives that are revered for their explanatory value. Even in the natural sciences and mathematics, equations and algorithms serve as a kind of universal language that allows scientists to tell a very complex story in almost visual terms. Biblical scholar John Dominic Crossan emphasizes the subtlety and complexity of symbolic religious language and praises the ingenuity of the writers who crafted and disseminated these sacred texts: "My point, once again, is not that those ancient people told literal stories and we are now smart enough to take them symbolically, but that they told them symbolically and we are now dumb enough to take them literally. They knew what they were doing; we don't."[22] Harari's dismissal of religious language as "fictions" describing an "imagined reality," with little or no value for understanding the true nature of things, betrays a major blind spot in scientific rationalism: that scientific discourse is itself metaphorical and imaginative.[23]

As Elizabeth Johnson's recent theological reflections on Darwinian evolution reveal, the very concepts upon which Darwin developed his theory are a series of extended—and sometimes inadequate—metaphors employed in describing complex natural processes.[24] Darwin labeled "the blind evolutionary processes that operate without goal or purpose" (Harari) with the clumsy metaphor "natural selection," an image that implies some intelligently directed *telos* or goal, as in the intentional breeding strategies of animal husbandry desiring to preserve certain physiological or behavioral categories while eliminating others. Darwin carried out just such a selective breeding program on

22. John Dominic Crossan and Richard G. Watts, *Who Is Jesus? Answers to Your Questions about the Historical Jesus* (Louisville, KY: Westminster John Knox Press, 1996), 79.

23. See Gregory Moore, *Nietzsche, Biology and Metaphor* (New York: Cambridge University, 2002) for a study of the genesis and development of nineteenth-century evolutionary theory that seeks to displace the false dualism between positivist descriptions of nature and the more metaphorical descriptions of the natural philosophers. Also see Robert M. Young, *Darwin's Metaphor: Nature's Place in Victorian Culture* (Cambridge: Cambridge University Press, 1985), 79–125. The author notes how "Anthropomorphic, voluntarist descriptions of natural selection occur throughout *On the Origin of Species*" (93) while arguing that "Darwin insists that his phrase is merely a metaphorical expression, which is 'almost necessary for brevity.' It is difficult to avoid personifying natural selection and nature itself, but these terms really refer only to the aggregate action and product of many natural laws" (97).

24. Elizabeth A. Johnson, *Ask the Beasts: Darwin and the God of Love* (London: Bloomsbury Publishing, 2014), 27–29.

domesticated pigeons and in his book *On the Origin of Species* (1859) drew upon this process of "artificial" selection in developing his theory of evolution by means of "natural" selection. However, the analogy falls apart, insofar as the very word "selection" implies intentionality, agency, and purpose, whereas what Darwin was attempting to describe was a blind, undirected, natural process: "We see nothing of these slow changes in progress, until the hand of time has marked the long lapse of ages, and then so imperfect is our view into long past geological ages, that we only see that the forms of life are now different from what they formerly were."[25] Through random mutations, as well as the preservation of favorable traits resulting from the natural competition of courtship, Darwin counters the dominant view of his day, "that each species has been independently created,"[26] with an elegant narrative that not only accounts for biological diversity, but also explains how complex life forms evolved from simpler organisms: "But on the view that groups of species have descended from other species, and have been modified by natural selection, I think we can obtain some light."[27] Despite the inexact quality of Darwin's overarching metaphor—and as Johnson points out, all metaphors contain "a strong note of dissimilarity"[28]—the explanatory value of natural selection overcomes its linguistic limitations, demonstrating how poetic language and narrative structure can be employed to communicate verifiable truths about complex realities. Natural selection is a metaphor—a creation of the human imagination—yet it is much more than a "fiction," and its metaphorical quality describes not just some "imagined reality" but a coherent understanding of the natural order that makes better sense of the existing fossil record than competing narratives: "I look at the natural geological record as a history of the world imperfectly kept, and written in a changing dialect."[29] Although the empirical evidence is incomplete, Darwin's narrative still provides the best explanation for the survival, adaptation, diversification, and evolution of species based on a close examination of the geological record. Furthermore, despite making room for random chance through mutation in understanding the evolution of species, Darwin was not completely opposed to teleology (understood as design and purpose in the

25. Charles Darwin, *On the Origin of Species: By Means of Natural Selection or the Preservation of Favored Races in the Struggle for Life*, reprint (New York: Cosimo Inc., 2007), 53.
26. Ibid., 4.
27. Ibid., 96.
28. Johnson, *Ask the Beasts*, 28.
29. Darwin, *On the Origin of Species*, 195.

universe) as evidenced by his letter to Asa Gray (an American botanist who sought to reconcile the Christian faith with Darwinian evolution): "I am inclined to look at everything as resulting from designed laws, with the details, whether good or bad, left to the working out of what we may call chance. . . . I cannot think that the world as we see it is the result of chance, yet I cannot look at each separate thing as the result of Design."[30] In other words, only a fundamentalism of science too narrowly conceived—a scientism[31]—would dismiss the metaphorical dimension of successful scientific descriptions. Not surprisingly, Darwin himself described the natural observations he made in the Scottish Highlands as a "kind of geological novel," no doubt shaped by his understanding of the historical novels of Sir Walter Scott as "a series of narrative episodes that change how we understand the world through complexity and contradiction."[32] Recognizing the explanatory value of narrative structure and metaphorical language for scientific description hopefully opens the door to other types of explanatory narratives, like theology, becoming contributors to the broader public discourse on what it means to be human.

4.2 ANALOGICAL APPREHENSION OF THE HIDDEN GOD

In *Philosophy for Understanding Theology* (1985), Diogenes Allen identifies the doctrine of creation—the belief that the world has a beginning and that God is its maker—as what distinguishes Christian theology from the god of classical Greek philosophy.[33] According to this doctrine the world is created *ex nihilo* ("out of nothing"), and the Creator is not part of the created universe—that is, God is ontologically distinct from the universe. As such, since the eternal and transcendent God cannot be subsumed under the categories of finite and contingent being, God's very being is unknowable to human reason. However, this essential "unknowability" does not relieve reason from

---

30. Cited in Moritz, *Science and Religion*, 144–45.

31. See Tom Sorell, *Scientism: Philosophy and the Infatuation with Science*, reprint (London: Routledge Books, 1991), in which the author rejects the post-Enlightenment tendency to overvalue the scientific method to the detriment of the arts and the humanities while arguing for a greater interrelationship between science, philosophy, art, poetry, history, and morality.

32. Devin Griffiths, *The Age of Analogy: Science and Literature between the Darwins* (Baltimore, MD: Johns Hopkins University Press, 2016), 236. The author argues that nineteenth-century poets, novelists, and historians profoundly influenced Darwin and that he sought to inculcate a more literary narrative style for naturalist and scientific writing.

33. Diogenes Allen, *Philosophy for Understanding Theology*, rev. ed. (Louisville, KY: Westminster John Knox Press, 1985), 1–14.

the task of reflecting on the nature and being of God; it simply limits our ability to *fully* comprehend God. Despite the vast ontological difference between God and contingent creation, the Christian theological tradition—notwithstanding Karl Barth's visceral rejection of natural theology—has always held that philosophical examination of creation can yield some knowledge of the Creator given the biblical assertion that humankind is created in the image of God (Gen. 1:27; Ps. 8).

Still, Christian theology has been cautious concerning its ability to comprehend the divine essence. Thomas Aquinas, in the *Summa Contra Gentiles*, argues that (given God's transcendence) we cannot know God's essence but can have some notion of it by stating what it is not.[34] This approach has been described as apophatic theology, or *via negativa*, and its origins can be traced to the work of Pseudo-Dionysius, who said that every positive statement made about God must be balanced with a negative statement in order to avoid turning our language about God into a false idol.[35] Use of *via negativa* implies what Kierkegaard in the modern era has called the "infinite qualitative difference" between the Creator and the creation. Accordingly, our language about God can never be reduced to the categories and concepts developed in our study of the creation; and unlike our understanding of nature, a clear idea of God's essence cannot be established by a series of empirically verifiable positive predicate statements. Instead, we reach some notion of God's essence negatively—through the denial of predicates—not because God lacks any of the perfections predicated, but because God infinitely exceeds the limited perfections of natural human reason.

By contrast, cataphatic theology, or *via positiva*, asserts that while we cannot know God's essence we can still make analogical predications about God. The positive way assumes that God, as the Creator and ultimate source of the universe, possesses all the qualities of creatures to the highest degree, implying a quantitative rather than qualitative difference between God and God's creatures. That is, to say that God is all-powerful implies God is more powerful than anything else. On the other hand, predicate statements such as "immutable" and "infinite" suggest by their very form an association with the negative way. "God is immutable" implies God is *not* mutable; "God is infinite" implies God is *not* finite. Nevertheless, there are statements that make positive

34. Thomas Aquinas, *Summa Contra Gentiles, Book One: God*, trans. Anton C. Pegis (Notre Dame, IN: University of Notre Dame Press, 1975), chap. 30, 139–41.

35. See Pseudo-Dionysius, *Pseudo-Dionysius: The Complete Works*, trans. Colm Luibheid with Paul Rorem (New York: Paulist Press, 1987), 49–58.

claims about God, such as "God is wise," which cannot be understood merely as the negation or removal of something from the divine essence. When positive statements such as this are predicated of God they say "something" about God, yet none of the positive statements by which we conceive the nature of God are able to represent God perfectly. For example, when we say, "God is wisdom," God's wisdom is not identical to how humans experience wisdom: God is wisdom in a sense that shares in yet transcends our experience of wisdom.

Thomas Aquinas, building upon the patristic exegetical tradition while adapting Aristotelian philosophy for Christian theology, developed a doctrine of analogy that allows us to speak of God. In developing his analogical method Aquinas uses the *via positiva* and *via negativa* together to conclude that through the use of analogies we can make true statements about God in order to gain an opaque but nonetheless genuine knowledge of God (1 Cor. 13:12). Since God and creatures differ so much, however, perfections must be attributed of God by analogy: "Therefore it must be said that these names are said of God and creatures in an analogous sense, that is according to proportion."[36] Aquinas recognizes two types of analogy: (1) analogy of proportion, in which the likeness between God and creatures is based on their proportionate participation in the same attribute (in virtue of the creature's relation and likeness to God as God's creation); and (2) analogy of proportionality, in which there exists a similarity of relations. Concerning the latter, reflecting on the relation of the eye to the mind when someone says, "I see," in a moment of comprehension, it is evident that the mind does not "see" in the same way as the eye and yet the eye is related to vision in the same way that the mind is related to comprehension. A simple conclusion can be reached from the above discussion: *all theological language is analogical language.* Focusing on the distinction established by Aquinas between knowledge and faith in order to explicate how Aquinas uses analogy to establish some knowledge of God, followed by a quick look at Karl Barth's critique of Aquinas's use of analogy, helps us to better understand how we can make true statements about God.

If we define natural theology as what can be known about God solely by the light of natural human reason, then systematic or dogmatic theology is that enterprise that, while using reason, accepts its guiding principles from revealed truth. That is, truths that are proper

---

36. Thomas Aquinas, *Introduction to Saint Thomas*, ed. Anton C. Pegis (New York: The Modern Library, 1948), 107.

to theology cannot be known by reason and are known only by revelation. For this reason Aquinas argues that it is impossible to have *faith* and *knowledge* concerning the same object at the same time by the same person, though something can be true for faith while false in philosophy (though not the other way around). The implication drawn from Aquinas's distinction is that the philosopher is limited to the range of human rationality while the theologian accepts truth that transcends the limits of nature. By this understanding, it is a matter of faith that God creates human beings for a supernatural end—perfect happiness attainable only in the next life through the grace of God—yet human beings can achieve an *imperfect* happiness in this life through the exercise of natural reason. This is the highest good of philosophy, to attain some knowledge of God through philosophical reflection on the created order for the purposes of attaining and exercising the natural virtues. Accordingly, "that truth that the human reason is naturally endowed to know cannot be opposed to the truth of the Christian faith."[37] But according to Aquinas (again from the *Summa Contra Gentiles*), since humankind is created for a supernatural end, natural knowledge of God cannot fully satisfy—it is imperfect and points beyond itself—leading the rational mind from philosophy to theology: "Yet it is useful for the human reason to exercise itself in such arguments, however weak they may be, provided only that there be present no presumption to comprehend or to demonstrate. For to be able to see something of the loftiest realities, however thin and weak the sight may be, as our previous remarks indicate, a cause of the greatest joy."[38]

The philosopher can demonstrate the existence of God from studying God's effects in nature, thus attaining some analogical knowledge of God. This knowledge can then be used to define the natural virtues and the means for attaining them; however, the philosopher cannot discover humanity's *divine* vocation: "As for false and earthly felicity, it contains no more than a shadow of that most perfect felicity."[39] Furthermore, in the *Summa theologica* Aquinas writes, "It was necessary for man's salvation that there should be a knowledge revealed by God, besides the philosophical sciences investigated by human reason."[40] This raises a host of questions for both the philosopher and the theologian: Does natural theology yield salvific knowledge of God? Does

---

37. Aquinas, *Summa Contra Gentiles*, chap. 7, 74.
38. Ibid., chap. 8, 76.
39. Ibid., chap. 102, 303.
40. Aquinas, *Introduction to Saint Thomas*, 4 (1.1.1).

this knowledge have the power to redeem and regenerate? What are the effects of sin on the human capacity to know God's will and our capacity to obey?

Aristotle defines particular objects in the world as *primary substances,* "that horse" or "my friend Bob," and these possess *qualities* that do not exist independent of primary substances. For example, color is not an object in itself but a quality belonging to an object ("the car is green"). Hence, we can *predicate* a quality of any primary substance, and according to Aristotle, the *genus* and *species* of a primary substance tells us its *essence* ("my friend Bob is a man") while other predicates tell us its *accidental* qualities ("my friend Bob has blonde hair"). The Bible predicates certain characteristics to God, and one of theology's tasks is to explicate their meaning: "God created the heavens and the earth" (Gen. 1:1); "The LORD is my shepherd" (Ps 23:1); "God is love" (1 John 4:8); "For God's foolishness is wiser than human wisdom, and God's weakness is stronger than human strength" (1 Cor. 1:25). Aquinas teaches that when a quality is applied to God—wisdom, for example—its use is not *univocal* (exact meaning) when the same quality is applied to human beings: "Whatever is predicated of various things under the same name but not in the same sense is predicated equivocally. But no name belongs to God in the same sense that it belongs to creatures. . . . Therefore whatever is said of God and of creatures is predicated equivocally."[41] Yet the fact that analogical knowledge of God is *equivocal* (ambiguous in meaning, open to more than one interpretation) does not mean philosophy and theology cannot speak about God with confidence. Rather, theology must struggle to communicate the similarity between divine wisdom and human wisdom by the use of *analogy.* Specifically, Aquinas uses analogy (when referring to God's attributes) as an *analogy of proportion,* in which the same trait is applied to two different things but to each according to its nature. Hence, the qualities of all finite creatures are themselves finite while God as infinite possesses these qualities in absolute perfection. Accordingly, the natural world provides some knowledge of God from God's effects, but it is important to recall that a creature is "like" God *only* in a diminished capacity, since God created the universe and the creation shares some of God's attributes. Yet, when we talk about God by projecting human perfections metaphorically onto God (wisdom, goodness, being, etc.), we are aware that, at best, the doctrine of analogy results in very limited

---

41. Ibid., 106 (13.5.3).

knowledge. Complementing this positive predication is *via negativa*, which allows speech about God by using human qualities to describe God in terms of their opposite; for example, humans are finite/God is infinite. Here Aquinas follows Pseudo-Dionysius in teaching that "what He is not is clearer to us than what He is."[42]

Paul Tillich's correlational method, in which theology answers the questions raised by culture yet every answer proposed by theology is inevitably an expression of a particular culture at a concrete time in history, presumes that no dogmatic statement is immune from criticism and revision. In many ways, Tillich has taken *via negativa* to its logical extreme, denying the very possibility of speaking about God: "one can only speak of the ultimate in a language which at the same time denies the possibility of speaking about it."[43] Karl Barth, on the other hand, began an attack against natural theology in the second edition of his Romans commentary inspired by Kierkegaard's "infinite qualitative difference" between the Creator and the creation. Barth rejects natural theology because its god is a philosophical construction and not the God of the Bible—the God who is self-revealed and can be known only by revelation and not apart from it. As a creation of human reason the god of natural theology is by definition an idol: paraphrasing Ludwig Feuerbach, this god is a projection of human subjectivity. According to Barth there is no way to reach the living God from human reasoning; this God must come to us as a self-revealing subject and is not an object constrained by human reason, "on the assumption that revelation itself creates of itself the necessary point of contact in man."[44] Given the infinite qualitative difference between God and humanity, even in God's self-revelation God remains hidden, a reality captured in Barth's oft-repeated phrase from the *Church Dogmatics*: "The veil is thick."[45] Does the hiddenness of God lead to incomprehensibility? No. How does one identify the hidden God who is self-revealing? By God's own actions. In other words, Barth is methodologically committed to limiting human knowledge of God to that which is revealed by God, as circumscribed by the written witness of the prophets and apostles in the sacred Scriptures. Yet this is a dogmatic axiom that is itself grounded in an act of human reasoning, for the Scriptures seem more accommodating to

---

42. Ibid., 17 (1.10.3); see *Pseudo-Dionysius: The Complete Works*, trans. Colm Luibhéid and Paul Rorem (New York: Paulist Press, 1987), 47–132.

43. Tillich, *Dynamics of Faith*, 60.

44. Barth, *Church Dogmatics*, I.1, 29.

45. Ibid., 165.

the possibility of natural knowledge of God than Barth is willing to grant: "For what can be known about God is plain to them. Ever since the creation of the world his eternal power and divine nature, invisible though they are, have been understood and seen through the things he has made. So they are without excuse" (Rom. 1:19–20). Admittedly, human sinfulness obscures the natural evidence, often leading to idolatry: "For all people who were ignorant of God were foolish by nature; and they were unable from the good things that are seen to know the one who exists, nor did they recognize the artisan while paying heed to his works; but they supposed that either fire or wind or swift air, or the circle of the stars, or turbulent water, or the luminaries of heaven were the gods that rule the world" (Wis. 13:1–2). Still, Scripture contains a consistent message concerning the human ability to know God from God's works in nature: "When I look at your heavens, the work of your fingers, the moon and the stars that you have established; what are human beings that you are mindful of them, mortals that you care for them?" (Ps. 8:3–4).

The difference between Aquinas's use of the *analogia entis* ("analogy of being") and Barth's use of *analogia fidei* ("analogy of faith") is that for the latter theology cannot treat God as a being—theology cannot ignore the infinite qualitative difference between God and humanity. By natural theology Barth means a theology that, in every positive or negative formulation, has independent subject matter and differs from God's self-revelation in Scripture: "Natural theology is the doctrine of a union of humanity with God existing outside God's revelation in Jesus Christ."[46] Given this definition, it is not surprising that Barth regards "the *analogia entis* as the invention of the Antichrist" in the opening volume of the *Church Dogmatics*.[47] However, as evidenced by the above reading of Aquinas, Barth's use of *analogia fidei* is not far removed from Aquinas's use of analogy. In the *Dogmatics* Barth speaks of God's being (essence) as God's actions and of God's actions as God's being; the difference is that for Barth all predicate statements made about God must originate and be interpreted in terms of God's self-revelation. This means we know God only as God is self-disclosed to us. For Barth, one of the tasks of theology is to relate what God is in essence with what God is for us. Is there a correspondence between creaturely events

---

46. Barth, *Church Dogmatics*, II.1, 168.
47. Barth, *Church Dogmatics*, I.1, xiii.

and God? Yes, but these analogies originate in God's self-revelation and—according to Barth—must be interpreted christologically. Thus, for Barth the analogy of faith tests and limits theological language by always relating it to God's self-revelation in Jesus Christ. Clearly, Barth is not an enemy of analogy in theological discourse. He does, however, seem closed to the possibility of human reason and experience as independent viable sources of knowledge of God.

Returning to the earlier premise, that all theological language is analogical language, analogical predication is defined as the use of likeness or proportionality to relate something known to something unknown. Aquinas used analogy to indicate how the same qualities could be ascribed to both God (who is infinite) and humans (who are finite). Ontologically, when something is attributed to both God and creatures it is attributed *primarily* of God and only *secondarily* of creatures for being belongs essentially to God and derivatively to God's creatures, since their being is received, dependent, finite, and contingent. Nevertheless, epistemologically, we know creatures *before* we come to know God, so we tend to attribute the thing signified first to creatures and then to God. However, given God's ontological primacy, the foundation of all analogy is the likeness of creatures to God, and this is only a one-way likeness, since the creature is like to God but we cannot properly say that God is like the creature. The limits of analogical language result from the ontological difference between the Creator and the creation, meaning that creatures are only like God *imperfectly*—they cannot bear a perfect resemblance to God—yet they *are* images of God (Gen. 1:26–28). As philosopher Eleonore Stump has argued, despite the presumption "among contemporary theologians and philosophers to suppose that the God of the Bible is radically different from the God of the philosophers,"[48] this seems an arbitrary and historically insupportable stereotype. To those, like Barth, who posit an unassailable chasm between theology and philosophy, Stump counters that the God of classical theism (as articulated by the three Abrahamic traditions of Averroes, Maimonides, and Aquinas) "really is the personal biblical God."[49] The use of analogical language that says something is both like and unlike by both Barth and Aquinas suggests that the theologies of Karl Barth and Thomas Aquinas have more in common than Barth is willing to admit.

---

48. Eleonore Stump, *The God of the Bible and the God of the Philosophers* (Milwaukee, WI: Marquette University Press, 2016), 11.
49. Ibid., 19.

4.3 THE DOGMATIC BURDEN: "WHAT
WE CANNOT SPEAK ABOUT"

Perhaps the biggest challenge to the "meaningfulness" of religious language, however, is the attack of logical positivism in the twentieth century,[50] which established a standard for judging a predicate statement as true if and only if it corresponds to an empirically observable fact. For positivists, only language that is empirically verifiable ("it is raining today") has cognitive meaning; religious language that speaks of things not subject to empirical observation ("God exists") is by definition meaningless. By this criterion, the doctrine of analogy fails to provide substantive knowledge of God. Yet it is important to note that Aquinas did not develop his analogical doctrine as a method for attaining epistemological certainty (Descartes) but in the service of "faith seeking understanding" (Anselm). While we can attain limited knowledge of God from studying nature, Aquinas believes that faith *perfects* reason—ultimately, the most reliable knowledge of God is *above* human reason and is attainable only by God's transforming act of grace. By embracing such a narrow standard of verifiability, positivists limit knowledge to quantitative scientific description, reducing much of what makes human life "human"—including religious experience—to the level of incoherence.

Such sentiments apparently echo in the enigmatic closing words of Ludwig Wittgenstein's *Tractatus Logico-Philosophicus* (1921): "What we cannot speak about we must pass over in silence."[51] However, English philosopher Basil Mitchell responds to logical positivists by suggesting that theological language is meaningful in the same way historical claims are meaningful, insofar as theological truth claims *cannot* be empirically demonstrated to be *conclusively* false.[52] In other words, while the doctrine of analogy cannot give us God's *essence* it can perhaps reveal guideposts along the journey. A more generous reading of Wittgenstein suggests that he was not dismissing all religious claims as nonsensical, but given the "concerns of Wittgenstein's own life and thought," the man who "read Kierkegaard, Schopenhauer, Tolstoy, and

50. See Peter Achinstein and Stephen F. Barker, *The Legacy of Logical Positivism: Studies in the Philosophy of Science* (Baltimore: John Hopkins University Press, 1969); Michael Friedman, *Reconsidering Logical Positivism* (New York: Cambridge University Press, 1999); and Oswald Hanfling, *Logical Positivism* (New York: Columbia University Press, 1981).

51. Ludwig Wittgenstein, *Tractatus Logico-Philosophicus*, trans. D. F. Spears and B. F. McGuinness, reprint (London: Routledge Classics, 2001), 89.

52. See Basil Mitchell, *The Justification of Religious Belief*, reprint (New York: The Macmillan Press, 1973), 7–20.

Dostoevski does not wish to *eliminate* value, but, like Bultmann, to insure that it is *not reduced* to the level of empirical propositions."[53] Thus, the "tradition of the *Tractatus* is not that of Russell, Moore, Ayer, and Carnap, but of Kraus, Schopenhauer, Kierkegaard, and Tolstoy."[54] In other words, "Wittgenstein draws a contrast between the language which describes the world because it depends on elementary propositions about states of affairs, and a 'showing' of the mystical . . . which occurs not *in* language but *through* language."[55]

Wittgenstein's most direct influence on theological discourse comes via the postliberalism of George Lindbeck and Hans Frei, who embrace Wittgenstein's insight that "religious belief is intimately tied to a form of life"[56] in the process of articulating the distinctive grammar of Christian communities:

> According to Wittgenstein, we cannot grasp meaning and language without it working in our lives. To understand religious belief and God we need to look to the religious form of life, the retreat into innate principles or general reason misses what is meant to be understood. If you want to understand music, you must engage instruments, scores and performances. Wittgenstein brings us back from metaphysical flights back to our everyday world.[57]

However, unlike many popular theological interpretations of Wittgenstein,[58] this immersion into the distinctive world of a particular "form of life" need not lead to fideism or relativism. Rather, by emphasizing the hermeneutical dimension of all forms of rationality— from empirical scientific methods to narrative theologies to Mozart sonatas—a Wittgensteinian approach highlights both, the contextuality of our theoretical frameworks and the need for dialogue and cooperation between differing perspectives:

> Christianity is not a doctrine, not, I mean, a theory about what has happened and will happen to the human soul, but a description of something that actually takes place in human life. For 'consciousness

---

53. Anthony C. Thiselton, *The Two Horizons: New Testament Hermeneutics and Philosophical Description*, reprint (Grand Rapids, MI: Wm. B. Eerdmans Publishing Co., 1993), 360.

54. Ibid., 369.

55. Ibid., 370.

56. Tim Labron, *Wittgenstein and Theology* (London: T. & T. Clark, 2009), 84.

57. Ibid., 85.

58. See Kai Nielsen, "Wittgensteinian Fideism," *Philosophy* 42, no. 161 (1967): 191–209; Paul Holmer, *The Grammar of Faith* (San Francisco: Harper & Row, 1978); Richard Griffith Rollefson, *Thinking with Kierkegaard and Wittgenstein: The Philosophical Theology of Paul L. Holmer* (Eugene, OR: Pickwick Publications, 2014); D. Z. Phillips, *Faith after Foundationalism* (London: Routledge, 2013).

of sin' is a real event and so are despair and salvation through faith. Those who speak of such things (Bunyan for instance) are simply describing what has happened to them, whatever gloss anyone may want to put on it.[59]

Wittgenstein, greatly influenced by Kierkegaard, views faith as a matter of existential decision, not epistemological certainty, and like Kierkegaard (not to mention the liberationists) locates religious meaning in concrete praxis rather than doctrinal exactness:

How God judges a man is something we cannot imagine at all. If he really takes strength of temptation and the frailty of nature into account, whom can he condemn? But otherwise the resultant of these two forces is simply the end for which the man was predestined. In that case he was created so that the interplay of forces would make him either conquer or succumb. And that is not a religious idea at all, but more like a scientific hypothesis. So if you want to stay within the religious sphere you must *struggle*.[60]

Wittgenstein prefigures the pragmatic turn from epistemology to hermeneutics defended in Richard Rorty's *Philosophy and the Mirror of Nature* by reconceptualizing truth as "a matter of conversation and of social practice,"[61] a sound strategy for coping with the realities of radical pluralism. Thus, theological narratives ought to be part of the academic and public discourse alongside the empirical or social sciences, in recognition that the existential appropriation of *all* narrative traditions involves a high degree of lived commitment:

Christianity is not based on a historical truth; rather, it offers us a (historical) narrative and says: now believe! But not, believe this narrative with the belief appropriate to a historical narrative, rather: believe, through thick and thin, which you can do only as the result of a life. Here you have a narrative, don't take the same attitude to it as you take to other historical narratives! Make a quite different place in your life for it.—There is nothing paradoxical about that![62]

So when Wittgenstein admits he is unable to believe all the things his Catholic colleagues believe, especially about the Eucharist, something

59. Ludwig Wittgenstein, *Culture and Value*, ed. G. H. von Wright, trans. P. Winch, rev. ed. (Oxford: Basil Backwell, 1998), 28.
60. Ibid., 86.
61. Rorty, *Philosophy and the Mirror of Nature*, 171.
62. Wittgenstein, *Culture and Value*, 31.

fundamental about the nature of religious belief is revealed: "Catholics
believe as well that in certain circumstances a wafer completely changes
its nature, and at the same time that all evidence proves the contrary."[63]
Rather than disparaging their beliefs, Wittgenstein recognizes that faith
"could only be (something like) passionately committing oneself to a
system of co-ordinates," which, "although it's *belief,* it is really a way
of living, or a way of judging life."[64] In other words, his inability to
accept the Catholic understanding of the eucharistic mystery is more
a product of his own formation than it is about the empirical evidence
in front of him, since in crucial ways we are molded by the "language-
games" we inhabit: "For there it has its restricted application. . . . But as
soon as I say this sentence outside its context, it appears in a false light.
For then it is as if I wanted to insist that there are things I *know.* God
himself can't say anything to me about them."[65] The language of worship and belief is learned through the act of worship itself. As Diogenes
Allen has noted,

> The very fact that worship takes place at all is enough to show that
> Christianity can never be reduced to mere ideas. We do use ideas,
> and they are essential to the forging of a commitment to God and
> to the act of worship, but all our thought and study finds its cul-
> mination in worship of the divine reality. In this act of yielding our
> entire nature to divine love, the earthly and the divine realms meet,
> intersect, and become one.[66]

The belief that *in* the bread and the wine God *is* experienced and
known is not proven via empirical evidence about the physical nature
of the elements but is a conviction grounded in an encounter with
the divine "other" mediated by the sacrament. Therefore, the possibility exists Wittgenstein might come to accept the Catholic "picture of
the world" through a "kind of *persuasion,*"[67] given certain compelling
grounds (insofar as "knowledge is related to a decision"),[68] but first
Wittgenstein must participate in the existential appropriation of the
distinctly Catholic "language-game"—not only through catechetical
instruction, but through the act of worship itself—an event whose

63. Ludwig Wittgenstein, *On Certainty,* ed. G. E. M. Anscombe and G. H. von Wright, trans. Dennis Paul and
G. E. M. Anscombe (New York: Harper Torchbooks, 1969), 32e (§239).
64. Wittgenstein, *Culture and Value,* 73.
65. Wittgenstein, *On Certainty,* 73e (§554).
66. Diogenes Allen, *The Traces of God* (Princeton, NJ: Caroline Press, 1981), 99–100.
67. Wittgenstein, *On Certainty,* 34e (§262).
68. Ibid., 47e (§362).

verity there is no possibility of accepting without first experiencing it
(which in the language of faith entails an act of divine grace). Embracing a hermeneutical approach to theological truth claims is neither an
escape into fideism nor surrender to subjectivism but recognition that
there is "no risk-free method of grasping the truth. Nevertheless, there
is truth to be grasped, and what Kierkegaard [and I would add Witt-
genstein] wants us to see is that our subjectivity is not just a screen that
distorts the truth, but may become a medium that, when controlled
by the right kind of passion, opens up to an encounter with truth."[69]
Thus, while Barth is correct to mistrust human reason, he compensates
to such a high degree he leaves little room for grace to cooperate with
human reason in the divine-human encounter. By contrast, Kierkegaard and Wittgenstein suggest that while "no human situation can
provide a valid analogy," the use of the analogical imagination awakens
"the mind to an understanding of the divine."[70]

4.4 THE HIDDENNESS OF GOD AS
HERMENEUTICAL PRINCIPLE

Despite a long and troubled history of conflict, the historical and cultural ties between Judaism, Christianity, and Islam facilitate the task
of comparative theology.[71] All three monotheistic faiths employ some
form of the doctrine of "revelation," a technical term for the concept
that knowledge of God originates in a divine act whereby something
previously unknown (or ambiguously apprehended) about God is disclosed, along with the subjective assurance that the content of this revelation is reliable. Also characteristic of the three Abrahamic religions is
the preservation and transmission of this revealed message by means of
sacred texts. All three religious traditions preserve collections of "holy
Scripture" that are more than just narratives about past events important for preserving the community's identity, and more than merely
classic works of human literary creativity, but these traditions sacralize

69. Evans, *Passionate Reason*, 3.
70. Kierkegaard, *Philosophical Fragments*, 26.
71. See María Rosa Menocal, *The Ornament of the World: How Muslims, Jews, and Christians Created a Culture of Tolerance in Medieval Spain* (New York: Back Bay Books, 2002), for a history of the cultural dialogue that took place in Medieval Spain between Muslims, Christians, and Jews that created a culture of tolerance and peaceful coexistence. Also see Miroslav Volf, *Allah: A Christian Response* (New York: HarperOne, 2011), Irfan A. Omar, ed., *A Christian View of Islam: Essays on Dialogue* (Maryknoll, NY: Orbis Books, 2010), and Mahmoud Ayoub, *A Muslim View of Christianity: Essays on Dialogue by Mahmoud Ayoub*, ed. Irfan A. Omar (Maryknoll, NY: Orbis Books, 2007).

these texts on the belief that the human authors are conveying a divinely revealed communication. Ultimately, sacred texts receive the status of Scripture because they are trusted as human testimonies witnessing to and relating divine acts of self-revelation.

Underlying this shared doctrine of revelation is some form of the doctrine of divine hiddenness (*Deus absconditus*), which states that if God exists, God does not make this existence sufficiently clear and available to all. Whether in Judaism, Christianity, or Islam, some variance of the doctrine of divine hiddenness leads to the conclusion that the full mystery of God can never be contained by human theological constructs.[72] The seventeenth-century philosopher and mathematician Blaise Pascal (1623–1662) argued that God remains hidden in order to nurture the virtue of humility as a necessary first step on the path toward wisdom: "God being thus hidden, any religion that does not say that God is hidden is not true, and any religion that does not explain why does not instruct. Ours does all this. *Verily thou art a God that hidest thyself.*"[73] Accordingly, "We can understand nothing of God's works unless we accept the principle that he wished to blind some and enlighten others."[74] God remains hidden not just because God cannot be grasped by our senses, but also because God *chooses* to hide from those who lust after power or desire dominance over others. Pascal even chastises intellectuals and academics who seek to know God solely through reason and intellect, arguing that while reason enables one to know that God exists from the beauty, complexity and order of creation, knowing God as a rational possibility is not the same as knowing God intimately through faith: "God wishes to move the will rather than the mind. Perfect clarity would help the mind and harm the will. Humble their pride."[75]

Granted, many "people are perplexed that God should permit a situation in which human beings live in incomprehension and bewilderment regarding His existence, while all the time He could save humanity

---

72. For a discussion of the hiddenness of God in the three Abrahamic religions, see Walter Brueggemann, *Theology of the Old Testament: Testimony, Dispute, Advocacy* (Minneapolis, MN: Fortress Press, 1997), 333–57; David B. Burrell, *Knowing the Unknowable God: Ibn-Sina, Maimonides, Aquinas* (Notre Dame, IN: University of Notre Dame Press, 1986); John Dillenberger, *God Hidden and Revealed: The Interpretation of Luther's Deus Absconditus and Its Significance for Religious Thought* (Philadelphia, Muhlenberg Press, 1953); Martin Buber, *Eclipse of God: Studies in the Relation between Religion and Philosophy* (London: Victor Gollancz, 1953); and Ebrahim Azadegan, "Ibn 'Arabi on the Problem of Divine Hiddenness," *Journal of the Muhyiddin Ibn 'Arabi Society* 53 (2013): 49–67.

73. Blaise Pascal, *Pensées*, trans. A. J. Krailsheimer, rev. ed. (New York: Penguin Books, 1995), F 584 (all citations from the *Pensées* use the fragment numbers from this translation). Pascal here alludes to Isaiah 45:15, "Truly, you are a God who hides himself, O God of Israel, the Savior."

74. Ibid., F 232.

75. Ibid., F 234.

from such a predicament."[76] Furthermore, it is widely acknowledged that the hiddenness of God can contribute to loss of faith and atheism: "Many nontheists regard the hiddenness of God as salient evidence that the Jewish-Christian God does not actually exist."[77] Nevertheless, "there are some thoughtful mystics who put another gloss on the phenomenon and see the world in a completely different manner."[78] There is a strong tradition of divine hiddenness in the Hebrew Bible, most notably in the psalmists' lamentations: "O Lord, why do you cast me off? Why do you hide your face from me?" (Ps. 88:14). Psalm 10 goes so far as to accuse YHWH of intentionally hiding from humanity: "Why, O Lord, do you stand far off? Why do you hide yourself in times of trouble?" (Ps 10:1), and this theme is also found within the prophetic tradition: "Truly you are a God who hides himself, O God of Israel, the Savior" (Isa. 45:15). However, no Jewish narrative captures the frustration and inscrutability caused by divine hiddenness better than Job's complaint to the Creator: "Why do you hide your face and count me as your enemy?" (Job 13:24).

Christianity is deeply steeped in this aspect of the Hebraic biblical tradition, elements of which are echoed in the letters of the apostle Paul when he references God darkening the intellect of the ungodly:

For the wrath of God is revealed from heaven against all ungodliness and wickedness of those who by their wickedness suppress the truth. For what can be known about God is plain to them, because God has shown it to them. Ever since the creation of the world his eternal power and divine nature, invisible though they are, have been understood and seen through the things he has made. So they are without excuse; for though they knew God, they did not honor him as God or give thanks to him, but they became futile in their thinking, and their senseless minds were darkened. Claiming to be wise, they became fools; and they exchanged the glory of the immortal God for images resembling a mortal human being or birds or four-footed animals or reptiles.

Therefore God gave them up in the lusts of their hearts to impurity, to the degrading of their bodies among themselves, because they exchanged the truth about God for a lie and worshipped and served the creature rather than the Creator, who is blessed for ever! Amen. (Rm 1:18–25, NRSV)

---

76. Azadegan, "Ibn 'Arabi on the Problem of Divine Hiddenness," 49.

77. Daniel Howard-Snyder and Paul K. Moser, "Introduction: The Hiddenness of God," in *Divine Hiddenness: New Essays*, eds. Daniel Howard-Snyder and Paul K. Moser (Cambridge: Cambridge University Press, 2002), 3.

78. Azadegan, "Ibn 'Arabi on the Problem of Divine Hiddenness," 50.

For Martin Luther (1483–1546) human sinfulness is so decisive in determining whether or not humankind can know God apart from God's self-revelation that he develops the *Deus absconditus* as the methodological starting point for theological knowledge, rejecting scholastic theology's continuity between revelation and natural knowledge of God, in order to affirm that even in the act of revelation God remains "hidden and beyond understanding."[79] The Christian mystical tradition, embodied in John of the Cross's (1542–1591) "dark night of the soul" argues for the *necessity* of divine hiddenness, "Since love of God and attachment to creatures are contraries, they cannot coexist in the same will."[80] Expressing a sentiment later elaborated by Pascal, John of the Cross views divine hiddenness as God's means of overcoming human arrogance and humbling the intellect in order to bring the believer to faith: "Faith affirms what cannot be known by the intellect . . . for though faith brings certitude to the intellect, it does not produce clarity, but only darkness."[81] This mystical strand of theistic belief that affirms divine hiddenness as necessary to God's revelation is also found in Islam, most especially the Sufi path as articulated by Ibn 'Arabi (1165–1240), according to whom, "The being of the Essence is beyond being known, it is the most hidden secret (*aktam al-sirr*). As the absolutely absent being (*al-ghayb al-ghuyub*), no one can know God in Himself but Himself."[82] For Ibn 'Arabi, the Qur'an's emphasis on Divine Mercy is an accommodation by Allah to human limitations in order to overcome our ignorance and doubt:

> Say, "Unto whom belongs whatsoever is in the heavens and on the earth?" Say, "Unto God. He has prescribed Mercy for Himself. He will surely gather you on the Day of Resurrection, in which there is no doubt. Those who have lost their souls, they do not believe. Unto Him belongs all that dwells in the night and in the day, and He is the Hearing, the Knowing." (Sura 6:12–13)[83]

When those who believe in Our signs come to thee, say, "Peace be upon you! Your Lord has prescribed Mercy for Himself, that

79. Martin Luther, *Luther's Works* (St. Louis, MO: Concordia Publishing House, 1974), 10:118 (1514); 28:377 (1534).
80. St. John of the Cross, "The Ascent of Mt. Carmel" I,6, in *The Collected Works of St. John of the Cross*, trans. Kieran Kavanaugh and Otilio Rodriguez (Washington, DC: ICS Publications, 1964), 85.
81. Ibid., 119.
82. Azadegan, "Ibn 'Arabi on the Problem of Divine Hiddenness," 51.
83. Seyyed Hossein Nasr, ed., *The Study Quran: A New Translation and Commentary*, additional eds. Caner K. Dagli, Maria Massi Dakake, Joseph E. B. Lumbard, Mohammed Rustom (New York: HarperOne, 2015). Unless otherwise noted, all citations from the Qur'an are from this translation.

whosoever among you does evil in ignorance and thereafter repents and makes amends, He is truly Forgiving, Merciful." (Sura 6:54)

In other words, "God mercifully and lovingly reveals Himself to His creation in theophanies that cannot but conform themselves to the subjective limitations of the creature," as a process of drawing the human "into the divine, to the extent that the conceptually circumscribed form of belief gives way to the spiritual realization of the content of belief."[84]

Although the hiddenness of God can serve as a methodological principle for limiting the scope and universality of theological truth claims, thereby facilitating comparative theology and interfaith cooperation, there is much resistance within Christian theology (as well as Jewish and Muslim theologies) to claims of a coherent and unified revelation about God underlying the sacred Scriptures of all three Abrahamic faiths. Sadly, many theologians question whether or not Judaism, Christianity, and Islam believe in and worship the same God, as evidenced by the recent controversy at Wheaton College, an evangelical Christian university that requires its faculty to sign and adhere to the college's statement of faith, when Larycia Hawkins, a professor of political science, was placed on administrative leave for claiming that Muslims and Christians worship the same God.[85] This book presumes that, despite a history of enmity and conflict, the Abrahamic religions affirm belief in one God, and that this God has chosen to reveal God's self in distinct and culturally particular, though not mutually exclusive, ways. Despite tragic histories in which missionary and proselytizing theologies were used to justify acts of political violence, all three Abrahamic religions share a more fundamental theological belief—the hiddenness and mystery of the self-revealing God—that can enable genuine peaceful discourse between the religions. If God is ultimately understood as mystery—a mystery whose truth is known only through an act of divine self-revelation (whether mediated through Moses, Jesus, or Muhammad)—then the sacred Scriptures of each tradition are most properly understood as a *human* witness to a divine act. The implications for

---

84. Reza Shah-Kazemi, "Do Muslims and Christians Believe in the Same God," *Do We Worship the Same God? Jews, Christians, and Muslims in Dialogue*, ed. Miroslav Volf (Grand Rapids, MI: Wm. B. Eerdmans Publishing Co., 2012), 108.

85. Christine Hauser, "Solidarity With Islam at Christian College, Then Discipline," in *The New York Times* (December 17, 2015), A30, http://www.nytimes.com/2015/12/17/us/ wheaton-college-professor-larycia-hawkins -muslim-scarf.html?_r=0. In an opinion piece, Christian theologian Miroslav Volf offered a theological argument in defense of Prof. Hawkins: "Wheaton professor's suspension is about anti-Muslim bigotry, not theology," in *The Washington Post* (December 17, 2015), https://www.washingtonpost.com/news/acts-of-faith/wp/2015/12/17 /wheaton-professors-suspension-is-about-anti-muslim-bigotry-not-theology/.

comparative theology arising from these two doctrines—revelation and the hiddenness of God—coupled with the limits these doctrines place on human knowledge of God cannot be overstated.

In all three Abrahamic religions the doctrine of the hiddenness of God has methodological implications for theological discourse insofar as human talk about God cannot limit or constrain God. Complementarily, affirming that there is one God, that this God is known primarily through God's own action, and that even in God's self-disclosure God is not fully known but remains mystery, *demands* a conception of theology as an imperfect and incomplete human endeavor. However, while the claims of theology are viewed as limited, open-ended, and subject to continual revision, this in no way undermines the ontological ground (God) that gives rise to the human hermeneutical enterprise in the first place. Rather, it is an acknowledgment of the

> . . . epistemic situation where we human beings live in a world in which God is transcendent, we have limited cognitive faculties, and that knowledge of God is essential for our flourishing in this-worldly and otherworldly life; and where in addition it is supposed that God, the omniscient, omnipotent, and perfectly loving, has permitted us to live in bewilderment and perplexity regarding His attributes and existence, all the while knowing that it is essential for our well-being during our eternal life to believe in His existence and so to act according to His commandments.[86]

This "epistemic situation," the human inability to know and comprehend God fully, ought to serve as a guiding principle for theological reflection in all three Abrahamic faiths in acknowledgment of human sinfulness and in recognition that God intends believers to practice humility and compassion. The apostle Paul cautions against arrogance: "Where is the one who is wise? Where is the scribe? Where is the debater of this age? Has not God made foolish the wisdom of the world? For since, in the wisdom of God, the world did not know God through wisdom, God decided, through the foolishness of our proclamation, to save those who believe" (1 Cor. 1:20–21).

Jesus of Nazareth, when asked who is the greatest in the kingdom of heaven, "called a child, whom he put among them, and said, 'Truly I tell you, unless you change and become like children, you will never enter the kingdom of heaven. Whoever becomes humble like this child

---

86. Azadegan, "Ibn 'Arabi on the Problem of Divine Hiddenness," 49.

is the greatest in the kingdom of heaven. Whoever welcomes one such child in my name welcomes me'" (Matt. 18:2–5). The Qur'an also seeks to nurture humility and reliance on God's self-revelation:

> Their parable is that of one who kindled a fire, and when it lit up what was around him, God took away their light, and left them in darkness, unseeing. Deaf, dumb, and blind, they return not. Or a cloudburst from the sky, in which there is darkness, thunder, and lightning. They put their fingers in their ears against the thunderclaps, fearing death. And God encompasses the disbelievers. The lightning all but snatches away their sight. Whenever it shines for them, they walk therein, and when darkness comes over them, they halt. Had God willed, He would have taken away their sight. Truly God is Powerful over all things. O mankind! Worship your Lord, Who created you, and those who were before you, that haply you may be reverent: He Who made for you the earth a place of repose and the sky a canopy, and sent water from the sky by which He brought forth fruits for your provision. So do not set up equals unto God, knowingly. (Sura 2:17–22)

Consequently, in order to remain faithful to the scriptural sources of revealed religion, proponents of Judaism, Christianity, and Islam should proceed with a methodological humility that encourages tolerance, compassion, and patience, especially when making doctrinal proclamations.

In other words, God calls us together as communities of faith not to plot against one another, but to bring others into the community through our faithful witness: "O you who believe! If you converse in secret, then do not converse in secret with a view to sin, enmity, and disobeying the Messenger; converse in secret with a view to piety and reverence. And reverence God, unto Whom you shall be gathered" (Sura 58:9). Medieval Jewish philosopher Moses Maimonides (1135–1204) interprets the Torah as both the source of love and the means by which God disciplines believers that they might obey the Law:

> God declares in plain words that it is the object of all religious acts to produce in man fear of God and obedience to His word—the state of mind which we have demonstrated in this chapter for those who desire to know the truth, as being our duty to seek. . . . The two objects, love and fear of God, are acquired by two different means. The love is the result of the truths taught in the Law, including the true knowledge of the Existence of God; whilst fear of God is produced by the practices prescribed in the Law.[87]

---

87. Moses Maimonides, *Guide for the Perplexed*, trans. A. H. Friedlander (New York: Dover, 1956), bk. 3, ch. 42.

From a biblical perspective the problem of other religions proves a frustrating proposition. On the one hand, Christian evangelization is grounded in Christ's command to "Go therefore and make disciples of all nations, baptizing them in the name of the Father and of the Son and of the Holy Spirit, and teaching them to obey everything that I have commanded you" (Matt. 28:19–20). While there is a call to share the Gospel with the whole world, no mention is made of coercing unbelievers into conversion. Nonetheless, exclusivist claims abound in the New Testament: "Very truly, I tell you, anyone who does not enter the sheepfold by the gate but climbs in by another way is a thief and a bandit" (John 10:1); "I am the way, and the truth, and the life. No one comes to the Father except through me" (John 14:6). Miroslav Volf, in *Flourishing: Why We need Religion in a Globalized World* (2015), defends religious exclusivism in part because there is a certain degree of comfort provided by the certainty of religiously exclusivist claims that fortify people's "need for boundaries in an uncertain world."[88] Volf presents a reading of the development of Western democratic liberalism that is linked to the "firm convictions held by religious exclusivists about religious liberty and separation of church and state" that led to the formation of "political institutions that would embody and reinforce" those convictions.[89] The crux of Volf's argument is that the exclusive claims of the Christian faith nurture certain values that are conducive to political pluralism and religious tolerance. Such virtues can, for example, be traced to Jesus' instructions to his disciples as he sent them out to proclaim the gospel, heal the sick, and cast out demons: "Wherever you enter a house, stay there until you leave the place. If any place will not welcome you and they refuse to hear you, as you leave, shake off the dust that is on your feet as a testimony against them" (Mark 6:10–11). These instructions command Christian disciples to share the gospel, but it also contains an implied command for how to respond to rejection—even persecution—without recourse to coercion or violence. Admittedly, the connotation is that the disciples have done all that God requires of them in sharing the gospel and that the rejection by those who "will not welcome you" and "refuse to hear you" merits God's wrathful judgment (Matt. 10:15), but there is no implied command for Christian disciples to act in any way against those who reject the gospel. Similarly, during the apostle Paul's evangelical journeys he

---

88. Miroslav Volf, *Flourishing: Why We need Religion in a Globalized World* (New Haven, CT: Yale University Press, 2015), 145.
    89. Ibid., 152.

engaged in spirited but respectful debate with Jews in the synagogue and the marketplace (Acts 14:15–17; 18:1–17) as well as with pagan audiences in Athens (Acts 17:15–34), but even though he was stoned and left for dead once (Acts 14:19), arrested and brought before Roman tribunals several times (Acts 18:12–16; 22:22–29; 28:17–19), and endured thirty-nine lashes from a whip on three different occasions (2 Cor. 11:24–25), Paul never condoned violence as a legitimate response to persecution. Instead, echoing Christ's beatitudes, Paul challenged Christians to "Bless those who persecute you; bless and do not curse them. . . . Do not repay anyone evil for evil, but take thought for what is noble in the sight of all. If it is possible, so far as it depends on you, live peaceably with all" (Rom. 12:14, 17–18).

In claiming that Judaism, Christianity, and Islam all worship the same God, no attempt is made to argue that they are one and the same religion. Instead, this book advocates a model of comparative theology grounded in mutual respect of religious differences while encouraging conversation about shared beliefs and practices. As a result, a model of comparative theology is embraced that presumes we can know God better by studying religious traditions in their particularity while asserting that no single theological interpretation of divine revelation can claim absolute authority over another. Without postulating a neutral, confession-less conception of God that undermines the foundational truth claims of traditional theologies—such as the uniqueness of Christ in the doctrine of the Incarnation, or the Qur'an's affirmation that "There is no god except the one God" (Sura 5:73)—a methodological humility is called for in comparative theology that recognizes the truth that comes from God *in other religions*. Without asking different religions to surrender their religiously exclusivist claims, the argument is made that within each of the Abrahamic religions one finds a divine command for justice, compassion, and love of the other that leads to social and political structures that protect religious freedom and facilitate peaceful coexistence. Instead of viewing different doctrinal traditions as culture-specific "language games" (Wittgenstein as interpreted by Lindbeck), this book defends a view of revelation as sacramental encounter with the divine *through* the medium of human tradition. In other words, human cultures are capable of communicating transcendent truth because of the agency of the Holy Spirit, who bridges the perceived gap between revelation and culture under the rubric of divine initiative overcoming human epistemological doubts. The goal is a pluralistic theology that moves beyond language games in order to make meaningful claims about ultimate reality in critical, mutually beneficial conversation with all the world's religions. As Karl Barth observes, "A mute and obscure God would be an idol. The true and living God is eloquent and radiant."[90]

4.5 A TRINITARIAN PERSPECTIVE ON RELIGIOUS PLURALISM

The chapter began quoting a passage from Kurt Vonnegut's novel *Breakfast of Champions* (1973) in which the author asserts that a particular event in human history—the moment of silence marking the end of the First World War—is a manifestation of God, a theophany, the very Voice of God speaking through the silencing and cessation of human carnage. For Vonnegut this event provides evidence within living human memory of a time when human beings heard God speaking directly to them. *Deus dixit.* God speaks. The Christian doctrine of revelation is grounded on the presumption that God not only speaks but also that humanity can hear and understand this divine self-communication. The challenge for contemporary theologies is discerning what God says when the locus of that revelation is outside the church.

As Mark Heim has observed, a liberative, praxis-centered approach is perhaps "the most straightforwardly inclusivist form of pluralistic theology."[91] Because most discussions of religious pluralism are "strongly motivated by concern over historical conflict and violence among the religions,"[92] the appeal of a liberative approach seems self-evident, though as Heim points out, not without obstacles: "The moral imperative not to regard our own faith as distinctively truthful collides with the expectation that religion is to be enlisted in the struggle for liberation."[93] If "pluralistic theologies can best be advanced on particularistic grounds,"[94] then liberationist theologies are not immune from chauvinism and must tread lightly rather than impose a particular conception of justice on other religions. Nevertheless, if a religion advances a liberative agenda on its own internal theological rationalization and brings it into conversation with other religions that share a similar liberative vision—fighting poverty, emancipating oppressed

90. Barth, *Church Dogmatics*, IV.3.1, 79.
91. S. Mark Heim, *Salvations: Truth and Difference in Religion* (Maryknoll, NY: Orbis Books, 1995), 196.
92. Ibid., 185.
93. Ibid., 197.
94. Ibid., 190.

populations, overcoming racial hatreds, combating violence against women, etc.—the likelihood of interreligious cooperation is greatly increased. Liberative theologies do not stand outside and above more traditional theologies but work from within a particular tradition to affirm those foundational sources and teachings that link devotion, ritual, worship, and prayer to the faith community's social praxis as the concrete embodiment of such divine virtues as love, mercy, justice, and compassion. In other words, the liberative pluralist agenda does not seek to "substitute its specific social agenda for the tenets of the faiths" but originates from within each particular faith as "a series of parallel transformations in the traditions, where each on its own grounds gives greater weight to the social concerns of liberation."[95]

Barth, Hauerwas, and Milbank all insist that Christian theology does not speak about God in vague generalities but speaks concretely about God as revealed in the sacred Scriptures of the Christian faith. Given that Trinitarian doctrine developed from the collective Christian effort to understand God as revealed and encountered in the New Testament, Mark Heim argues for a Trinitarian pluralistic theology. Still, if the goal is to articulate a comparative theology of revelation in conversation with Judaism and Islam, it might seem counterproductive to focus on the distinctly Christian language of Trinitarian doctrine. Nevertheless, despite resistance from the more radical monotheisms of Judaism and Islam, Heim moves forward with a Trinitarian pluralistic theology on the basic premise that "Christians believe that the understanding of God as Trinity, the understanding whose catalyst is the incarnation of Christ, allows us to grasp key features of God's character and God's relation with us."[96] Heim's proposal embraces religious pluralism by means of the Trinity, emphasizing the work of the Holy Spirit in such a way that he preserves Christ's unique saving role *while* valuing the contribution of other faiths to this very thick and complex understanding of divinity. Heim argues that "Trinity provides a particular ground for affirming the truth and reality of what is different" by ruling out narrowly exclusivist conceptions of God as inauthentic since there "is an irreducible variety in what is true or of greatest significance. Christians can find validity in other religions because of the conviction that the Trinity represents a universal truth about the way the world and God actually are."[97] Of course, Trinitarian doctrine developed from

95. Ibid., 199.
96. Heim, *The Depth of the Riches*, 125.
97. Ibid., 127.

Christological questions since to "make sense of the fact that God was as decisively in Christ as Christians believed, it was necessary to hold that God was elsewhere than Christ also."[98] In other words, in order to make sense of how God could become incarnate in a particular person, Jesus of Nazareth, while still remaining God, is "perhaps the key pivot point of the Christian theology of religions" insofar as the Trinitarian economy of God's action preserves "God's active relation to creation in ways distinct from the event of the historical Jesus."[99]

The next chapter will expand the notion of revelation as a sacramental encounter facilitated by the Spirit in order to move beyond the impasse in North American academic theology that reacts to religious pluralism and doctrinal diversity with epistemological uncertainty and praxeological impotence. Recognizing that both theologies of manifestation (McFague) and theologies of proclamation (Milbank) are inadequate for dealing with the radical plurality of contemporary theological discourse, it has been argued that liberative and contextual theologies (De La Torre) find commonality across confessional boundaries by emphasizing the work of the Holy Spirit in preserving human dignity and emancipating the victims of oppression.[100] This pluralist tolerance has been present in liberation theology since its inception, as evidenced by key passages from Gutiérrez's *A Theology of Liberation* (1973): "The grace of the vision of God thus culminates a profound aspiration of the human spirit. Human beings fulfill themselves completely only in this communion, dependent upon God's free initiative. The natural and supernatural orders are therefore intimately unified."[101] Reflecting on Rahner's "anonymous Christianity," Gutiérrez locates divine revelation in the work of historical and political liberation: "This affirmation of the single vocation to salvation, beyond all distinctions, gives religious value in a completely new way to human action in history, Christian and non-Christian alike. The building of a just society has worth in terms of the Kingdom, or in more current phraseology, to participate in the process of liberation is already, in a certain sense, a salvific work."[102] Then in exegeting the parable of the Good Samaritan, Gutiérrez provides an important marker for tracking the work of the Holy Spirit in

98. Ibid., 131.

99. Ibid.

100. See Rubén Rosario Rodríguez, *Racism and God-Talk: A Latino/a Perspective* (New York: New York University Press, 2008), 212–35. In this book I argue that "God's presence is manifest in concrete liberating praxis" and "often found outside the faith community" (213). Accordingly, the work of the Holy Spirit is what enables us to recognize "God's action in the world *wherever* we find the work of liberation" (212, emphasis in the original).

101. Gutiérrez, *A Theology of Liberation*, 44.

102. Ibid., 46.

the world by answering the lawyer's question ("Who is my neighbor?"): "The neighbor was the Samaritan who approached the wounded man and made him his neighbor. The neighbor, as has been said, is not the one whom I find in my path, but rather the one in whose path I place myself, the one whom I approach and actively seek."[103]

Having rejected the false dichotomy characteristic of both anthropological and revelational theologies—which favor either experience or revelation but are unable to bring both together—the next chapter develops a doctrine of revelation grounded in the ongoing work of the Holy Spirit. Building on Jürgen Moltmann's attempts at bridging this gap, it is presumed that we cannot recognize God's self-communication as revelation without first experiencing the Spirit of God. Accordingly, though the continuity between human spirit and divine Spirit originates in and is preserved by divine initiative, this indwelling by the Spirit of God makes human knowledge and action possible despite our epistemological uncertainty because of the Christlike praxis it engenders. It follows from recognizing the presence of the Holy Spirit in liberating work—especially when such work is located outside the church—that, as in Heim's Trinitarian pluralism, God desires and values doctrinal diversity and theological pluralism. When this emphasis on liberative praxis is joined to a methodological humility that affirms the hiddenness of God in divine self-revelation, the resulting conception of theology is one in which no tradition speaks with absolute certainty or universal application, multiple doctrinal formulations are not only tolerated but encouraged, and theological truth claims are tested in comparative theological analysis.

---

103. Ibid., 113.

5

Pneumatology—Revelation as Sacramental Encounter

The dynamism and vitality expressed by "spirit" are accentuated when the human person is considered from the standpoint of God's action on it. Spirit and its derivates signify a life that is in accordance with God's will—that is, a life in accordance with the gift of divine filiation that finds expression in human fellowship.

—Gustavo Gutiérrez[1]

Citing Paul Knitter's contribution to a World Council of Churches dialogue on the "turn to pneumatology" within Christian theology of religions, Amos Yong affirms this methodological turn and suggests that "starting with pneumatology rather than with christology" opens theological reflection to the "possibility of the Spirit's 'saving presence' and 'saving power' in the non-Christian faiths."[2] As previously noted, late in his life Paul Tillich became interested in Christianity's dialogue with other religions, explicitly in his final lecture at the University of Chicago Divinity School, "The Significance of the History of Religions for the Systematic Theologian" (1965), and implicitly in the turn to pneumatology in the third volume of his *Systematic Theology* (1963): "The Spiritual Community contains an indefinite variety of expressions of faith and does not exclude any of them. It is open in all directions because it is based on the central manifestation of the Spiritual Presence."[3] Jürgen Moltmann, a Reformed theologian heavily influenced by both Tillich and Barth, identifies strong reluctance within mainline Protestantism to embrace the human experience of God in the world and praises Eastern Orthodoxy, the Spiritualist traditions of

1. Gustavo Gutiérrez, *We Drink from Our Own Wells: The Spiritual Journey of a People*, trans. Matthew J. O'Connell, reprint (Maryknoll, NY: Orbis Books, 2003), 62.

2. Amos Yong, *Beyond the Impasse: Toward a Pneumatological Theology of Religions* (Eugene, OR: Wipf & Stock, 2003), 84.

3. Paul Tillich, *Systematic Theology*, vol. 3, *Life and the Spirit, History and the Kingdom of God* (Chicago: The University of Chicago Press, 1963), 155.

the sixteenth-century Reformations, and the rising global Pentecostal movement for embracing this work of the Spirit. Reluctance, however, seems to typify Karl Barth's engagement with pneumatology:

> There is no reason why the attempt of Christian anthropocentrism should not be made, indeed ought not to be made. There is certainly a place for legitimate Christian thinking starting from below and moving up, from man who is taken hold of by God to God who takes hold of man. Let us interpret this attempt by the 19th-century theologians in its best light! Provided that it in no way claims to be exclusive and absolute, one might well understand it as an attempt to formulate a theology of the third article of the Apostles' Creed, the Holy Spirit. . . . But insofar as [this] theology was intended to be a theology of Christian self-understanding and not a theology of the Holy Spirit, it could not break through the general trend of the century.[4]

Despite Barth's hesitation to focus on the believer's subjective experience of the Spirit, however, his Trinitarian theological project does emphasize the work of the Spirit in the work of redemption, identifying "God's revelation as Spirit of promise" and the life of the redeemed as "the new life in hope, begotten of the Holy Spirit."[5]

From the perspective of Enlightenment rationalism, the popularity and success of the global Pentecostal and Charismatic movements defies explanation, insofar as the scientific worldview that came to dominance post-Enlightenment has systematically worked to eliminate the reality and experience of God from the canons of rational discourse. In other words, while scientific rationalism is willing to tolerate the Deist notion of an abstract and distant "Creator" (William Paley's "divine watchmaker"), or even endure fideistic claims about the historical Jesus *so long* as they remain relegated to the *private* sphere, the secular scientific worldview adamantly opposes any concrete and tangible notion of divine agency in the world. It is one thing to claim with Hegel, Schleiermacher, and Feuerbach that some aspect of human subjectivity concerns itself with *opinions* about a divine being, and quite another to claim that these beliefs make *factual claims* about the "natural" world. From the dominant modernist perspective, "it is too much to ask people to accept the claim that in God's Spirit God is near them, that in the

---

4. Karl Barth, "Evangelical Theology in the 19th Century," in *The Humanity of God*, trans. Thomas Wieser (Richmond, VA: John Knox Press, 1972), 24–25.

5. Karl Barth, *The Holy Spirit and the Christian Life: The Theological Basis of Ethics*, trans. R. Birch Hoyle (Louisville, KY: Westminster/John Knox Press, 1993), 2.

Spirit God is present among them and acts on them."[6] The astonishing success of the worldwide charismatic movement in its many variants stands as refutation to this secularizing trend in modernism through its "appeal to the powerful experience of the reality and presence of God in the Spirit."[7] Pneumatology—a theology of the Holy Spirit—challenges modernity by affirming God is a power that creates, intervenes, and directs the world. This concrete experience of God in everyday life offends the modern consciousness, which cannot adequately explain the miracle of Pentecostalism as "the largest religious movement in history" without declaring the movement (and the claims of its members) as some sort of mass delusion.[8] Nevertheless, this book argues that without recovering some means of rationally articulating the experience of the God who acts in human history, contemporary theologies remain mired at the impasse between revelational and anthropological approaches. To that end, this concluding chapter serves as an "attempt to change the secular world's habitual forms of experience in the direction of a greater openness to experience of the Spirit"[9] by exploring the Holy Spirit's historical manifestation in acts of human liberation that preserve human dignity and reveal an indispensable dimension of God's true nature.

5.1 SCRIPTURAL CONCEPTIONS OF SPIRIT

The temptation for a Christian believer is to subsume any and all work of the Spirit under the umbrella of a Trinitarian theology, which is why even a pluralistic Christian theology of religions like that put forth by S. Mark Heim might prove a stumbling block to the non-Christian interlocutor. Yet even the most cursory glance at the scriptural descriptions of the work of the Spirit in the Hebrew Bible reveals a plurality of conceptions that do not easily conform to a strictly Trinitarian framework. Broadly, the scriptural conception of Spirit refers to the "manifestation of divine presence and power perceptible especially in prophetic inspiration," loosely defined in "late biblical thought, but developed in early Judaism and Christianity to a fundamental dogma."[10] Nevertheless,

---

6. Michael Welker, *God the Spirit*, trans. John F. Hoffmeyer (Minneapolis, MN: Fortress Press, 1994), 5.
7. Ibid., 7.
8. Ibid., 1.
9. Ibid.
10. F. W. Horn, "Holy Spirit," in *The Anchor Bible Dictionary*, vol. 3, ed. David Noel Freedman, trans. Dietlinde M. Elliot (New York: Doubleday, 1992), 260. For a comprehensive study of biblical perspectives of the Spirit, see

the various conceptions of Spirit found therein yield a cohesive whole that can serve as the ground for a pluralistic and comparative theology capable of overcoming human epistemological uncertainty while engendering "righteousness and justice" (Gen. 18:19) across confessional boundaries.[11] Yet, in order to make the argument that the various sacred Scriptures share a similar notion of Spirit, it is necessary to look in some detail at the conceptions of Spirit in the sacred Scriptures of all three Abrahamic religions.

5.1.1 Spirit in the Tanakh

Despite the fact that the various references to the work of the Spirit in biblical Judaism do not conform to a single pattern, the Hebrew Bible is the logical starting point for a comparative study of Spirit insofar as the Hebraic worldview shaped the belief and praxis of Jesus and his earliest followers, which in turn contributed to the cultural milieu in which Muhammad received his revelation from God via the archangel Gabriel (Sura 17:106). This assumption is supported by the fact that the Septuagint (LXX), or Greek translation of the Hebrew Scriptures, served as the Bible for the first two generations of Christian believers prior to the composition and canonization of the New Testament, and by the Qur'an's citing of the Hebrew prophets and patriarchs from Abraham to Moses to David, as well as major figures from the Christian New Testament, like John the Baptist, Mary the mother of Jesus, and of course, Jesus himself, who in Islam is considered the last prophet and messenger of God prior to God's final and definitive self-revelation to Muhammad.

With the formation of creedal Christianity and the rise of rabbinic Judaism in the post-apostolic era, biblical conceptions of Spirit ossified into religiously exclusivist dogmas. Still, there exists within the biblical

---

George T. Montague, S.M., *The Holy Spirit: Growth of a Biblical Tradition* (New York: Paulist Press, 1976). For a historical study of the church's understanding of the work of the Holy Spirit from a Roman Catholic perspective, see Yves Congar, *I Believe in the Holy Spirit*, rev. ed., trans. David Smith (New York: Crosssroad Publishing Company, 1997). For systematic treatments of the doctrine of the Holy Spirit from a Christian perspective, see Clark H. Pinnock, *Flame of Love: A Theology of the Holy Spirit* (Downers Grove, IL: InterVarsity Press, 1996), Michael Welker, *God the Spirit*, trans. John F. Hoffmeyer (Minneapolis, MN: Fortress Press, 1994), and Veli-Matti Kärkkäinen, *Pneumatology: The Holy Spirit in Ecumenical, International, and Contextual Perspective* (Grand Rapids, MI: Baker Academic, 2002).

11. For a constructive proposal on the doctrine of the Spirit as enabling dialogue and cooperation in pluralistic context, see Veli-Matti Kärkkäinen, *A Constructive Christian Theology for the Pluralistic World*, vol. 4, *Spirit and Salvation* (Grand Rapids, MI: Wm. B. Eerdmans Publishing Co., 2016).

account an organic and un-systematized—yet surprisingly coherent—understanding of the work of the Spirit that reflects the Semitic conception of the natural and spiritual worlds. *Ruach* ("wind" or "breath"), most often translated as *pneuma* ("wind") in the LXX, is the primary Hebrew word used when referring to the Spirit, with some overlap with the words *neshamah* ("soul") and *nephesh* ("soul" or "life"), suggesting a strong relationship between the work of YHWH's Spirit in the world and the soul as the center of human sentience.[12] Most likely, the original meaning of *ruach* stemmed from descriptions of natural forces insofar as it described the movement of air as in either "wind" or "breath," which very quickly became connected to God's action in the world as both the source of life and the guiding force behind natural forces. In fact, in the opening verses of Genesis these two conceptions are intertwined and directly linked to God insofar as the divine *ruach* is both a "wind" from God sweeping across the as yet unformed waters, and the life-giving "breath" of God that creates life from the void (Gen. 1:2). While its original usage suggests an impersonal concept, throughout the Hebrew Bible *ruach* as a force of nature is linked to God's action in the world, reinforcing YHWH's dominion over all creation. So, for example, *ruach* is the term used to describe the gale wind that disperses the great flood (Gen. 8:1) and parts the Red Sea, turning "the sea to dry land" (Exod. 14:21).

Locating these uses of *ruach* within the creation story, it becomes necessary to acknowledge the polemical nature of much of what takes place in the book of Genesis as a distinctly Hebraic cosmology over against competing Near Eastern cosmologies like the Mesopotamian creation epic the *Enuma Elish*. One of the major points being argued by the author(s) of Genesis is that phenomena other cultures have labeled, and worshiped, as divinities are in fact natural forces created by and under the divine providence of the one true God:

> These mythical beings are variously designated Yam (Sea), Nahar (River), Leviathan (Coiled One), Rahab (Arrogant One), and Tannin (Dragon). . . . They have survived in the Bible solely as obscure, picturesque metaphors and exclusively in the language of poetry.

---

12. For a comprehensive survey of the various uses of "spirit" in the Hebrew Bible and the New Testament, as well as relevant ancient literature, see the article, "*Pneuma, pneumatikos,*" by Kleinknecht, Baumgärtel, Bieder, Sjöberg, and Schweizer, in *Theological Dictionary of the New Testament*, vol. 6, ed. Gerhard Kittel and Gerhard Friedrich, trans. by G. W. Bromiley (Grand Rapids, MI: Wm. B. Eerdmans Publishing Co., 1968), 332–455 (the discussion of *ruach* is found on pp. 359–67).

Never are these creatures accorded divine attributes, nor is there any-
where a suggestion that their struggle against God could in any way
have posed a challenge to His sovereign rule.[13]

This cosmological narrative reinforces the uniqueness and lordship of
God by defining rival cosmological powers as mere natural forces under
God's complete and total control, most clearly symbolized by God's
manifestation as a wind (*ruach*) sweeping over the primal waters of
chaos before beginning the work of creation. Therefore, when unpack-
ing the various conceptions of "spirit" in the Hebrew Bible it helps to
understand that even natural forces like "wind" serve as theophanies,
and that as far as the ancient Hebrew worldview is concerned there is
no chasm between the natural and supernatural realms. Rather, there
is only one phenomenal reality, divinely instituted and ordered to bear
witness to the fact that the "universe is wholly the purposeful product of
divine intelligence, that is, of the one self-sufficient, self-existing God,
who is a transcendent Being outside of nature and who is sovereign
over space and time."[14] Consequently, as we unpack the various uses
of *ruach*, we must acknowledge and maintain two distinct conceptions
in creative tension: (1) God's "spirit" is not just limited to the creative
power that once upon a time acted in the mythological prehistory of
Israel but continues to reveal God's self through direct manipulation
of the natural order, and (2) God's "spirit" acts on humanity in much
the same way it directs the natural order *without* violating the human
person's sense of self.

The former understanding of *ruach* as God's "spirit" directing the
natural order challenges the dominant modernist conception of the
natural order, which at best tolerates a Deist view of God as a necessary
First Cause that does not interfere directly with the world. The biblical
conception of God and God's relation to the creation, however, conveys
a very clear and unequivocal sense that God acts directly on human
lives and the world they inhabit. Furthermore, it is by means of the
ruach that God's agency in the world and God's impact on human lives
is known and experienced. The latter understanding of *ruach* as God's
"spirit" acting on human subjectivity also contains a sense of God's
"spirit" gifting humankind with its own individual "spirit," endowing
humanity with the distinct and unique role within God's Creation as
the *imago Dei* (Gen. 1:27). Notably, this interpersonal notion of the

---

13. Nahum M. Sarna, *The JPS Torah Commentary: Genesis* (Philadelphia: The Jewish Publication Society, 1989), 3.
14. Ibid., 4.

"spirit" of God interacting with our human "spirits" also contradicts modernist notions of self, especially the Enlightenment view of the human being as an autonomous, self-directed being. Of course, the biblical account acknowledges the "devastating impact of God on men and on their world"[15]—for example, the prophet Jeremiah describes the work of the Spirit in his life with the words "you have overpowered me" (Jer. 20:7), employing the Hebrew word *chazaq* that can connote assault and even rape (Deut. 22:25; Judg. 19:25; 2 Sam. 13:14)[16]—yet still manages to preserve some understanding that our most authentic self originates within this asymmetrical covenantal relationship with the divine *ruach* (however unsettling). In much the same way that God's mastery and control over the natural order is symbolized by *ruach* ("wind") as a natural force under divine control, the Hebrew Bible also preserves a conception of God as the source of both good and evil "spirits" as another means of asserting God's unchallenged sovereignty: "[the Hebrew Bible] can and does use *ruach* to speak of a good or evil influence coming from God and exerting an impact on the lives of individuals or groups."[17] This is illustrated well in Genesis when God troubles Pharaoh's dreams (Gen. 41:8), in the exodus narrative when God "hardened the heart of Pharaoh" (Exod. 9:12), and in the book of Samuel when "the spirit (*ruach*) of the LORD departed from Saul, and an evil spirit (*ruach*) from the LORD tormented him" (1 Sam. 16:14).

From this, we can conclude some things about the various uses of *ruach* in the Hebrew Bible: (1) *ruach* originated in the natural realm (as "wind" or "breath") but came to be used to describe God's action on the natural world; (2) *ruach* is also used to describe the principle of life that is a gift from God ("spirit" or "soul"), which makes us fully human as *imago Dei*; and (3) *ruach* ("spirit") is used to identify God's unique agency in the world. This last category sometimes appears to involve a separate being distinct from God, as in Christian Trinitarian conceptions of God, but in the Hebrew Bible the *ruach* ("spirit") of God "is not detachable, as it were, from Yahweh himself: it is his living impact here and now."[18] In other words, when the Hebrew Bible speaks about the "spirit" of God, it is addressing God's agency in the world similar

---

15. Alasdair I. C. Heron, *The Holy Spirit* (Philadelphia: The Westminster Press, 1983), 4.

16. Abraham J. Heschel, *The Prophets*, vol. 1 (New York: Harper & Row, 1969). Heschel argues, "The words used by Jeremiah to describe the impact of God upon his life are identical with the terms for seduction and rape in the legal terminology of the Bible" (114).

17. Heron, *The Holy Spirit*, 5.

18. Ibid., 8.

to the way other biblical images metaphorically describe the "arm" (Ps. 89:13) or "hand" (Isa. 66:2) of God, and even talk of God's presence as the "face" (Num. 6:25) of God, without intending a separate divine entity. Yes, the *ruach* ("spirit") of God manifests God's presence in the world, but not as a distinct agent. Rather, these manifestations— whether in the natural world or in human consciousness—simply *are* God for us. Accordingly, "The personal categories used to describe the activity of the Spirit [in the Hebrew Bible] are not designed to present Him as a special heavenly being but rather to bring out the fact that He is an objective divine reality which encounters and claims man."[19] Whether through natural forces, like the whirlwind (Job. 38:1), or in the still small voice (1 Kgs. 19:12) we have come to call our conscience, God is present: "it is precisely because he transcends earth and heaven that he can be directly and immediately *present* in that place, though not *contained* in it or limited by it."[20] Nevertheless, there remains in the biblical uses of *ruach* some sense that God's Spirit is external to us even as it acts upon us to transform us.

Consequently, the *ruach* is best conceived as a charismatic power (from *charis* meaning "grace" or "favor," the Greek translation of the Hebrew *hanan* meaning "to show favor"), at least when discussing the work of the Spirit of God on human beings, insofar as it is viewed as a gift from God that comes from without yet transforms the inner self. The paradigm for this understanding of the biblical concept of *ruach* is the powerful work of the Judges in pre-monarchic Israel and the anointing by the Spirit of the Lord in the prophetic books. George Montague, in his comprehensive study of biblical uses of Spirit, *The Holy Spirit: Growth of a Biblical Tradition* (1976), focuses on the Deuteronomic History (the books of Joshua, Judges, Samuel, Kings, and of course Deuteronomy) as a key interpretive framework for understanding the Hebrew Bible's conception of the work of the Spirit because, "while their final editing and publication may have been only in the 5th century B.C., the narrative they contain goes all the way back to Israel's conquest of the 'Holy Land,' and scribes began to write down these traditions during the period of the monarchy long before the Babylonian exile in 587 B.C."[21] Montague argues that the material having to do with the *ruach* ("spirit") of God as charismatic gift in particular "gives every evidence of belonging to

19. Kittel and Friedrich, ed., *Theological Dictionary of the New Testament*, vol. 6, 387.
20. Ibid.
21. George T. Montague, *The Holy Spirit: Growth of a Biblical Tradition* (New York: Paulist Press, 1976), 17.

an early stratum of the materials in the Deuteronomic history."[22] Furthermore, the "major contribution of the book of Judges to the understanding of the spirit lies in its very graphic interpretation of the charismatic leadership of this period as the work of the *ruah Yahweh*, the spirit of the Lord."[23]

As a charismatic power, conceptions of the work of the Spirit in the Deuteronomic History connote an overpowering of the person by the *ruach* of YHWH, often times enabling that person to carry out powerful—even supernatural—works (Judg. 3:10; 6:34; 14:6; 1 Sam. 16:13; Ezek. 3:12). Considering that these earliest accounts pre-date the monarchy and describe a time when Israel was barely a nation (more a loose confederation of tribes), the Deuteronomic History drives home the point that it is YHWH, not any single political leader (however personally accomplished that leader might be), who, under the Mosaic covenant, rules over the people of Israel. This pattern of being visited by the *ruach YHWH* ("spirit of the Lord") as a sign of both empowering and anointing to lead is repeated several times in the book of Judges: Othniel, sent by God in response to the prayers of Israel (Judg. 3:10); Gideon, who defeated the Midianites despite being greatly outnumbered as a show of God's sovereignty (Judg. 6:34); Jephtha, chosen by YHWH to deliver the Israelites from the Ammonites despite being the son of a prostitute, also as a show of God's absolute sovereignty (Judg. 11:29); and Samson, whose legendary feats are attributed to and made possible by the Spirit of the Lord (Judg. 13:25). Even Deborah, whose time as judge over Israel is not explicitly attributed to the work of the Spirit, nevertheless falls under this charismatic anointing by the *ruach YHWH*, as evidenced by her title of "prophetess" (Judg. 4:4). From the Deuteronomic History we receive a pattern of the *ruach YHWH* acting in response to the prayers of the people of Israel, inspiring great acts that are always intended for the good of the nation of Israel as a whole, and acknowledgment that this anointing of an individual by the Spirit is "not tied to any institution or rite."[24] In other words, not only are the various feats of YHWH's judges, prophets, priests, and eventually kings, made possible *solely* by the power of the Spirit, the very selection of YHWH's human agents is itself an act of the Spirit meant to undermine any sense of hereditary entitlement or elevated social status being granted to YHWH's servants:

22. Ibid.
23. Ibid.
24. Ibid., 18.

With the story of Saul's anointing by Samuel, the monarchy is linked at its very beginning from the prophetic office, so that kingly authority in Israel is shown from the very beginning to derive from the "spirit of the Lord," not from mere dynastic succession. The account shows both the continuity of Israelite monarchy with the prophetic movement and also the limitation of its power to the spiritual aims of Yahweh—a point which the Deuteronomist makes repeatedly in his history of the kings.[25]

This theme is continued in the preexilic prophets as in the calling of Amos, who "was among the shepherds of Tekoa" (Amos 1:1) and only reluctantly accepted the mantle of prophet when called by YHWH: "I am no prophet, nor a prophet's son; but I am a herdsman, and a dresser of sycamore trees, and the LORD took me from following the flock, and the LORD said to me, 'Go, prophesy to my people Israel'" (Amos 7:14–15).

The link between the monarchy and prophecy dates to the very foundation of the kingdom of Israel, with Saul prophesying under the influence of the *ruach YHWH* (1 Sam. 10:6; 19:24), and not only is this early understanding of prophecy linked to divine charismatic anointing, the very act of prophecy is described as "a state of wild, ecstatic possession which was ascribed to the influence of God's *ruach*: 'prophet' meant much the same as the Islamic 'dervish.'"[26] This work of the Spirit is chronicled in frightening terms: "Then the Spirit of the LORD will possess you, and you will be in a prophetic frenzy along with them and turned into a different person" (1 Sam. 10:6). When David witnessed Samuel's frenzy among the prophets he too was overcome by the Spirit of the Lord, which caused him to strip naked and dance before Samuel "all that day and all that night" (1 Sam. 19:24). Ecstatic prophecy characterizes this earliest layer of Hebrew prophecy, though it became muted in the preexilic prophets, only to return during the exile, most vividly in the apocalyptic visions of Ezekiel attributed to the *ruach YHWH* (Ezek. 2:1–2; 3:12–15), which at one point left Ezekiel stunned "for seven days" (Ezek. 12:15). This ecstatic dimension of spiritual anointing would persist through the late apocalyptic literature and into the intertestamental period, only to be appropriated later into the early Christian understanding of prophecy and spiritual anointing in the New Testament. What unites these various prophetic acts,

25. Ibid., 19.
26. Heron, *The Holy Spirit*, 13–14.

whether involving extreme ecstatic behavior or limiting itself to the preaching of the prophet, is that all prophecy finds its source and efficacy in its divine origin: the *ruach* of the Lord. Thus, while Amos correctly grounds his authority as prophet not in some pre-existing office but in the divine act of calling the prophet to speak the word of the Lord (*dābhar YHWH*),[27] what remains constant is that "all true prophecy had been inspired by that same *ruach*."[28] In other words, prophecy is God's chosen tool to instruct, guide, reprimand, and when necessary, even punish Israel, and no stronger proof of Israel's rebellion exists than when it disobeys—and even attacks and kills—God's chosen prophets, who are manifestations of God's *ruach* in the world.

The Spirit's role in establishing righteousness and justice is most evident in the preaching of the Hebrew Prophets.[29] The book of the prophet Isaiah explicitly links the work of liberation to the *ruach YHWH*:

> The spirit of the Lord God is upon me,
>> because the Lord has anointed me;
> he has sent me to bring good news to the oppressed,
>> to bind up the brokenhearted,
> to proclaim liberty to the captives,
>> and release to the prisoners;
> to proclaim the year of the Lord's favor,
>> and the day of vengeance of our God;
>> to comfort all who mourn;
> to provide for those who mourn in Zion—
>> to give them a garland instead of ashes,
> the oil of gladness instead of mourning,
>> the mantle of praise instead of a faint spirit.
> They will be called oaks of righteousness,
>> the planting of the Lord, to display his glory.
>> (Isa. 61:1–3)

Not surprisingly Jesus, "filled with the power of the Spirit" (Luke 4:14), quotes this passage from Isaiah when he preaches his first sermon in Nazareth only to receive a rather hostile reception: "When they heard this, all in the synagogue were filled with rage" (Luke 4:28). Drawing on the preaching of the preexilic and exilic prophets, liberation theologian

---

27. W. H. Schmidt, "Dābhar," in *Theological Dictionary of the Old Testament*, vol. 3, rev., ed. G. Johannes Botterweck and Helmer Ringgren (Grand Rapids, MI: Wm. B. Eerdmans Publishing, 1977), 122–25.
28. Heron, *The Holy Spirit*, 15.
29. Kittel and Friedrich, *Theological Dictionary of the New Testament*, vol. 6, 383.

Gustavo Gutiérrez interprets the covenant with YHWH through the lens of establishing God's righteousness and justice: "Israel's identity, or what it means to belong to the Hebrew people, consists in doing justice to the poor and restoring their trampled rights."[30] This interpretation of the covenant with YHWH predates the nation of Israel and is present as far back as the Abrahamic covenant, which commands, "keep the way of the LORD by doing righteousness and justice" (Gen. 18:19); it is a particular concern of the preexilic prophets like Amos, "For I know how many are your transgressions, and how great are your sins—you who afflict the righteous, who take a bribe, and push aside the needy in the gate" (Amos 5:12) and Micah, "Hear this, you rulers of the house of Jacob and chiefs of the house of Israel, who abhor justice and pervert all equity, who build Zion with blood and Jerusalem with wrong!" (Mic. 3:9–10); and finds its most mature expression in the preaching of Jeremiah:

> Thus says the LORD: Act with justice and righteousness, and deliver from the hand of the oppressor anyone who has been robbed. And do no wrong or violence to the alien, the orphan, and the widow, or shed innocent blood in this place. For if you will indeed obey this word, then through the gates of this house shall enter kings who sit on the throne of David, riding in chariots and on horses, they, and their servants, and their people. But if you will not heed these words, I swear by myself, says the LORD, that this house shall become a desolation. (Jer. 22:3–5)

Thus, the outpouring of the divine *ruach* is not exclusively experienced in terms of ecstatic and visionary experiences, though these are clearly part of the biblical tradition, but are most properly located in the ethical and moral realm, both *individually* as believers and *corporately* as the people of God.

Though it is easy to see how the early Christian church would take these accounts of the divine agency of God revealed by the works of the Spirit and develop them into an explicitly Trinitarian theology in which the Holy Spirit is viewed as a distinct and independent agent, it is important to note that there are only three instances in the entire Hebrew Bible in which the phrase "the Holy Spirit" (*ha ruach ha kodesh*) is uttered (Isa. 63:10–11; Ps. 51:13), and in all three instances "this *ruach* is nothing other than God's own active presence."[31] The

---

30. Gustavo Gutiérrez, *The God of Life*, trans. Matthew J. O'Connell (Maryknoll, NY: Orbis Books, 1991), 22.
31. Heron, *The Holy Spirit*, 19.

pattern that remains consistent throughout the history of Israel's inter-action with the divine Spirit is that it is by an act of God's Spirit that Israel is shown special favor in the first place, that the working of the Spirit is intended to help Israel live within the bounds of the covenant with YHWH, and that YHWH withdraws the Spirit from the nation as a result of Israel's rebellion in an effort to bring them back into the covenant, usually by means of prophetic preaching. Not surprisingly, the later prophetic books preserve an apocalyptic hope among the peo-ple of Israel that there will be a new outpouring of the *ruach YHWH* among the people of God: "Then afterward I will pour out my spirit on all flesh; your sons and your daughters shall prophesy, your old men shall dream dreams, and your young men shall see visions. Even on the male and female slaves, in those days, I will pour out my spirit" (Joel 2:28–29). Historically, this hope is undoubtedly wrapped up in the national desire for the restoration and renewal of the nation of Israel after the Babylonian exile: "It is very much a *corporate* hope that is offered here; the *ruach* of God's presence is the power of the restored life of Israel, not merely the inspiration of individuals."[32] Nevertheless, it doesn't take much imagination to see how the early church, exiled from both the Temple (before its destruction in 70 CE) and the syna-gogue, would embrace this "end-time" prophecy from Joel that dates to the fourth century BCE and reimagine it as both a renewal of the covenant and a re-inauguration of ecstatic prophetic preaching offered to both Jews and Gentiles.

5.1.2 Spirit in the New Testament

The Greek word *pneuma* ("spirit"), the most common translation of the Hebrew word *ruach* in the LXX, appears 379 times in the New Tes-tament but only three times (John 3:8; 2 Thess. 2:8; Heb. 1:7) does it connote the original meaning of *ruach* as "wind" or "breath." In approx-imately 275 of these passages *pneuma* connotes the "spirit of God," and 92 of these textual references speak explicitly about the *pneuma hagion*, or "Holy Spirit."[33] Despite this preponderance of New Testament uses of *pneuma* that speak chiefly about the spirit of God, there remains a continuity with the Hebrew Bible's varied understanding of *ruach*, such

---

32. Ibid., 20 (italics in the original).
33. Horn, "Holy Spirit," in *The Anchor Bible Dictionary*, vol. 3, 265.

as when speaking of the human being as possessing a "soul," or when speaking about the human "spirit" (though the terms *soma* and *psyche* are more common). Roughly 40 times the word *pneuma* is used to refer to the center of human personal identity, and in most of these instances, "the spirit of a human being is that aspect of a man or a woman through which God most immediately encounters" the human person (Rom. 8:16; Gal. 6:18; Phil. 4:23; Heb. 4:12), though "in several instances it is not absolutely clear whether the word refers to the human spirit or the divine Spirit" (Matt. 5:3; Luke 1:47; Rom. 1:9; 1 Pet. 3:4).[34] Furthermore, as in the Hebrew Bible, the New Testament also speaks of good and evil spirits (Mark 3:22–30; 5:1–13), though mostly in terms of a spiritual battle between good and evil, which nevertheless reinforces God's—and Jesus Christ as God's agent in the world—complete sovereignty over all Creation.

Still, it becomes evident when surveying the New Testament uses of *pneuma* that the early Christians adopted then transformed the Hebraic understandings of *ruach* in such a way that the Spirit of God became an increasingly distinct and separate agent of divine action who is "now seen and shown to be inherently involved in what God has done in Jesus Christ."[35] In other words, while sharing the same Semitic worldview as the Hebrew Bible, what distinguishes the New Testament is its predominately christological and Trinitarian conception of the work of the Spirit as "the Spirit of your Father" (Matt. 10:20), "the Spirit of God" (Matt. 12:28), "the Spirit of Jesus" (Acts 16:7), and "the Spirit of Christ" (Rom. 8:9). Thus, even the assertion that God is sovereign and has dominion over all spiritual realities—even demonic powers, as in the encounter with the Gerasene demoniac in the Gospel of Mark—becomes an occasion for a christological confession when Jesus rebukes the demon by saying, "Come out of the man, you unclean spirit," prompting the possessed man to shout, "What have you to do with me, Jesus, Son of the Most High God?" (Mark 5:7).

There is a tendency within Christian pneumatology to begin reflection on the work of the Spirit with the birth of the Christian church at Pentecost (Acts 2), a clear example of the charismatic and ecstatic dimensions of the *ruach YHWH* recast for a Christian context in which the apostles "were filled with the Holy Spirit and began to speak in other languages, as the Spirit gave them ability" (Acts 2:4), an ecstatic

---

34. Kärkkäinen, *Pneumatology*, 28.
35. Heron, *The Holy Spirit*, 39.

fervor that also affected the crowd, consisting of Jews from across the Mediterranean world (in Jerusalem to celebrate the feast of Pentecost), who repented and were baptized: "that day about three thousand persons were added" (Acts 2:41). Yet to approximate the earliest Christian beliefs about the work of the Spirit, it makes sense to begin not with the Gospels (including the Acts of the Apostles, given Luke-Acts is a literary whole) but with the letters of Paul. What we find in this earliest layer of Christian literature is that by 51 CE, when Paul wrote his first letter to the Thessalonians, there already existed within Christian circles a tendency to speak of the spirit of the Lord (*ruach YHWH*) as "the Holy Spirit" (*pneuma hagion*), that, as in the Hebrew Bible, the theme of being elected and anointed by the Spirit was widely accepted (1 Thess. 1:4), and that, as in the more ecstatic prophetic and apocalyptic texts of the Hebrew Bible, the work of the Spirit was accompanied by miraculous signs: "because our message of the gospel came to you not in word only, but also in power and in the Holy Spirit and with full conviction" (1 Thess 1:5). This first appearance of the Holy Spirit in Christian writing, written some two generations *before* the Acts of the Apostles, contains the same emphasis on the charismatic power and ecstatic joy that characterizes the paradigmatic pneumatology of Pentecost grounded in a Christian appropriation of the Messianic eschatological hopes of the prophet Joel (Acts 2:17–21): "Then afterward I will pour out my spirit on all flesh; your sons and your daughters shall prophesy, your old men shall dream dreams, and your young men shall see visions. Even on the male and female slaves, in those days, I will pour out my spirit" (Joel 2:28–29).

What we find in the letters of Paul is a wide range of divine actions attributable to the work of the Spirit that include "freedom from the law of sin and death" (Rom. 8:2), "a spirit of adoption" that leads to becoming "joint heirs with Christ" of the resurrection (Rom. 8:15, 17), and intercession in prayer since "the Spirit helps us in our weakness; for we do not know how to pray as we ought, but that very Spirit intercedes with sighs too deep for words . . . because the Spirit intercedes for the saints according to the will of God" (Rom. 8:26–27). Furthermore, for the believer who has received the gift and power of the Holy Spirit, discernible and tangible fruits ensue: "By contrast, the fruit of the Spirit is love, joy, peace, patience, kindness, generosity, faithfulness, gentleness, and self-control. There is no law against such things" (Gal. 5:22–23). Thus we find that Paul's earliest audience, the church in Thessalonica, was able to rejoice in the good news of Jesus Christ "in spite of persecution" because they were filled "with joy inspired by the Holy Spirit" (1 Thess. 1:6). In other words, acceptance of the gospel message, the ability to confess, "Jesus is Lord" (1 Cor. 12:1–3), also brings with it a spirit of humility that breaks down differences and builds community: "If we live by the Spirit, let us also be guided by the Spirit. Let us not become conceited, competing against one another, envying one another" (Gal. 5:25–26). Remembering that Paul's letters were written out of pastoral concern addressing specific problems affecting a particular congregation, the first letter to the Corinthians attempts to resolve a disagreement over the community's understanding of the charismatic gifts of the Spirit that has led to "jealousy and quarreling among you" (1 Cor. 3:3). Paul responds by appealing to the Spirit of fellowship (*koinōnia*), "For in the one Spirit we were all baptized into one body—Jews or Greeks, slaves or free—and we were all made to drink of one Spirit" (1 Cor. 12:13), in order to overcome strife and division, for the Holy Spirit is "the upbuilder of the Christian community."[36] Accordingly, the reason for the gifts of the Spirit (*charismata*) is to build up the community, especially in the context of persecution, that they might witness to the good news of Jesus Christ through their corporate life together. To that end, just "as in one body we have many members, and not all the members have the same function, so we, who are many, are one body in Christ, and individually we are members one of another" (Rom. 12:4–5). Not only are there multiple gifts from the Spirit—healing, leadership, prophecy, speaking in tongues, and interpretation—each of these gifts serves a purpose within the one body, "To each is given the manifestation of the Spirit for the common good" (1 Cor .12:7).

It is evident that Paul did not want to restrict or curtail the practice of charismatic gifts within the life of the church (1 Cor. 14:39–40), though he did warn against the zeal to outdo one another in the exercise of the spiritual gifts by reminding the church in Corinth that even though he excelled at speaking in tongues, "in church I would rather speak five words with my mind, in order to instruct others also, than ten thousand words in a tongue" (1 Cor. 14:19). Without reducing the fruits of the Spirit to morality, Paul links the gifts of the Spirit to divine righteousness (Gal. 5:5), the peace of God (Rom. 15:13), and above all else, selfless love (Rom 5:5; 1 Cor. 13; 2 Cor. 6:6; Gal. 5:22), in order to develop the argument that the greatest of all the gifts of the Spirit is love:

36. Ibid., 50.

Now you are the body of Christ and individually members of it. And God has appointed in the church first apostles, second prophets, third teachers; then deeds of power, then gifts of healing, forms of assistance, forms of leadership, various kinds of tongues. Are all apostles? Are all prophets? Are all teachers? Do all work miracles? Do all possess gifts of healing? Do all speak in tongues? Do all interpret? But strive for the greater gifts. And I will show you a still more excellent way. (1 Cor. 12:27–31)

According to Alasdair Heron, Paul's thought "here is in line with the Old testament link between the Spirit of God and the human spirit," and "at its inmost core is formed by participation in a movement of communication, recognition and response issuing from the heart of God himself."[37] Yet for Paul the work of the Spirit is unambiguously christological, since the *ruach YHWH* is explicitly interpreted as the Spirit of Christ: "you are in the Spirit, since the Spirit of God dwells in you. Anyone who does not have the Spirit of Christ does not belong to him" (Rom. 8:9). Furthermore, it is by the Spirit of Christ that the believer is received into the community as body of Christ: "And because you are children, God has sent the Spirit of his Son into our hearts, crying, 'Abba! Father!'" (Gal. 4:6). Thus, it is best to understand Paul's teaching on *charismata* within the context of God's covenant with Israel, with love as the chief gift of the Spirit: "a still more excellent way" (1 Cor. 12:31). In other words, the Spirit of God produces among its many fruits a distinct way of life: "The Lord's dealing with his people in the Old Testament was not only a matter of revealing to them a way to live in his covenant . . . it was a road that led to rest and blessing."[38] In a passage that suggests some familiarity with Jesus' Sermon on the Mount (Matt 5:1–7:29), Paul delineates the "marks" of the true Christian: "Let love be genuine; hate what is evil, hold fast to what is good; love one another with mutual affection; outdo one another in showing honor. Do not lag in zeal, be ardent in spirit, serve the Lord. Rejoice in hope, be patient in suffering, persevere in prayer. Contribute to the needs of the saints; extend hospitality to strangers" (Rom. 12:9–13). Just as Jesus commanded the disciples to love their enemies, Paul instructs Christians to "Bless those who persecute you; bless and do not curse them," and "if it is possible, so far as it depends on you, live peaceably with all" (Rom. 12:14, 18). And just as Christ taught

---

37. Ibid.
38. Montague, *The Holy Spirit*, 163.

that "if anyone strike you on the right cheek, turn the other cheek also" (Matt. 5:39), Paul sums up the Christian ethos by saying, "Do not be overcome by evil, but overcome evil with good" (Rom. 12:21).

Paul, writing at the time of Emperor Nero's persecution of Christians in 64 CE, advised Christians to remain true to the way of Christ. History suggests that early Christian communities paid close attention and embodied Paul's vision of life in the Spirit, as evidenced by the second-century Letter to Diognetus describing the communities of persecuted Christians:

> They marry, like everyone else, and they beget children, but they do not cast out their offspring. They share their board with each other, but not their marriage bed. It is true that they "are in the flesh," but they do not live "according to the flesh." They busy themselves on earth, but their citizenship is in heaven. They obey the established laws, but in their own lives they go far beyond what the laws require. They love all men, and by all men are persecuted. They are unknown, and still they are condemned; they are put to death, and yet they are brought to life. They are poor, and yet they make many rich; they are completely destitute, and yet they enjoy complete abundance. They are dishonored, and in their very dishonor are glorified; they are defamed, and are vindicated. They are reviled, and yet they bless; when they are affronted, they still pay due respect. When they do good, they are punished as evildoers; undergoing punishment, they rejoice because they are brought to life. They are treated by the Jews as foreigners and enemies, and are hunted down by the Greeks; and all the time those who hate them find it impossible to justify their enmity.[39]

The theme of persecution, especially persecution endured in the name of Christ, is present throughout the New Testament, from Paul's sufferings during his missionary journey (Acts 16:16–24; 2 Cor. 11:16–33), to Jesus' apocalyptic warning about persecution from the synagogue and the state (Mark 13:9–13), to the prophetic visions of the martyred church in Revelation (Rev. 6:9–11). As Robin Darling Young argues, all early Christian literature was written with the intention of preparing Christians to endure persecution, suffering, and even martyrdom: "Those in training to become martyrs are shaped by the letters of people who have previously trained for and thought about this

---

39. "The So-called Letter to Diognetus," in *Early Christian Fathers*, ed. and trans. Cyril C. Richardson, 33–73 (New York: Collier Books, 1970), 217.

contest. In early Christianity this begins with Paul and continues in the Apocalypse."[40]

In the Apocalypse of John (Revelation) there is an equally strong link between Christ and Spirit, though not always employing the same language as the rest of the New Testament. Instead, the text bears many similarities to the prophetic texts of the Hebrew Bible, and its author identifies himself as a (Christian) prophet (Rev. 10:7), so it is safe to assume continuity with the Pauline theology of *charismata* that included prophecy among the gifts of the Spirit, which in turn demonstrates continuity with the Hebrew Bible and its emphasis on prophecy as one of the principal works of the *ruach YHWH*. Furthermore, as in the charismatic tradition that began with the judges and came to include the prophets, the "revelation of Jesus Christ" received by John (Rev. 1:1) is also marked by ecstatic frenzy and revelatory visions (Rev. 1:10; 4:2; 17:3; 21:10). The assurance of John's words is grounded in the source of revelation, the one true God: "These words are trustworthy and true, for the Lord, the God of the spirits of the prophets, has sent his angel to show his servants what must soon take place" (Rev. 22:6). So when John writes, "the mystery of God will be fulfilled, as he announced to his servants the prophets" (Rev. 10:7), he is affirming his place as one of Israel's prophets by referencing the prophet Amos: "Surely the Lord GOD does nothing, without revealing his secret to his servants the prophets" (Amos 3:7). As Richard Bauckham notes in his study of Revelation, John is clothing himself with the authority of YHWH's prophets in order to make the theological claim that Christ and YHWH are one, not only echoing the pneumatology of the whole of the New Testament, but also expressing it in its most mature form. Bauckham interprets the repeated assertion that Jesus Christ is the one "who is and who was and who is to come" (Rev. 1:4) as a profoundly theological statement defining the distinctly Christian doctrine of God. By affixing the title Lord (*Kyrios*) to Jesus the Christ, as in the Pauline literature, John "places Jesus Christ with God on the divine side of the distinction between the divine Giver of blessings and the creaturely recipient of blessings. It shows how naturally early Christians implicitly included Jesus in the divine, because he was the source of salvation that comes from God to humans, even if they had no way of conceptualizing in ontological terms this relation of Jesus

40. Robin Darling Young, *In Procession Before the World: Martyrdom as Public Liturgy in Early Christianity*, The Père Marquette Lecture in Theology 2001 (Milwaukee, WI: Marquette University Press, 2001), 9.

to God."[41] By having both YHWH and Christ speak in one voice, repeating the same formula by which their divine identity and unity is maintained, John makes a bold theological statement. First God speaks, "'I am the Alpha and the Omega', says the Lord God, who is and who was and who is to come, the Almighty," then Jesus Christ, "I am the Alpha and the Omega, the first and the last, the beginning and the end" (Rev. 1:8; 22:13). In effect, while the Hebrew prophets spoke about the Spirit of God, and Paul gave precedence to the Spirit of Christ, John conflates them into one and the same Spirit of life, reaffirming the universal scope of YHWH's covenant, as did the later prophets of the Hebrew Bible (Isa. 2:2–4), by proclaiming, "You must prophesy again about many peoples and nations and languages and kings" (Rev. 10:11).

5.1.3 Spirit in the Qur'an

Rū, the Arabic word translated as "spirit," shares the same root meaning, "wind" or breath," as ruach in Hebrew and pneuma in Greek while also carrying the theological connotation of "life force" or "supernatural being."[42] In the Qur'an the word appears twenty-one times, with the great majority of these instances employing the sense of "spirit" rather than the more literal "wind," analogous to the variety of meanings for ruach in the Hebrew Bible. Thomas O'Shaughnessy attributes this emphasis on "spirit" rather than "wind" within the Qur'an to the Hellenistic influence, especially from Gnostic Christian texts that preserved a dualism between the material and the spiritual: "the echo of certain notions, common in the centuries preceding the rise of Islam among the Judeo-Christian, heretical, and Gnostic sects which undoubtedly influenced the religious environment of Arabia in Mohammad's time."[43] Jürgen Moltmann, in his constructive pneumatological proposal, argues the same point and commends a critical retrieval of the Semitic understanding of ruach and rū as a natural force ("wind" or "breath") over against the more hellenized reading: "If we wish to understand the Old Testament word ruach, we must forget the word 'spirit', which

41. Richard Bauckham, *The Theology of the Book of Revelation* (Cambridge: Cambridge University Press, 1993), 23–24.
42. Michael Sells, "Spirit," in *Encyclopedia of the Qur'ān*, vol. 5 (Si-Z), ed. Jane Dammen McAuliffe (Leiden, NLD: Brill, 2006), 114–17.
43. Thomas O'Shaughnessy, S.J., *The Development of the Meaning of Spirit in the Koran* (Rome: Pontifical Oriental Institute, 1953), 19.

belongs to Western culture. The Greek word πνευμα, the Latin *spiritus*, and the Germanic *Geist*/ghost were always conceived as antithesis to matter and body. They mean something immaterial."[44]

Admittedly, there is no fully developed pneumatology within the Qur'an, perhaps attributable to the Islamic rejection of Christian Trinitarian thought as polytheistic: "They certainly disbelieve, those who say, 'Truly God is the third of three,' while there is no god save the one God. If they refrain not from what they say, a painful punishment will befall those among them who disbelieved" (Sura 5:73). Also, "Say, 'He, God, is One, God, the Eternally Sufficient unto Himself, He begets not; nor was He begotten. And none is like unto Him'" (Sura 112:1–4). Regardless, by the time the Hadith, an oral tradition of sayings and anecdotes by and about the Prophet, was compiled in the late eighth and early ninth centuries, there was a clear emphasis on radical monotheism (*Tawhid*) emphasizing the "oneness" of God and subsuming all other "spiritual" beings under God's absolute sovereignty. Consequently, orthodox Islamic doctrine teaches that references to the Holy Spirit (*Rūh al-Qudus*) in the Qur'an do not indicate a separate divine agent, but are veiled references to the work of the angel Gabriel, who is Allah's chief messenger, serving not only as the vehicle of divine revelation, but also as Allah's primary means of providing succor to prophets and other righteous people striving on the path of Allah. So, for example, when the Spirit visits Mary the Mother of Jesus, Islamic tradition identifies the Spirit and messenger of the Lord as Gabriel (Sura 19:16–36). Nevertheless, despite this later orthodoxy, the text of the Qur'an itself—at all stages of Muhammad's prophetic career—reveals a multiplicity of meanings and uses for the word *rū*. Michael Sells acknowledges that most "classical commentaries identify the holy spirit with Gabriel. Nowhere in the Qur'ān is such an identification made explicit and the name Gabriel appears in only two verses in the Qur'ān."[45] He then identifies three major works of the Spirit in the Qur'an: (1) the work of Creation, (2) the sending of prophetic revelation, and (3) the work of divine judgment and resurrection on the day of reckoning (*yawm al-dīn*).[46]

Not only conceptually, but also scripturally and culturally, the Qur'an affirms the Jewish and Christian Scriptures that preceded it,

44. Moltmann, *The Spirit of Life*, 40.
45. Sells, "Spirit," in *Encyclopedia of the Qur'ān*, vol. 5, 115.
46. Ibid., 114.

not least by employing the term "the Holy Spirit" (*Rūh al-Qudus*) in describing God's act of revelation: "And indeed We gave unto Moses the Book and caused a succession of messengers to follow him. And We gave Jesus son of Mary clear proofs, and strengthened him with the Holy Spirit" (Sura 2:87). Furthermore, as in the Tanakh and New Testament, the Qur'an understands prophetic revelation as the chief work of the Spirit: "Among them are those to whom God spoke, and some He raised up in ranks. And We gave Jesus son of Mary clear proofs and strengthened him with the Holy Spirit" (Sura 2:253). Also: "Say, 'The Holy Spirit has brought it down from thy Lord in truth, to make firm those who believe, and as guidance and glad tidings for those who submit'" (Sura 16:102). Thus, the pattern found in the Qur'an for conceptualizing and describing the work of the Spirit is similar to the *ruach YHWH* in the Hebrew Bible insofar as the Spirit is the force from God that animates life by breathing into creatures, and all prophecy takes place through the Spirit by the command of God. Interestingly, there are only a handful of times when Spirit is used as "to breathe" or "to blow" in the Qur'an: "the bringing to life of Adam; the conception of Jesus; Jesus' bringing the material forms of birds to life; and (in twelve different places) the day on which the trumpet will be blown, that is, the day of reckoning and resurrection."[47]

While Islamic orthodoxy rejected the notion of the Spirit as a distinct divine agency, O'Shaughnessy traces a development in the Qur'an from an earlier conception of the Spirit as "a personal being set above the angels" to what later becomes "an impersonal thing, a breath of life, originating with Allah and animating the human body."[48] Throughout these conceptual developments, however, the Qur'an consistently affirms the Spirit's *unique mediatory role*, as not only the source of revealed prophecy, but as the means by which this revelation is trusted as coming from God, and confirmed as true in the life of the believer: "Then we breathed therein of Our Spirit, and she confirmed the Words of her Lord and His Books; and she was among the devoutly obedient" (Sura 66:12). Furthermore, the Qur'anic concept of justice is inseparable from the revelatory work of the Spirit insofar as conversion and acceptance onto the path of Allah brings a renewal of the believer onto the ways of divine righteousness: "He it is Who sent among the unlettered a Messenger from among themselves, reciting unto them His signs, purifying

---

47. Ibid., 117.
48. O'Shaughnessy, *The Development of the Meaning of Spirit in the Koran*, 25.

them, and teaching them the Book and Wisdom, though before they were in manifest error" (Sura 62:2). The Qur'an also says, "O People of the Book! Our Messenger has come onto you, making clear to you much of what you once hid of the Book, and pardoning much. There has come unto you, from God, a light and a clear Book, whereby God guides whosoever seeks His Contentment unto the ways of peace, and brings them out of darkness into light, by His leave, and guides them onto a straight path" (Sura 5:15–16). This principle is reinforced by the Qur'anic instruction to treat others as you would treat your closest kin: "O you who believe! Be steadfast for God, bearing witness to justice, and let not hatred for a people lead you to be unjust. Be just; that is nearer to reverence. And reverence God. Surely God is Aware of whatsoever you do" (Sura 5:8). In other words, the Qur'an emphasizes the role of justice and good deeds in the worship of God, and this work of establishing justice is linked to the work of the Spirit as in the Hebrew Bible:

> It is made quite clear by the Qur'an that apostles are selected from amongst the people themselves and they impart wisdom to them and guide them to fight against oppression and exploitation. The prophet Moses is projected by the Qur'an as a liberator of the Israelis who were being oppressed by Pharaoh. The Israelis were the oppressed and weak *mustad'ifun* on earth. Moses was the man of the people who fought for their liberation from the oppressive establishment.[49]

These brief glances at the conceptual development of the work of the Spirit in the Tanakh, the New Testament, and the Qur'an reinforces the book's underlying thesis that God desires that all humankind live peaceably together guided by God's compassionate justice. By exploring scriptural views of the work of the Spirit in each of the three Abrahamic religions *before* these conceptions calcified into exclusivist doctrines, it is argued that the work of the Spirit serves as a theological locus for pluralistic dialogue and cooperation because the sacred Scriptures of all three faiths share an ethical norm grounded in the themes of liberation, justice, and compassion. Furthermore, despite great variances in how the work of the Spirit is conceptualized and described, all three faiths share a conception of Spirit as the *historical* manifestation of God in the world *through* acts of liberation that preserve human dignity.

---

49. Asghar Ali Engineer, "On Developing Liberation Theology in Islam," in *Voices from the Margin: Interpreting the Bible in the Third World,* new ed., ed. R. S. Sugirtharajah (Maryknoll, NY: Orbis Books, 1995), 400.

5.2 LIBERATION AS THE HISTORICAL
EXPERIENCE OF THE SPIRIT

This book began with the question, "Is Babel a problem to be solved?" In other words, what happens to doctrinal language when we accept theological diversity as normative? Accordingly, it has been argued that *all* theological claims remain open-ended and provisional since the self-revealing God remains mystery *even* in the act of revelation (*Deus absconditus*), a foundational reality that hopefully engenders religious tolerance and encourages a more comparative methodology. However, if all dogmatic statements are relativized, how can theology make meaningful claims about God? Christine Helmer argues that doctrine has lost its referential point of contact with the divine, its "living connection to the reality of God."[50] In response, this book maintains that dogmatic certainty is not an epistemological possibility and that seeking such certainty only steers us toward theological totalitarianism. Rather, theological knowledge arises from the interpersonal encounter with the divine and is more a matter of personal and communal spiritual formation than of detached scientific observation. Sadly, the dominant culture has embraced an unreflective scientism that elevates empirical methods above all other intellectual discourses, thus excluding approaches that might provide an alternative rational accounting of divine action in the world. The language of faith, without limiting itself to an empirical methodology, nevertheless strives to make intelligible "God's objective and concrete presence to the human knower."[51] Focusing on the work of the Spirit within all three Abrahamic religions reveals how God can be known in human history through divinely inspired acts of justice, compassion, and liberation.

In *The Spirit of Life* (1992), Jürgen Moltmann defends the historical experience of God as "an experience of God which happens to people in the medium of history through historical events, and which is perceived in terms of time."[52] Moltmann argues that the Hebrew Bible always links Israel's experiences of God to concrete historical persons and events, as evidenced by the formulaic phrase, "I am the God of your father, the God of Abraham, the God of Isaac, and the God of Jacob" (Exod. 3:6), which immediately calls to mind "the various experiences

---

50. Helmer, *Theology and the End of Doctrine*, 61.
51. Marga, *Karl Barth's Dialogue with Catholicism*, 59.
52. Moltmann, *The Spirit of Life*, 39.

of God associated with their names."[53] Accordingly, the Scriptures can and ought to be read as a historical narrative because the encounter with God is always an event in human history, whether one refers to the original revelatory event or the contemporary encounter mediated by the reading of sacred Scripture: "Through historical remembrance, the God of the Exodus, the covenant and the promised land becomes present to such a degree that as the Creator of the world and the Lord of human liberty he determines the present."[54] As Mark Taylor frames the contemporary theological situation, we are challenged by a postmodern "trilemma" that demands theologians simultaneously acknowledge tradition, celebrate plurality, and resist domination.[55] The very language of dogmatics is grounded in tradition: though this work aims at a comparative theology, it cannot help but speak from within the particularity of the Christian tradition and only from that concrete historical location *then* seek to engage the reality of pluralism. However, Taylor's third criterion, resisting domination, is as historically concrete as any tradition, yet contemporary theologies do not always find an adequate vocabulary for speaking about human struggles for liberation *as* the historical experience of God. To that end, Taylor commends certain strategies for tracking the work of the Spirit in the world today:

> The "spirit" at issue is a notion that is variously invoked in the midst of cultural practices like popular artistic expression (not only Springsteen and Speech, but also Madonna, Public Enemy and many others), political movements, or debates over urban policy— all expressions and developments that are rarely termed "spiritual" or "religious" . . . In cultural and political domains, in social action and intellectual discourse, therefore, some notion like "spirit" often persists. To observe this entails no claim that the users' concerns are only or primarily "spiritual." Nor do I intend any kind of defense of the spiritual in cultural domains or for the benefit of anyone else. I begin simply by noting the persistence of the reference to spirit in diverse cultural spheres.[56]

Without giving preference to a theological understanding of "spirit," Taylor surveys instances of "spirit" language in popular cultural

---

53. Ibid.
54. Ibid.
55. Mark Kline Taylor, *Remembering Esperanza: A Cultural-Political Theology for North American Praxis* (Maryknoll, NY: Orbis Books, 1990), 23–45.
56. Mark Lewis Taylor, "Tracking Spirit: Theology as Cultural Critique in America," in *Changing Conversations: Religious Reflection and Cultural Analysis*, ed. Dwight N. Hopkins and Sheila Greeve Davaney (New York: Routledge, 1996), 124.

expression and practice in order to identify "three dynamics of cultural practices which I propose as signaling a spiritual dimension" under the rubric of liminality, integrative vision, and emancipatory desire.[57] These three distinct yet interrelated moves describe the work of the Spirit and provide a theological framework for "tracking spirit" in culture *without* adhering to any one confessional or ideological tradition, which in turn facilitates a certain kind of "body politic" that embodies the emancipatory practices of spirit in the public arena. A contemporary example of the kind of body politic Taylor envisions as giving flesh to the work of the Spirit in culture is the Black Lives Matter movement that came to national prominence in the aftermath of the murder of African American youth Michael Brown by a white police officer in Ferguson, Missouri, on August 9, 2014.

Though not explicitly theological—and definitely not linked to any single confessional tradition—the Black Lives Matter (BLM) movement has often invoked Martin Luther King Jr. to differentiate, situate, and defend itself from external criticism. Specifically, the movement's founders have responded to criticisms that their involvement in the rioting in Ferguson betrayed the nonviolent legacy of Dr. King, arguing instead that they are "recovering the radicalism of King's methods and message for the twenty-first century"[58] by retrieving and reclaiming King's "Letter from a Birmingham City Jail" (1963) and his infamous address at Riverside Church in New York City, "A Time to Break Silence" (1967), in order to drive home the urgency of the current situation in which black lives continue to be brutalized and murdered by agents of the state. Therefore, BLM stands on the same principled call to "direct action" that brought Dr. King to Birmingham in 1963, because there "comes a time when the cup of endurance runs over, and men are no longer willing to be plunged into an abyss of injustice where they experience the blackness of corroding despair."[59] With Dr. King, they have learned from "painful experience that freedom is never voluntarily given by the oppressor; it must be demanded by the oppressed";[60] like Dr. King, they do not shy away from controversy by affirming their unapologetic "blackness" in a white supremacist culture in much

57. Ibid., 127.

58. Jermaine M. McDonald, "Ferguson and Baltimore according to Dr. King: How Competing Interpretations of King's Legacy Frame the Public Discourse on Black Lives Matter," *Journal of the Society of Christian Ethics* 36, no. 2 (Fall/Winter 2016): 150–51.

59. Martin Luther King Jr., "Letter from a Birmingham City Jail," in *A Testament of Hope: The Essential Writings of Martin Luther King, Jr.*, ed. James Melvin Washington (San Francisco: HarperSanFrancisco, 1991), 293.

60. Ibid., 292.

the same way Dr. King refused to back down when he was criticized for using his fame to address issues beyond civil rights in order to condemn the U.S. war in Vietnam: "A nation that continues year after year to spend more money on military defense than on programs of social uplift is approaching spiritual death."[61]

Founded in 2013 by three radical Black organizers—Alicia Garza, Patrisse Cullors, and Opal Tometi—in response to the acquittal of George Zimmerman, a neighborhood watch coordinator for a gated community in Sanford, Florida, who had murdered African American teenager Trayvon Martin (a guest at a town home in the gated community) with a 9mm semi-automatic pistol. According to the movement's mission statement, BLM is "an ideological and political intervention in a world where Black lives are systematically and intentionally targeted for demise," committed to affirming "the lives of Black queer and trans folks, disabled folks, undocumented folks, folks with records, women, and all Black lives along the gender spectrum. Our network centers those who have been marginalized within Black liberation movements."[62] When Michael Brown was murdered in 2014, BLM worked with local organizers in Ferguson, Missouri, to coordinate a series of nonviolent protests (that led to civil unrest) designed to draw international attention to the systemic pattern of brutalization of African Americans by law enforcement. While the movement has since become an international network with over thirty local chapters, their involvement in Ferguson highlights the founders' desires to work as a decentralized network without a formal hierarchy. It is worth noting that despite the growth of the movement and subsequent incidents of police fatal violence targeting African Americans in places like Baltimore and Minneapolis-St. Paul, the BLM website still credits local organizers and activists in Missouri for their ongoing frontline work: "the folks in St. Louis and Ferguson who put their bodies on the line day in and day out, and who continue to show up for Black lives."[63] As theological ethicist Jermaine M. McDonald has noted, much of the backlash from within the African American civil rights establishment directed at Black Lives Matter stems from the fact that BLM is "primarily composed of younger activists, it conflicts with elders in the black community over tactics and strategies, and it is not committed to any

61. Martin Luther King Jr., "A Time to Break Silence," in *A Testament of Hope: The Essential Writings of Martin Luther King, Jr.*, ed. James Melvin Washington (San Francisco: HarperSanFrancisco, 1991), 241.
62. See https://blacklivesmatter.com/about/ and https://blacklivesmatter.com/about/herstory/, for an introduction to and defense of the movement (accessed on October 13, 2017).
63. Ibid.

particular religious worldview."[64] Employing Mark Taylor's paradigm for "tracking spirit" in culture, I contend that these "confession-less" yet profoundly spiritual movements of liberation have become the new *loci theologici* ("places of theology") for understanding and encountering the work of the Spirit in history, and these new spiritual-but-not-religious social movements are causing the church to rethink its understanding of *ecclesia* ("assembly") and its views on sacramentality.

Taylor uses liminality in much the same way this book employs the concept of the hiddenness of God, or David Tracy discusses hermeneutical ambiguity in the religious classic: "a realm of ultimate incomprehensibility and real, fascinating and frightening mystery. When religious persons speak the language of revelation, they mean that something has happened to them that they cannot count as their own achievement."[65] A term borrowed from anthropology, liminality (from the Latin *limen* meaning "a threshold"), refers to our inadequacy to define an experience, not because it is any less real, but because the very nature of the experience defies conceptual boundaries since it inhabits multiple conceptual spaces simultaneously: "Liminal experiences are not experiences outside temporal and spatial matrices, but betwixt-and-between typical ways of organizing both. They exist, in other terms, in the interstices or within some overlapping of these domains, within some dense, textured interaction of them."[66] Yet this sense of being "at the limit," what Karl Jaspers called "boundary situations,"[67] need not deter the theologian from naming what is in essence unnameable. Rather, it ought to serve as a hermeneutical principle that acknowledges and embraces the *provisional* nature of dogmatic claims because we are dealing with "limit questions,"[68] which for Tracy is liberating insofar as it allows us to live more comfortably within ambiguity while still affirming the objective reality of liminal experiences "through some personal sense of the uncanny"[69] that we recognize originate in "a power not one's own."[70]

While the Spirit inhabits, and is very often encountered, in these interstitial spaces that frustrate the human tendency to limit and

64. McDonald, "Ferguson and Baltimore according to Dr. King," 149.
65. Tracy, *The Analogical Imagination*, 173.
66. Taylor, "Tracking Spirit," 127.
67. See Kurt Salamun, "Karl Jaspers on Human Self-Realization: Exintenz in Boundary Situations and Communication," in *Karl Jaspers's Philosophy: Expositions and Interpretations*, ed. Kurt Salamun and Gregory J. Walters (Amherst, NY: Humanity Books, 2008), 243–62.
68. See Stephen Toulmin, *An Examination of the Place of Reason in Ethics* (Cambridge: Cambridge University Press, 1950)), 204–11.
69. Tracy, *The Analogical Imagination*, 371.
70. Ibid.

define, Mark Taylor also identifies an equally compelling dimension of encountering the Spirit in human history and culture: "*a penchant for the integrative,* a drive that seeks some holistic vision."[71] Taylor recognizes a simple point elaborated in the theologies of Lindbeck and Frei, that within established religions "there is reliance on a narrative to provide this, to tell a story from beginning to end."[72] Recognizing that "spirit" is not always connected to specific beliefs or convictions, Taylor nevertheless affirms that particular practices and expressions delineate a culture's unique "spiritual" dimension as a way of providing an integrative vision without necessarily becoming a "totalizing" metanarrative. In some popular movements ("body politic") there is only the "barest suggestion of such an integrating vision," which Taylor illustrates by referencing the lyrics of Speech, the main songwriter for the 1990s hip-hop group Arrested Development, whose interweaving of personal trauma with the history of African American suffering and repression Taylor describes as "a reach for breadth, a desire for a holistic standpoint—laboring against all odds to put some things together, to make a little bit of sense of things."[73] This integrative drive, however indeterminate, is the source of the community's "united front," which, in the kind of "body politic" Taylor is envisioning, leads to a shared revolutionary practice that is a manifestation of Spirit when the liminal experience gives way to a *liberative* holistic vision: "The liminal and the integrative thus abide, but the greatest is the emancipatory concern, pulsing as the power in both."[74]

Accordingly, a movement like Black Lives Matter eschews traditional religion and focuses primarily on advocating for those who have been marginalized within established black liberation movements yet presents itself as an emancipatory spirituality for all black lives. Recognizing that their revolutionary goals necessitate tactics that might not meet with the approval of the older, ecclesiocentric civil rights movement, the founders of BLM have struggled to differentiate their movement and its goals while nonetheless locating themselves within the rich history of African American struggles for liberation. In an interview for *Teen Vogue* magazine, Patrisse Cullors, one of the three founders of Black Lives Matter, expressed the resistance she and her two comrades experienced: "The first challenge was making sure that people knew who *actually* were the

---

71. Taylor, "Tracking Spirit," 129 (emphasis in the original).
72. Ibid.
73. Ibid., 130.
74. Ibid., 133.

creators of Black Lives Matter—pushing back against our own erasure. I
have never felt the grips of patriarchy and its need to erase black women
and our labor . . . so strongly until the creation of Black Lives Matter."[75]
However, the greatest resistance came from the white mainstream, which
has labeled Black Lives Matter a terrorist group.[76] Thus, even supposed
white allies come under the critical lens of BLM and its consistent message that racism is alive and well in post-Obama America: "We forced
folks to look at the Democratic Party as a party that has historically said
it's on the side of black people but instead it hasn't been, and the policies
have shown that."[77] George Wayne Smith, the tenth Anglican Bishop
of Missouri, focuses the vague spiritual urge underlying the activism of
groups like BLM within an explicitly theological framework with the
suggestion that the site of Michael Brown's murder on Canfield Avenue
in Ferguson has become a shrine:

> People go to that place and weep, or they rage, or they sing, or they
> stand in slack-jawed silence. The place allows people to express deep
> emotion, and it lets them hope. Some even pray. The pavement is
> still visibly marked by Michael Brown's blood. Protestors sometimes
> paraphrase Genesis 4 in saying that his blood cries out for justice.
> But the place is also saturated by the anger, the hopes, and the
> prayers of thousands. It is an important place. Dare I call it holy?[78]

This spiritual urging that gives voice to an entire people's history
of suffering and dehumanization occupies the liminal space where the
love of God coexists with innocent human suffering but in place of
theodicy—a rational explanation for the existence of evil—the Spirit
offers *mystery*, turning the tragedy of Michael Brown into a sacramental encounter with God in the midst of human history. The need
to track the work of the Spirit in the popular culture does not mean
that systematic theologies or the creedal formulations of the church
are wrong so much "as they are incomplete; that is, they may satisfy

---

75. Lincoln Anthony Blades, "Patrisse Cullors of Black Lives Matter Discusses the Movement," in *Teen Vogue* (August 24, 2017), https://www.teenvogue.com/story/patrisse-cullors-of-black-lives-matter-discusses-the-movement.

76. Currently there is a popular movement petitioning the White House to declare BLM a terrorist group on par with ISIS and Al-Qaeda; the White House responded saying, "The White House plays no role in designating domestic terror organizations," nor does the U.S. government "generate a list of domestic terror organizations." See Erroll Barnett, "White House responds to petition to label Black Lives Matter a 'terror' group," CBS News (July 17, 2016), https://www.cbsnews.com/news/white-house-responds-to-petition-to-label-black-lives-matter-a-terror-group/.

77. Ibid.

78. George Wayne Smith, "Blood Cries Out from the Ground: Reflections on Ferguson," *Anglican Theological Review* 97, no 2 (Spring 2015): 261.

a certain kind of integrative reach of spirit, but not so much spirit's liminal and liberating desires."[79] In the Hebrew Bible, the New Testament, and the Qur'an the work of the Spirit always gives voice to this unarticulated human desire for liberation, and almost exclusively by means of the prophetic, which in all three Abrahamic traditions is inextricably entwined with God's work for justice, compassion, and liberation. The argument articulated in these pages is simple: faith ought not be reduced to human emancipation, but faith without the liberating works of the Spirit has lost all "living connection to the reality of God."[80] Marc Ellis, Jewish liberation theologian, confronts the challenge of speaking about God in the shadow of the Holocaust and other more recent acts of genocide: "For who can easily speak of God in a century of mass death, where millions have been condemned to the precincts of the dead and the living dead?"[81] It is difficult to speak of God in any age given God's divine hiddenness, but near impossible in the present age where not only is the dominant culture predisposed to reject discourses about transcendence and divine agency, but also because of the radically pluralist contemporary situation characterized by a plethora of competing religious perspectives. In this context, the work of the Spirit embodied by the prophetic tradition of protest and lamentation, serves as "a way of anchoring our personal and communal life in a structure that lends meaning and support. In a time of crisis our unfinishedness takes on another dimension of hope that a future beyond crisis is open. Speech about God may in the final analysis be speech about hope, *that history is open, that humanity is possible, that community rather than empire has the last word.*"[82]

5.3 THE SACRAMENT OF HISTORY

A focus on the work of the Spirit in human history—especially through works of compassion and liberation—indicates a possible strategy for moving past the impasse between the *theologies of the Word* that take a fideistic stance on Scripture as God's self-revelation without subjecting their dogmatic claims to external criticism, and the *theologies of culture* that contend God can only be known through the medium of culture

---

79. Taylor, "Tracking Spirit," 142.
80. Helmer, *Theology and the End of Doctrine*, 61.
81. Marc H. Ellis, *Revolutionary Forgiveness: Essays on Judaism, Christianity, and the Future of Religious Life* (Waco, TX: Baylor University Press, 2000), 143.
82. Ibid., 143–44 (emphasis in the original).

but lack criteria for differentiating revelation from the cultural status quo. The argument has been made that God is encountered in history *in* works of justice, compassion, and liberation, even when the locus of this spiritual work is a body politic not historically associated with any religion whose members describe their emancipatory work without appealing to explicitly theological language. Furthermore, it has been argued that this position is warranted after a critical reading of the foundational sacred Scriptures of the three Abrahamic religions, since there exists a theological affirmation *within* all three faiths that *wherever* the work of establishing justice, extending compassion, and facilitating human liberation occurs, *there* is the true Spirit of God. In effect, these emancipatory movements in history share in this revelatory sacramental dimension because they embody the divine will for all humankind regardless of confessional or creedal origin. In other words, focusing on the work of the Spirit opens the door to the notion of history as sacrament, not only providing a phenomenological vocabulary for describing divine agency in human history but also affirming the work of the Spirit in the religious and cultural "other."

The immediate objection raised to the notion of emancipatory movements interpreted as *sacramental* encounters with the self-revealing God is the use of the term sacrament itself. In Western Christianity the focus on particular, community-defining sacraments as "authorized" means of grace—i.e., as officially recognized media of divine self-communication—has actually worked to undermine tolerance, pluralism, and cooperation. No better example exists than the five-hundred-year schism between Roman Catholic and Protestant Christianity over the number and efficacy of the sacraments. Specifically, disagreements over the sacrament of Communion, or the Eucharist (from the Greek *eukharistia* meaning "thanksgiving"), which for Roman Catholicism is the focal point of the mass while in some Protestant traditions is only celebrated infrequently, have perpetuated and escalated confessional strife. Admittedly, there has been an increased rapprochement between Protestant and Roman Catholic governing bodies since the Second Vatican Council (1962–65), as evidenced by the ecumenical statement from the Commission on Faith and Order of the World Council of Churches in 1982, *Baptism, Eucharist, and Ministry* (BEM),[83] and the more recent *Joint Declaration on the Doctrine*

---

83. See *Baptism, Eucharist, and Ministry* (Geneva: World Council of Churches, 1982). Also see Max Thurian, ed., *Churches Respond to BEM* (Geneva: World Council of Churches, 1986); and *Baptism, Eucharist, and Ministry 1982–1990* (Geneva: World Council of Churches, 1990).

of Justification (1999) issued by the Lutheran World Federation and the Roman Catholic Church.[84] Still, these efforts at ecumenical reconciliation are far from achieving "full ecclesiastical communion," given the Vatican statement *Dominus Iesus* (2000) that described Protestant communions as "not Churches in the proper sense."[85] Nevertheless, Latin American liberation theologian Gustavo Gutiérrez, in his seminal *A Theology of Liberation* (1973), envisions the church as a universal sacrament of salvation in human history, a point also found in the work of his Protestant counterpart, Rubém Alves, a Brazilian Presbyterian theologian who was actually the first to coin the term "liberation theology."[86]

Gutiérrez begins from the assumption that the church's position in the world today is being challenged and its status eroded to the point that a "radical revision of what the Church has been and what it now is has become necessary," and while the Second Vatican Council marks a promising move in a more inclusive direction, the church's *aggiornamento* with the forces of secularization "has not suppressed the challenges that they bring with them. Rather it has strengthened and deepened them."[87] According to Gutiérrez, the position that the church is the *only* visible community manifesting the work of the Holy Spirit in the world is no longer tenable: "we must avoid reducing the salvific work to the action of the Church."[88] Instead, Gutiérrez challenges the church to "uncenter" itself by ceasing to consider "itself the exclusive place of salvation and orient itself towards a new and radical service of people," which "presupposes a new awareness that the action of Christ and his Spirit is the true hinge of the plane of salvation."[89] The new ecclesiological understanding coming out of Vatican II was to view the church as sacrament (*Lumen Gentium*, nos. 1, 9, 48, 59; *Gaudium et spes*, no. 45; *Sacrosanctum concilium*, nos. 5, 26; and *Ad gentes*, no. 9); this new "communion ecclesiology" drew upon the biblical image of

84. "Joint Declaration on the Doctrine of Justification" by the Lutheran World Federation and the Catholic Church (1999), http://www.vatican.va/roman_curia/pontifical_councils/chrstuni/documents/rc_pc_chrstuni _doc_31101999_cath-luth-joint-declaration_en.html.

85. Congregation for the Doctrine of the faith, "Declaration *Dominus Iesus* on the Unicity and Salvific Universality of Jesus Christ and the Church," 4.17 (August 6, 2000), http://www.vatican.va/roman_curia /congregations/cfaith/documents/rc_con_cfaith_doc_20000806_dominus-iesus_en.html.

86. See Enrique Dussell, *A History of the Church in Latin America: Colonialism to Liberation (1492–1979)*, trans. Alan Neely (Grand Rapids, MI: Wm. B. Eerdmans Publishing Co., 1981), 261. Dussell points out that Alves published *Religión ¿opio o instrumento de liberación?* (Montevideo: Tierra Nueva, 1968) a year earlier than Gutiérrez's landmark essay, *Hacia una teología de la liberación* (Montevideo: Servicio de Documentación, JECI, 1969).

87. Gutiérrez, *A Theology of Liberation*, 141.

88. Ibid., 143.

89. Ibid., 143–44.

the church as the body of Christ (1 Cor. 12; Rom. 12:4–8; Eph. 2:11–3:6) in order to affirm our participation in the life of Christ via mystical union with Christ. A central feature of post-Vatican II communion ecclesiology is the appeal to Paul's discussion of the community as the mystical body of Christ in the context of the Lord's Supper (1 Cor. 10:16–22; 11:17–34), which leads Catholic theologian Susan K. Wood to conclude, "Where the Eucharist is, there is church."[90]

Despite Wood's strong statement, however, communion ecclesiology affirms the sacramental presence of Christ without reducing the church to the Eucharist by building upon a Trinitarian understanding of God as a divine community (*perichoresis*), thus grounding the very possibility of human communion with Christ and with one another as inseparable from the "elements of grace and sacrament that ultimately identify ecclesial communities in terms of their relationship to Christ."[91] Though this emphasis on the real presence in the Eucharist can create doctrinal barriers with those churches unable to affirm the same sacramental practice, Catholic theologians still view communion ecclesiology as a potential avenue for ecumenical reconciliation by emphasizing the work of the Spirit as mediating this central relationship to Christ. Latin American liberation theology presents a model of communion ecclesiology that holds much promise for articulating a genuinely ecumenical understanding of *ecclesia* by challenging the Roman Catholic Church to look beyond its current liturgical focus in order to affirm the sacramental dimension of the work of human liberation—a universal sacrament that extends Christ's redemptive work to all humankind by means of the Spirit.

Returning to the scriptural roots of the concept of *sacramentum*, the Latin translation of the Greek word *misterion*, Gutiérrez cites the apostle Paul—whose understanding of mystery means "*the fulfillment and the manifestation of the salvific plan*"[92]—who says, "the mystery that has been hidden throughout the ages and generations but has now been revealed to his saints" (Col 1:26, NRSV). Ultimately, this mystery is God's call, by the Spirit, to all humanity to live in communion with God and with one another: "Human beings are called together, as a community and not as separate individuals, to participate in the life of the Trinitarian community, to enter into the circuit of love that unites

90. Susan K. Wood, "Communion Ecclesiology: Source of Hope, Source of Controversy," *Pro Ecclesia: A Journal of Catholic and Evangelical Theology* 2, no. 4 (Fall 1993): 425.
91. Ibid.
92. Gutiérrez, *A Theology of Liberation*, 146 (emphasis in the original).

the persons of the Trinity."[93] Vatican II called the church the "visible sacrament of this saving unity"[94] whose historical manifestation is a visible sign of "the unity of all humankind."[95] Furthermore, *Lumen gentium* affirms that the church as constituted by the Spirit is "the universal sacrament of salvation,"[96] which leads Gutiérrez to conclude:

> . . . outside the action of the Spirit which leads the universe and history towards its fullness in Christ, the Church is nothing. Even more, the Church does not authentically attain consciousness of itself except in the perception of this total presence of Christ and his Spirit in humanity. The mediation of the consciousness of the "other"—of the world in which this presence occurs—is the indispensable precondition of its own consciousness as community-sign. Any attempt to avoid this mediation can only lead the Church to a false perception of itself—to an ecclesiocentric consciousness.[97]

In other words, while the Constantinian church has focused on expanding its institutional power and cultural influence as the most expedient means to carry out its mission, in doing so it has forgotten the underlying spiritual reality that called and named the church "church" in the first place. In contrast, the Holy Spirit chooses to live and inhabit the most humble of places:

> God loves the whole world. But God clearly shows a partiality to those who are suffering. Jesus declares himself present in the prisoner, but is silent about the imprisoners. He says he suffers with the hungry, but has no joy with those who are overstuffed with food. It appears that things are hard for the rich and powerful from the perspective of the Kingdom of God. What do you think about this?[98]

Accordingly, liberation theology challenges the church, as a "sign of the liberation of humankind," to alter its concrete existence such that it becomes "a place of liberation."[99]

In spite of the universal scope of Christ's lordship, unity remains one of the desired characteristics of the new spiritual community described

---

93. Ibid.

94. "Dogmatic Constitution on the Church: *Lumen gentium*," Solemnly Promulgated By His Holiness Pope Paul VI (November 21, 1964), no. 9, http://www.vatican.va/archive/hist_councils/ii_vatican_council/documents /vat-ii_const_19641121_lumen-gentium_en.html (accessed October 16, 2017).

95. Ibid., No. 1.

96. Ibid., No. 48.

97. Gutiérrez, *A Theology of Liberation*, 147.

98. Rubem Alves, *I Believe in the Resurrection of the Body* (Philadelphia: Fortress Press, 1986), 56–57.

99. Gutiérrez, *A Theology of Liberation*, 147.

by Paul. In Corinth he found a community divided over the Eucharistic meal, and Paul's words to that community provide a strong challenge to those traditions that do not affirm a real sacramental presence in the celebration of the Lord's Supper, and to all who persist in accepting doctrinal divisions without working toward a historical unity: "The cup of blessing that we bless, is it not a sharing in the blood of Christ? The bread that we break, is it not a sharing in the body of Christ? Because there is one bread, we who are many are one body, for we all partake of the one bread" (1 Cor. 10:16–17). Paul distinguishes between a shared common meal and the Eucharistic fellowship by arguing that the Lord's Supper embodies a unity of spirit characterized by the sharing of common resources for the well-being of all. This dying of self-interest and living for others—"Do not seek your own advantage, but that of the other" (1 Cor. 10:24)—is essential for a genuine celebration of the sacramental meal in which the many become one in Spirit with the risen Christ. Furthermore, Paul warns, "Whoever, therefore, eats the bread or drinks the cup of the Lord in an unworthy manner will be answerable for the body and blood of the Lord. Examine yourselves, and only then eat of the bread and drink of the cup" (1 Cor. 11:27–28). Therefore, this fellowship initiated and preserved by the work of the Spirit cannot take place without "a real commitment against exploitation and alienation," for in a society without solidarity and justice, "the Eucharistic celebration is an empty action."[100] Rubém Alves defines a sacrament as a "longing remembrance" born from the love of things now absent:

> When things awaken longing remembrance and cause the memory of love and the desire for return to grow in the heart, we say that they are *sacraments*. This is a sacrament: visible signs of an absence, symbols which make us think about return. Like what happened with Jesus who, just before his departure, carried out a memorial of longing remembrance and of awaiting. He gathered his friends, followers, broke the bread and gave it to them to eat, took the wine and drank it with them saying that after that would come separation and longing remembrance.[101]

This sacramental fellowship is possible because it is a gift of the Spirit—a divine grace given to center our lives on hope and life instead of fear and death—and as people living in the Spirit we strive to live in

100. Ibid., 150.
101. Alves, *I Believe in the Resurrection of the Body*, 13.

grace: "Theologians gave the name of grace to this uncontrollable and unpredictable wind [*pneuma*] in which our body-kites fly, playfully. Mysterious wind, beyond what we can, when we can not, despite our not being able, when our arms fall, impotent. And he comes, making the world spin and live, Spirit of God."[102] For Alves, our rigid insistence on right-doctrine runs counter to the work of the Spirit: "Life is lost when we no longer float at the mercy of God's goodness."[103] Yet, despite knowing that we live in grace and ought to trust the guidance of the Spirit, we still need concrete reminders of this grace: "But, in my hunger, I need visible signs of your invisible grace. Serve me your sacraments, the first fruits of this Kingdom."[104]

Gustavo Gutiérrez speaks as a Catholic priest and theologian, appealing to the dogmatic statements proceeding from the Second Vatican Council in order to make the claim that the possibility of universal salvation is mediated by the sacrament of Communion, properly understood, and "thus the efficacious revelation of the call to communion with God and to the unity of all humankind."[105] However, with the understanding that God is the God of all people, all nations, and all religions; so while the Roman Catholic Church—much like Israel—has a distinct dogmatic relationship with God, there is no basis within the scriptural foundations of this covenantal relationship to exclude the possibility that God's relationship to other peoples can take different dogmatic paths. In other words, if God is truly God, then religious pluralism is not a challenge or affront to God but simply revelatory of the myriad ways God has chosen to reveal God's self to all people. Then how are dogmatic claims to be tested and evaluated? How can dogmatic statements speak to the reality undergirding our subjective claims—"to the externality of the linguistic referent"?[106]

This book has argued, through an appeal to Søren Kierkegaard's epistemological critique of modernism in which revelation is defended as a historical possibility by means of the existential appropriation of faith mediated by the interpersonal encounter with God in history (which in turn influenced Barth's neo-orthodoxy and Lindbeck's postliberalism), that God *is* knowable: "God is an irremovable subject that can never be confused with an object," so God's "revelation consists of the fact

102. Ibid., 61.
103. Ibid.
104. Ibid., 78.
105. Gutiérrez, *A Theology of Liberation*, 146.
106. Helmer, *Theology and the End of Doctrine*, 152.

that he himself encounters us, that we see ourselves set before God."[107] Accordingly, the most apt analogy for evaluating dogmatic claims is the human-divine relationship as presented in Kierkegaard's image of the lover reading a letter from the beloved: "a lover who has received a letter from his beloved—I assume that God's Word is just as precious to you as this letter is to the lover. I assume that you read and think you ought to read God's Word in the same way the lover reads this letter."[108] In other words, our hermeneutical endeavors ought to be grounded in a methodological humility that withholds judgment, allows God to speak, and is receptive to the work of the Spirit wherever it manifests itself for, "The wind [*pneuma*] blows where it chooses, and you hear the sound of it, but you do not know where it comes from or where it goes. So it is with everyone who is born of the Spirit [*pneuma*]" (John 3:8). Nevertheless, in this mysterious act of divine self-communication God does indeed speak—clearly and unequivocally—through the work of the Spirit that reveals God's justice and righteousness (*tzedakah*) as summed up in the commandments (*mitzvah*). A comparative study of the work of the Spirit in the Hebrew Bible, New Testament, and the Qur'an has demonstrated that the Spirit is most often and most clearly encountered *in the prophetic*.

Unfortunately, the prophetic office is one that has disappeared or been greatly muted in the three Abrahamic religions. Within Judaism, the rabbis have superseded the prophets within YHWH's covenant with Israel: "In fact, for the rabbis, prophecy ended with the destruction of the Temple and the exile. How could there be prophecy if God had withdrawn?"[109] If the "prophets spoke the unmediated word of God, the rabbis used the record of God's instruction [Torah, Talmud] to help guide the community in the present."[110] Within Christianity, Reformed theologian John Calvin defines prophecy in his commentary on 1 Corinthians: "I take the term *prophecy* to mean that unique and outstanding gift of revealing what is the secret will of God, so that the prophet is, so to speak, God's messenger to [humankind]."[111] However, Calvin also believed that the need for a distinct prophetic office came to an end with God's most perfect self-revelation in Christ: "Christ is the only teacher

107. Barth, *The Göttingen Dogmatics*, 327.

108. Kierkegaard, *For Self-Examination/Judge for Yourself*, 26.

109. Marc H. Ellis, *Toward a Jewish Theology of Liberation: The Challenge of the 21st Century*, 3rd exp. ed. (Waco, TX: Baylor University Press, 2004), 34.

110. Ibid.

111. John Calvin, *Calvin's New Testament Commentaries*, vol. 9, *The First Epistle of Paul to the Corinthians*, ed. David Wishart Torrance and Thomas Forsyth Torrance, trans. John W. Fraser (Grand Rapids, MI: Wm. B. Eerdmans Publishing Co., 1959), 263.

of the Church."[112] This despite the fact that the apostle Paul recognized the office of prophet as a gift (*charismata*) of the Holy Spirit (1 Cor. 12:7–11; 14:1–40), but as Calvin notes, Paul also recognizes two permanent offices, pastors and teachers. Concerning prophets, God "now and again revives them as the need of the times demands," but this office "either does not exist today or is less commonly seen."[113] At least Calvin's lukewarm acknowledgment that God might once again reinstate the office of prophecy remains open to the possibility of a renewed age of prophecy "as the need of the times demands." Within Islam, the Qur'an is unequivocal in its affirmation concerning Muhammad's unique role as the final and definitive prophet of God: "Muhammad is not the father of any man among you; rather, he is the Messenger of God and the Seal of the prophets. And God is Knower of all things" (Sura 33:40).[114] Nevertheless, early in the twenty first century a prophetic stance is called for since it "is not possible to remain neutral in the face of poverty and the resulting just claims of the poor; a posture of neutrality would, moreover, mean siding with the injustice and oppression in our midst."[115] Both Alves and Gutiérrez affirm the work of the Spirit in human liberation as a living sacrament, a visible sign of God's justice and compassion manifest in concrete ecclesial practices, which demands that the church "must make the prophetic *denunciation* of every dehumanizing situation, which is contrary to fellowship, justice and liberty," and must also "criticize every sacralization of oppressive structures to which the Church itself might have contributed."[116] Consequently, whatever else the church decides defines its distinctive dogmatic "grammar," *unless* the church is actively decrying and opposing the dehumanization of human beings in solidarity with Syrian refugees, Black Lives Matter, Palestinian Arabs, Rohingya Muslims in Myanmar, gay men in Chechnya, or undocumented immigrants in the United States, its doctrines and practices are "an empty action" (Gutiérrez).

Dogmatic theology strives for clarity and concreteness in developing its explanatory narratives, striving to rationally defend divine agency

---

112. John Calvin, *Calvin's New Testament Commentaries*, vol. 4, *The Gospel according to St John: 1–10*, ed. David Wishart Torrance, trans. Thomas Henry Louis Parker (Grand Rapids, MI: Wm. B. Eerdmans Publishing Co., 1996), 37.

113. John Calvin, *Institutes of the Christian Religion*, ed. John T. McNeill, trans. Ford Lewis Battles (Philadelphia: Westminster Press, 1960), 4.3.4, 1056–57.

114. See *The Study Quran: A New Translation and Commentary*, Seyyed Hossein Nasr, editor-in-chief, 1031–32. The commentators state that the phrase "Seal of the prophets" is "understood to mean he is the last Prophet sent to humanity" (1031).

115. Gutiérrez, *A Theology of Liberation*, 159.

116. Ibid., 152.

in the natural world and the human social order, yet rarely leaving the swamp of contested orthodoxies and fideistic opinions. Daniel Migliore, in his introduction to the discipline of theology, *Faith Seeking Understanding* (1991), presumes that faith is faith in the one true God who by definition "remains a mystery beyond human comprehension."[117] That said, theology still receives truth and is able to speak truth, so true "faith must be distinguished from fideism. Fideism says we reach a point where we must stop our inquiry and simply believe; *faith keeps on seeking and asking*."[118] Accordingly, "Theology is strenuous inquiry, a process of seeking, contending, wrestling, like Jacob with the angel until dawn, wanting to be blessed and limping away from the struggle (Gen. 32:24ff.)."[119] Modern theology has tended to limit this struggle to the intellectual or spiritual planes, to which liberation theology responds by emphasizing praxis. Here liberation theology stands with some of the more vocal nineteenth-century critics of Christianity, Nietzsche and Kierkegaard. After all, it was Nietzsche, perhaps the harshest critic of Christianity, who questioned the emphasis on correct doctrine and stated, "It is false to the point of nonsense to find the mark of the Christian in a 'faith,' for instance, in the faith in redemption through Christ: only Christian *practice*, a life such as he *lived* who died on the cross, is Christian."[120] Central to Nietzsche's critique of Christianity is the church's mistaken emphasis on doctrinal orthodoxy, so he aims his venom at the priestly architects of the Christian religion who replace Christlike praxis with "faith" understood as rational assent to doctrinal claims: "To reduce being a Christian, Christianism, to a matter of considering something true, to a mere phenomenon of consciousness, is to negate Christianism."[121] These views are harmonious with the critique of liberationists like Gutiérrez and Alves, who view dogmatic claims through the lens of praxis: "The goal is to balance and even to reject the primacy and almost exclusiveness which doctrine has enjoyed in Christian life and above all to modify the emphasis, often obsessive, upon the attainment of an orthodoxy which is often nothing more than fidelity to an obsolete tradition or a debatable interpretation."[122] Rubém Alves wrestles with Nietzsche fully aware that for Nietzsche Christianity is

---

117. Daniel L. Migliore, *Faith Seeking Understanding: An Introduction to Christian Theology* (Grand Rapids, MI: Wm. B. Eerdmans Publishing Co., 1991), 2.
118. Ibid., 2 (emphasis added).
119. Ibid., 5.
120. Nietzsche, *The Antichrist*, in *The Portable Nietzsche*, 612.
121. Ibid., 613.
122. Gutiérrez, *A Theology of Liberation*, 8.

the enemy, yet optimistic that this encounter with Nietzsche's virulent atheism will "become the occasion for radical self-criticism on both sides . . . which could make man freer than he was before. A true dialogue thus requires full awareness of the radical opposition."[123] Alves is thus capable of engaging Nietzsche's genealogical critique because, "in order to be free for history and for the transformation of society one has to unlearn the language of theology,"[124] and nowhere has this been attempted "in a more forcible and passionate manner than in the writings of Nietzsche. He welcomed the death of God—and with it the end of theological language—as a joyful liberating reality."[125] Neither Alves nor Gutiérrez truly wish to see an end to theological language, but they both hope to eclipse the narrow, sectarian language of theological totalitarianism that prevents the church from embracing its prophetic call as a universal sacrament of salvation and liberation for all humanity.

For some within the church the move toward religious pluralism, comparative theology, and interreligious cooperation is positive—a flowering of the Spirit—but for others it signals a failure of doctrinal purity and ecclesial unity. The church in the twenty-first century finds itself increasingly irrelevant, grasping to the old Constantinian ways of being church within the existing power structures without realizing that the dominant powers have relegated the church to a sectarian and intellectual ghetto. This book has argued that the way forward begins with a return to the scriptural past by embracing the prophetic work of the Spirit as that which defines *ecclesia* ("assembly"). Only when the Christian church recognizes that God has always worked *extra muros ecclesiae* ("beyond the walls of the church"), and that God's covenantal relationship has always included all peoples and nations, will Christian theology find a sure footing for engaging the complexities of globalized Christianity in a radically pluralist world. Only when we abandon the historical impulse to label the other either "heretic," "apostate," or "pagan," and approach the religious other as a fellow pilgrim on the same journey of "faith seeking understanding," can we Christians then say that we are faithful to the divine will revealed in our sacred Scriptures. Alves reminds us that to "talk about God is to speak of *God's promises* of joy to humankind."[126] These promises extend to all humanity, a point driven home by one of the parables of Søren Kierkegaard:

---

123. Rubem Alves, *A Theology of Human Hope* (St. Meinrad, IN: Abbey, 1972), 30.
124. Ibid., 29.
125. Ibid., 30.
126. Alves, *I Believe in the Resurrection of the Body*, 41.

If someone lives in the midst of Christianity and enters, with knowledge of the true idea of God, the house of God, the house of the true God, and prays, but rays in untruth, and if someone lives in an idolatrous land but prays with all the passion of infinity, although his eyes are resting upon the image of an idol—where, then, is there more truth? The one prays in truth to God although he is worshipping an idol; the other prays in untruth to the true God and is therefore in truth worshipping an idol. The distance between objective reflection and subjectivity is indeed an infinite one.[127]

Without advocating cultural relativism or sectarian fideism, truth has been defined as an existential appropriation and practical application of the prophetic work of the Spirit to love the neighbor as oneself, recognizing that religious traditions elaborate complex and expansive narratives that cover a lot of ground. At the same time, fidelity to the self-revealing God of the Abrahamic traditions demands a life of justice, compassion, and solidarity with fellow human beings who have been denied their basic dignity as creatures made in the image of God. Dogmatic claims made *in the absence of* this historical and sacramental praxis of love are devoid of meaning.

127. Kierkegaard, *Concluding Unscientific Postscript*, 201.

Conclusion

From Babel to Pentecost

"We have to condemn publicly the very *idea* that some people have the right to repress others. In keeping silent about evil, in burying it so deep within us that no sign of it appears on the surface, we are *implanting* it, and it will rise up a thousandfold in the future. When we neither punish nor reproach evildoers, we are not simply protecting their trivial old age, we are thereby ripping the foundations of justice from beneath new generations. It is for this reason, and not because of the 'weakness of indoctrinational work,' that they are growing up 'indifferent.' Young people are acquiring the conviction that foul deeds are never punished on earth, that they always bring prosperity.

It is going to be uncomfortable, horrible, to live in such a country!"

—Aleksandr Solzhenitsyn[1]

A spirituality of liberation emphasizes life in community marked by concrete works that strive for *universal* human liberation. Accordingly, identifying guiding parameters in Scripture for our "life together" is imperative, and also revelatory of the inherently political dimension of theological thought. As Mahatma Gandhi once commented, "those who say religion has nothing to do with politics do not know what religion is."[2] So when George W. Bush was chided for naming Jesus Christ as the most influential political philosopher during a presidential debate, my reaction was not to join in the ridicule but to push back by asking, "Then why do your policies not reflect the justice, compassion, and love of Jesus?"[3] If, as Aristotle contends, the human being is by nature a "political animal,"[4] then any account of human existence—be it scientific, historical, or theological—ought to provide some normative description of corporate life. The biblical narratives, some dating back to human prehistory, present just such an accounting, even when they fail to provide the level of exactness demanded by political philosophers.

1. Aleksandr Solzhenitsyn, *The Gulag Archipelago 1918–1956: An Experiment in Literary Investigation*, 2 vols., trans. Thomas P. Whitney (New York: Harper & Row, Publishers, 1973), 177–78.
2. Mahatma Gandhi, *Gandhi's Experiments with Truth: Essential Writings by and about Mahatma Gandhi*, ed. Richard L. Johnson (Lanham, MD: Lexington Books, 2006), 69.
3. Hanna Rosin, "Bush's 'Christ Moment' Is Put to Political Test by Christians: Act of Faith or Partisan Ploy, It Draws Faithful's Attention," in *The Washington Post* (Thursday, December 16, 1999): A14.
4. See Aristotle, *The Politics*, reprint, ed. Stephen Everson (Cambridge: Cambridge University Press, 1988), book 1, section 1253a.

The language of Scripture is often the language of myth. Accordingly, many of its stories are heavily etiological, providing—through
the use of imaginative and poetic language—some explanation for
how things in the world came to be as they are. As Nahum Sarna notes
in his commentary on Genesis, the "work of God's Creation has been
termed 'very good'; the idyllic life of man and woman in the Garden
of Eden has been described," yet one pressing question remains unanswered: "How did evil come into existence?"[5] Consequently, "Genesis
3.14–19 contains not merely one but a whole series of aetiologies,
and this is typical of the Yahwist's narratives in Genesis 1–11, explain-
ing why serpents crawl on their bellies, female labour pains and subordination to men, the labouriousness of man's toil, and apparently
death."[6] The story of Babel stands as yet another of these etiological
myths, written to explain "the geographic dispersal imposed by God"
on humanity, by a narrator clearly "disturbed by the vast diversity of
languages that characterizes the human race" given the Creation story's
account that all humanity "constitutes one great family traceable to a
common ancestry."[7]

Latino theologian Luis G. Pedraja, in *Jesus Is My Uncle* (1999),
approaches the Babel narrative from a linguistic perspective, arguing
that language "is essential to the establishment of a community. As
a result, the role of language is central to the establishment of the
community of faith."[8] Implied in the biblical Babel story is the claim
"that they are able to accomplish the building of the city and tower
because they share a common language," so that when "they cease
to share a language they not only abandon the construction of the
tower, they also abandon the city as well."[9] Consequently, traditional
interpretations view the confusion of languages as divine punishment
for the sin of pride, insofar as when the people of Babel are working
together "nothing that they propose to do will now be impossible
for them," therefore God acted to confuse their language then "scattered them abroad from there over the face of all the earth" (Gen.
11:6–7). According to such interpretations, Babel is "a story of general hubris and prideful human rebellion,"[10] when humanity, "who

---

5. Sarna, *The JPS Torah Commentary: Genesis*, 24.
6. John Day, *From Creation to Babel: Studies in Genesis 1–11* (London: Bloomsbury T. & T. Clark, 2013), 45.
7. Sarna, *The JPS Torah Commentary: Genesis*, 80.
8. Luis G. Pedraja, *Jesus Is My Uncle: Christology from a Hispanic Perspective* (Nashville, TN: Abingdon Press, 1999), 110–11.
9. Ibid., 111.
10. Bill T. Arnold, *Genesis: The New Cambridge Bible Commentary* (Cambridge: Cambridge University Press, 2009), 118–19.

has been made for God and made to exercise power responsibly under God, seeks to overstep the limits of [its] creatureliness."[11] However, Pedraja is dissatisfied with such traditional explanations, instead arguing, "Babel is about more than the confusion of languages. It is about community, sharing, and human pride. Without diversity in our communities, we easily lose sight of our place in creation and fancy ourselves to be the definitive standard for everything."[12] Pedraja contends that the people of Babel were intolerant of cultural and linguistic diversity. Consequently, they did not lose community when they lost their common language because they "never had a sense of community in the first place!"[13]

Though coming at the problem from a very different angle, liberationist Miguel A. De La Torre reaches similar conclusions about the cultural intolerance present in the Babel narrative by accentuating the interpretations of segregationist Christians during the civil rights movement: "during the time of Jim and Jane Crow in the U.S. South, it was used to advocate God's divine will to maintain segregation among the races and ethnicities."[14] Bigoted, hateful claims twist the text into a justification for racial segregation: "[the confusion of languages] was an act of Divine Providence to frustrate the mistaken efforts of godless men to assume the permanent integration of the peoples of the earth."[15] They argue that God's punishment at Babel—the confusion of languages and the dispersion of peoples "over the face of all the earth" (Gen. 11:8)—was God's "penalty for their attempt at racial integration."[16] The main implication stemming from this convoluted eisegesis suggests that humanity was not just randomly scattered by God, but scattered into distinct ethnic and racial groupings, each group meant to live in unified isolation from the other, thereby maintaining racial purity. Thankfully, this racist script cannot be maintained in light of the Genesis text itself, nor in light of later acts of God: namely, God's actions on the Day of Pentecost in the New Testament.

Luis Pedraja envisions the Babel and Pentecost stories as bookends that when read together provide real insight into the nature of genuine community:

11. Robert Davidson, *Genesis 1–11* (Cambridge: Cambridge University Press, 1973), 107.
12. Pedraja, *Jesus Is My Uncle*, 111.
13. Ibid.
14. Miguel A. De La Torre, *Genesis* (Louisville, KY: Westminster John Knox Press, 2011), 136.
15. G. T. Gillespie, *A Christian View on Segregation* (Winona, MS: Association of Citizen's Councils, 1954), 9. Cited in De La Torre, *Genesis*, 136.
16. Everett Tilson, *Segregation and the Bible* (New York: Abingdon Press, 1958), 27. Cited in De La Torre, *Genesis*, 136.

At Pentecost, the opposite occurs: God forms a true community out of diversity. Unlike Babel, where the people attempted to build a community through a common language, at Pentecost *the community is built upon sharing God's spirit*. Through the Holy Spirit, God affirms our diverse languages and cultures, *without* the imposition of one language upon everyone. The miracle of Pentecost is not the creation of a common language that everyone understands. The miracle of Pentecost is that everyone is able to hear God's word in their own tongue (Acts 2:1–11).[17]

For that reason the stories of Babel and Pentecost help us understand how "true community requires an ability to bridge our differences without dissolving them."[18] Though previous exegetes have not made the point as explicitly as Pedraja, there is a subtext within traditional exegeses of the Babel story that suggests God's divine punishment is not motivated by the building of the tower into the heavens (Gen. 11:4) nor by a perceived threat to divine sovereignty from human hubris (Gen. 11:6) but because of an earlier disobedience to the divine command to "Be fruitful and multiply, and fill the earth and subdue it" (Gen. 1:28), which was repeated to the sons of Noah after the flood in God's first covenant with humankind: "And you, be fruitful and multiply, abound on the earth and multiply in it" (Gen. 9:7). Thus, according to the etiologies that characterize the book of Genesis, all of humanity is descended from Shem, Ham, and Japheth, the three sons of Noah: "and from these the whole earth was peopled" (Gen. 9:19). Consequently, the sin of Babel is that rather than dispersing and populating the whole of the earth, humanity came together in one big city under a single language and culture in defiance of God, for "otherwise we shall be scattered abroad upon the face of the whole earth" (Gen. 11:4).

Mennonite theologian Theodore Hiebert names the Babel story "the Bible's foundational text about cultural diversity," and identifies John Calvin's sixteenth-century exegesis of Genesis 11:1–9 as "the seminal Reformed interpretation," which can serve as a resource for "meeting the challenge of cultural diversity in our own generation."[19] Calvin has both Jewish and Christian precursors who identify cultural diversity as one of the "problems" addressed by the biblical Babel story. For example,

---

17. Pedraja, *Jesus Is My Uncle*, 112 (emphasis added).
18. Ibid.
19. Theodore Hiebert, "Babel: Babble or Blueprint? Calvin, Cultural Diversity, and the Interpretation of Genesis 11:1–9," in *Reformed Theology, Identity and Ecumenicity II: Biblical Interpretation in the Reformed Tradition*, ed. Wallace M. Alston Jr. and Michael Welker (Grand Rapids, MI: Wm. B. Eerdmans Publishing Co., 2007), 127.

according to the rabbinic tradition, humanity was once united in language (Hebrew), but when God confused all the languages, those who no longer spoke Hebrew were "at a disadvantage, since only Hebrew words 'fully express the purpose of the heart,' and since the angels cannot understand or attend to human communications in other languages (*Zohar* 1, 75b)."[20] Cultural diversity is a problem insofar as it challenges the traditional claim in Genesis that all peoples were descended from the sons of Noah because the world contains a plurality of languages, cultures, and religions. Augustine exhibits a similar intolerance for cultural diversity, albeit from a Christian exegetical perspective: "Like the rabbis, Augustine spends some time reflecting on the punishment for this godless pride, the division of languages. And like the rabbis, he regards this division as a tragic event in biblical history."[21] In other words, cultural diversity is for Augustine "the fate of sinners alone."[22] According to Hiebert, despite the fact that John Calvin's exegesis adopts many of the same conclusions as these traditional precursors, Calvin differs in one very important way: "he does not exempt a righteous line of descent (which continued to speak Hebrew, the original common language) from Babel and its punishment, as did Augustine, Luther, and some rabbinic interpreters. He thus does not raise the righteous above diversity, relegating diversity only to the unrighteous segment of humanity."[23] In other words, while Calvin still views God's actions at Babel as a punishment, he does not view the dispersion of humanity as part of that punishment: "Men had already been spread abroad; and this ought not to be regarded as a punishment, seeing it rather flowed from the benediction and grace of God."[24]

As Hiebert notes, John Calvin reads chapters 10 and 11 of Genesis chronologically, which means that by the time the events of Babel unfold humanity had already been scattered over the whole earth and had multiplied into many different languages, cultures, and nationalities, as evidenced by the genealogies of the sons of Noah (Gen. 10:5, 20, 31). Therefore, even though Calvin stands within the dominant exegetical traditions of Judaism and Christianity that view the confusion of languages as "a catastrophe for the human race,"[25] Calvin's

---

20. Ibid., 130.
21. Ibid., 131.
22. Ibid.
23. Ibid., 135.
24. John Calvin, *Calvin's Commentaries Vol. 1: Genesis*, trans. The Rev. John King, M.A., reprint ed. (Grand Rapids, MI: Baker Books, 2003), 332.
25. Hiebert, "Babel: Babble or Blueprint?" 137.

interpretation is distinguished by its acceptance of cultural, ethnic, and linguistic diversity as part of God's divine plan for humanity from the Creation. On what does John Calvin base this interpretation? First, on the fact that the Table of Nations (Gen. 10) lists a multiplicity of languages and nationalities *prior* to the events of Babel, as many commentators note: "Instead of the present arrangement, the ethnic map of chapter 10 with its multifarious families and languages seems more naturally to *follow* the Tower of Babel episode as effect follows cause."[26] Second, the very actions of the people of Babel, who clearly acted in defiance of God's command to "fill the earth" (Gen. 1:28):

> They knew that the earth was formed to be inhabited, and would every where supply its abundance for the sustenance of men; and the rapid multiplication of mankind proved to them that it was not possible for them long to remain shut within their present narrow limits; wherefore, to whatever other places it would be necessary for them to migrate, they design this tower as a witness of their origin.[27]

In other words, the sin being punished is their arrogant attempt to set themselves up as great or greater than God by erecting a monument to their ambition and ingenuity. The irony is that they *were* remembered, not for their building project but for God's response to their act of rebellion—their great city forever linked to the confusion of languages: "Therefore it was called Babel [*bābel*], because there the LORD confused [*bālal*] the language of all the earth" (Gen. 11:9). As Calvin comments, "Behold what they gained by their foolish ambition to acquire a name!"

Admittedly, John Calvin himself never argued for cultural diversity and tolerance, but the fact remains he bucked the exegetical trend by affirming cultural, linguistic, and ethnic diversity *as part of* God's plan for creation, a perspective now commonly articulated by contemporary exegetes: "The Table of Nations in its current location fulfills the divine command 'to be fruitful and multiply, and fill the earth' (9:1, reflecting also 1:28), and is therefore predominately a positive appraisal of human dispersion."[28] Unfortunately, as Miguel De La Torre has pointed out, there is a long and tragic history of this text (and others, like the Curse of Ham)[29] being manipulated to justify racial hatred and division. As with

26. Arnold, *Genesis*, 119.
27. Calvin, *Commentary on Genesis*, 328–29.
28. Arnold, *Genesis*, 119.
29. See Rubén Rosario Rodríguez, *Racism and God-Talk: A Latino/a Perspective* (New York University Press, 2008), 35–39.

the segregationists in the Southern United States during the civil rights movement, Dutch Reformed supporters of apartheid in South Africa interpreted this text as a divine mandate for maintaining distinct and separate races—in other words, as establishing the apartheid state: "We must not forget that Gen. 11 also tells us of man's attempt to establish a (forced) unity of the human race."[30] Supporters of apartheid employed "the creation narratives and the proto-history of Genesis 1–11" in order to argue that "the Scriptures teach and uphold the essential unity of mankind and the primordial relatedness and fundamental equality of all peoples,"[31] while at the same time defending the stratified and rigidly segregated South African state: "In specific circumstances and under specific conditions the New Testament makes provision for the regulation on the basis of separate development of the co-existence of various peoples in one country."[32] As both John Calvin and the liberationists Pedraja and De La Torre exegete Genesis 11:1–9, "the story of Babel in fact directly and radically *opposes* the Report's attempt to make so much of cultural identity and achievement,"[33] suggesting that it is precisely the idolatrous elevation of Afrikaner *volk* culture, paralleling the arrogance of the people of Babel, that brings down the wrath and judgment of God. Not surprisingly, a similar critique is employed in the Belhar Confession (1982), a joint statement from Dutch Reformed, Presbyterian, and Congregationalist pastors and theologians, under the leadership of black Reformed liberation theologian Allan Boesak, that called upon their churches to "recognize apartheid as a heresy and to unite in opposing it."[34] Therefore, the opening paragraph of the Belhar Confession contains an explicit rejection of the Dutch Reformed exegesis of Genesis 11:1–9 as articulated in the Landman report:

> Therefore, we reject any doctrine which absolutizes either natural diversity or the sinful separation of people in such a way that this absolutization hinders or breaks the visible and active unity of the Church, or even leads to the establishment of a separate church formation. . . . Therefore, we reject any doctrine which, in such a

30. *Human Relations and the South African Scene in the Light of Scripture* (Cape Town: Dutch Reformed Church Publishers, 1976), 18. This document came to be called the Landman report after its primary author, Dr. W. A. Landman, who also wrote an apology for his church's defense of apartheid directed at American Reformed critics of the Dutch Reformed Church in South Africa: W. A. Landman, *A Plea for Understanding: A Reply to the Reformed Church in America* (Cape Town: NG Kerk-Uitgewers, 1968).

31. John W. de Gruchy with Steve de Gruchy, *The Church Struggle in South Africa*, 25th anniversary ed. (Minneapolis, MN: Fortress Press, 2005), 69 (citing *Human Relations and the South African Scene*).

32. Ibid., 70 (citing *Human Relations and the South African Scene*).

33. Hiebert, "Babel: Babble or Blueprint?" 144.

34. De Gruchy, *The Church Struggle in South Africa*, 192.

situation, sanctions in the name of the gospel or of the will of God
the forced separation of people on the grounds of race and color and
thereby in advance obstructs and weakens the ministry and experience of reconciliation in Christ.[35]

Though controversial at the time, the Belhar Confession (like the Barmen Declaration under the Third Reich) is now widely acknowledged
to represent a moment of *status confessionis* in the history of the Christian church, when the church is called to make a concrete and binding
doctrinal stance on sociopolitical questions under the guidance of the
Holy Spirit.

Veli-Matti Kärkkäinen, in his recently completed five-volume systematic theology, *A Constructive Christian Theology for the Pluralistic
World* (2013–2017), traces the breadth and depth of the Spirit's work
in the contemporary pluralistic world guided by certain key theological
questions: Who is the Spirit? Where is the Spirit? How do we discern
the Spirit(s)? This book has attempted to provide one answer—though
surely not the only avenue for tracking the work of the Spirit in our
religiously pluralistic world—by tracing the work of the Spirit in God's
preferential option for the poor, oppressed, and powerless over against
those who exploit, repress, and dehumanize the inherent dignity of
their fellow human beings. Specifically, the work of the Spirit in preserving the inherent dignity of humankind made in the image of God is
the foundation for genuine community, the basis for hope in the face of
hopelessness, and the concrete pattern for unity in plurality by bridging
"our differences without dissolving them."[36] Not the forced unity of
Babel, nor the confusion of languages in the aftermath of God's punishment, but a community made possible by the work of the Spirit in
which unity is maintained by respecting and affirming particularity *and*
diversity. However else this new community is defined, the prophetic
biblical witness is clear that a spirit-led community embodies the divine
imperatives to extend compassion, justice, and hospitality to all, but
especially those in greatest need. As Gutiérrez contends, the "gratuitous
love of God requires that we establish authentic justice for all, while
giving privileged place to a concern for the unimportant members of

35. This is a translation of the original Afrikaans text of the confession as it was adopted by the synod of the
Dutch Reformed Mission Church in South Africa in 1986. In 1994 the Dutch Reformed Mission Church and the
Dutch Reformed Church in Africa united to form the Uniting Reformed Church in Southern Africa (URCSA).
This inclusive language text was prepared by the Office of Theology and Worship, Presbyterian Church (U.S.A.).
https://www.rca.org/resources/confession-belhar?pid=304 (accessed November 11, 2017).
36. Pedraja, *Jesus Is My Uncle*, 112.

society—that is, for those whose rights are not recognized either in theory (by a set of laws) or in practice (in the way society conducts itself)."[37] Who is our neighbor? The one we go out of our way to help simply because they need our help. This is intentional community in its truest sense; an *ecclesia* ("assembly") brought together by the work of the Spirit for human liberation and not because its members have shared interests and mutually beneficial ends.

37. Gutiérrez, *The God of Life*, 117.

Bibliography

Achinstein, Peter, and Stephen F. Barker. *The Legacy of Logical Positivism: Studies in the Philosophy of Science.* Baltimore: John Hopkins University Press, 1969.

Allen, Diogenes. *Christian Belief in a Postmodern World: The Full Wealth of Conviction.* Louisville, KY: Westminster John Knox Press, 1989.

———. *Philosophy for Understanding Theology.* Rev. ed. Louisville, KY: Westminster John Knox Press, 1985.

———. *Three Outsiders: Pascal, Kierkegaard, Simone Weil.* Princeton, NJ: Caroline Press, 1983.

———. *The Traces of God.* Princeton, NJ: Caroline Press, 1981.

Allen, John L., Jr. *The Future Church: How Ten Trends Are Revolutionizing the Catholic Church.* New York: Image, 2009.

Allen, Paul L. *Theological Method: A Guide for the Perplexed.* London: T. & T. Clark, 2012.

Alter, Robert. *The Art of Biblical Narrative.* Rev. ed. New York: Basic Books, 2011.

Alves, Rubem. *I Believe in the Resurrection of the Body.* Philadelphia: Fortress Press, 1986.

———. *Protestantism and Repression: A Brazilian Case Study.* Translated by John Drury. Reprint, Eugene, OR: Wipf & Stock Publishers, 2007.

———. *A Theology of Human Hope.* St. Meinrad, IN: Abbey, 1972.

———. "Towards a Theology of Liberation: An Exploration of the Encounter Between the Languages of Humanistic Messianism and Messianic Humanism." PhD diss., Princeton Theological Seminary, 1968.

Aquinas, Thomas. *Introduction to Saint Thomas.* Edited by Anton C. Pegis. New York: The Modern Library, 1948.

———. *Summa contra Gentiles, Book One: God.* Translated by Anton C. Pegis. Notre Dame, IN: University of Notre Dame Press, 1975.

Aristotle. *The Politics.* Reprint. Edited by Stephen Everson. Cambridge: Cambridge University Press, 1988.

Arnold, Bill T. *Genesis: The New Cambridge Bible Commentary.* Cambridge: Cambridge University Press, 2009.

Ayoub, Mahmoud. *A Muslim View of Christianity: Essays on Dialogue by Mahmoud Ayoub.* Edited by Irfan A. Omar. Maryknoll, NY: Orbis Books, 2007.

Azadegan, Ebrahim. "Ibn 'Arabi on the Problem of Divine Hiddenness." *Journal of the Muhyiddin Ibn 'Arabi Society* 53 (2013): 49–67.

Balthasar, Hans Urs von. *The Glory of the Lord: A Theological Aesthetics.* Vol. 1, *Seeing the Form.* Edited by John Riches. Translated by Erasmo Leiva-Merikakis. Edinburgh: T. & T. Clark, 1982.

———. *Love Alone: The Way of Revelation.* London: Sheed & Ward, 1977.

Baptism, Eucharist, and Ministry 1982–1990. Geneva: World Council of Churches, 1990.

Baptism, Eucharist, and Ministry. Geneva: World Council of Churches, 1982.

Barnett, Erroll. "White House responds to petition to label Black Lives Matter a 'terror' group." CBS News (July 17, 2016), https://www.cbsnews.com/news/white-house-responds-to-petition-to-label-black-lives-matter-a-terror-group/.

Barth, Karl. *Church Dogmatics.* Edited by G. W. Bromiley and T. F. Torrance. 13 vols. Edinburgh: T. & T. Clark, 1936–1969.

———. *Church Dogmatics.* Vol. I.1. Edited by G. W. Bromiley and T. F. Torrance (Edinburgh: T. & T. Clark, 1936).

———. *Church Dogmatics.* Vol. I.2. Edited by G. W. Bromiley and T. F. Torrance (Edinburgh: T. & T. Clark, 1988).

———. *Church Dogmatics.* Vol. II.1. Edited by G. W. Bromiley and T. F. Torrance. Translated by T. H. L. Parker, W. B. Johnston, Harold Knight, and J. L. M. Haire. (Edinburgh: T. & T. Clark, 1957).

———. *Church Dogmatics.* Vol. II.2. Edited by G. W. Bromiley and T. F. Torrance. Edinburgh: T. & T. Clark, 1957.

———. *Church Dogmatics.* Vol. III.3. Edited by G. W. Bromiley and T. F. Torrance. Translated by G. W. Bromiley and R. J. Ehrlich. London: T. & T. Clark, 1960.

———. *Church Dogmatics.* Vol. IV.1. Edited by G. W. Bromiley and T. F. Torrance. Translated by G. W. Bromiley. Edinburgh: T. & T. Clark, 1956.

———. *Church Dogmatics.* Vol. IV.3.1. Edited by G. W. Bromiley and T. F. Torrance. Edinburgh: T. & T. Clark, 1961.

———. *Church Dogmatics.* Vol. IV.3.2. Edited by G. W. Bromiley and T. F. Torrance. Translated by G. W. Bromiley. Edinburgh: T. & T. Clark, 1962.

———. "Concluding Unscientific Postscript on Schleiermacher." In *Karl Barth: Theologian of Freedom.* Edited by Clifford Green. Minneapolis, MN: Fortress Press, 1991.

———. *The Epistle to the Romans.* Translated by Edwyn C. Hoskins. Oxford: Oxford University Press, 1968.

———. "Evangelical Theology in the 19th Century." In *The Humanity of God.* Translated by Thomas Wieser. Richmond, VA: John Knox Press, 1972.

———. *The Göttingen Dogmatics: Instruction in the Christian Religion.* Vol. 1. Edited by Hannelotte Reiffen. Translated by Geoffrey W. Bromiley. Grand Rapids. MI: Wm. B. Eerdmans Publishing Co., 1991.

———. *The Holy Spirit and the Christian Life: The Theological Basis of Ethics.* Translated by R. Birch Hoyle. Louisville, KY: Westminster/John Knox Press, 1993.

―――. "Interview." *Time* (May 31, 1963).

―――. "No! Answer to Emil Brunner." In *Karl Barth: Theologian of Freedom.* Edited by Clifford Green. Minneapolis: Fortress Press, 1991.

―――. *The Word of God and Theology.* Translated by Amy Marga. London: T. & T. Clark International, 2011.

Bauckham, Richard. *The Theology of the Book of Revelation.* Cambridge: Cambridge University Press, 1993.

Beilby, James K., and Paul Rhodes Eddy, eds. *The Historical Jesus: Five Views.* Downers Grove, IL: InterVarsity Press, 2009.

"Belhar Confession." *https://www.rca.org/resources/confession-belhar?pid=304.*

Bell, Daniel M., Jr. *Liberation Theology After the End of History: The Refusal to Cease Suffering.* London: Routledge, 2001.

―――. "Postliberalism and Radical Orthodoxy." In *The Cambridge Companion to Christian Political Theology.* Edited by Craig Hovey and Elizabeth Phillips. Cambridge: Cambridge University Press, 2015.

Betances, Emelio. *The Catholic Church and Power Politics in Latin America: The Dominican Case in Comparative Perspective.* Lanham, UK: Rowman & Littlefield, 2007.

Bevans, Stephen B. *Models of Contextual Theology.* Maryknoll, NY: Orbis Books, 1992.

Bevans, Stephen B., and Roger P. Schroeder. *Constants in Context: A Theology of Mission for Today.* Maryknoll, NY: Orbis Books, 2004.

Black Lives Matter website, https://blacklivesmatter.com/about/.

―――, https://blacklivesmatter.com/about/herstory/.

Blades, Lincoln Anthony. "Patrisse Cullors of Black Lives Matters Discusses the Movement." In *Teen Vogue* (August 24, 2017), https://www.teenvogue.com /story/patrisse-cullors-of-black-lives-matter-discusses-the-movement.

Blake, Elizabeth A., and Rubén Rosario. "Journey to Transcendence: Dostoevsky's Theological Polyphony in Barth's Understanding of the Pauline KRISIS." *Studies in East European Thought* 59, no. 1/2, Dostoevskij's Significance for Philosophy and Theology (June 2007): 3–20.

Bloesch, Donald G. *A Theology of Word and Spirit: Authority and Method in Theology.* Downers Grove, IL: InterVarsity Press, 1992.

Blomberg, Craig. *Can We Still Believe the Bible? An Evangelical Engagement with Contemporary Questions.* Ada, MI: Brazos Press, 2014.

Bonhoeffer, Dietrich. *Act and Being: Transcendental Philosophy and Ontology in Systematic Theology.* Edited by Wayne W. Floyd and Hans-Richard Reuter. Translated by H. Martin Rumscheidt. Minneapolis, MN: Fortress Press, 1996.

―――. *Letters and Papers from Prison: Dietrich Bonhoeffer Works.* Vol. 8. English ed. Edited by John W. de Gruchy. Translated by Isabel Best, Lisa E. Dahill, Reinhard Krauss, and Nancy Lukens. Minneapolis, MN: Fortress Press, 2010.

Borges, Jorge Luis. "The Library of Babel." In *Collected Fictions*. Translated by Andrew Hurley. New York: Penguin Books, 1998.

Boyarin, Daniel. "A Broken Olive Branch." Special issue *Symposium on John Milbank's Theology and Social Theory, Arachne* 2, no.1 (1995): 124–30.

Bradbury, Ray. *Fahrenheit 451*. New York: Ballantine Books, 1953.

Brooks, David. "The Benedict Option." In *The New York Times* (March 14, 2017).

Brown, Delwin. *Boundaries of Our Habituations: Tradition and Theological Construction*. Albany, NY: SUNY Press, 1994.

———. "Public Theology, Academic Theology: Wentzel van Huyssteen and the Nature of Theological Rationality." *American Journal of Theology and Philosophy* 22, no. 1 (January 2001): 88–101.

Bruegel, Pieter. *The Tower of Babel*. C. 1563. Oil painting.

Brueggemann, Walter. *Theology of the Old Testament: Testimony, Dispute, Advocacy*. Minneapolis, MN: Fortress Press, 1997.

Buber, Martin. *Eclipse of God: Studies in the Relation between Religion and Philosophy*. London: Victor Gollancz, 1953.

Burnett, D. Graham. *Descartes and the Hyperbolic Quest: Lens Making Machines and Their Significance in the Seventeenth Century (Transactions of the American Philosophical Society)*. Philadelphia, PA: American Philosophical Society, 2005.

Burrell, David B. *Analogy and Philosophical Language*. New Haven, CT: Yale University Press, 1973.

———. *Knowing the Unknowable God: Ibn-Sina, Maimonides, Aquinas*. Notre Dame, IN: University of Notre Dame Press, 1986.

Burrows, William R., Mark R. Gornik, and Janice A. McLean, eds. *Understanding World Christianity: The Vision and Work of Andrew F. Walls*. Maryknoll, NY: Orbis Books, 2011.

Calvin, John. *Calvin's Commentaries*. Vol. 1, *Genesis*. Translated by The Rev. John King. M.A. Reprint. Grand Rapids, MI: Baker Books, 2003.

———. *Calvin's New Testament Commentaries*. Vol. 4, *The Gospel according to St John: 1–10*. Edited by David Wishart Torrance. Translated by Thomas Henry Louis Parker. Grand Rapids, MI: Wm. B. Eerdmans Publishing Co., 1996.

———. *Calvin's New Testament Commentaries*. Vol. 9, *The First Epistle of Paul to the Corinthians*. Edited by David Wishart Torrance and Thomas Forsyth Torrance. Translated by John W. Fraser. Grand Rapids, MI: Wm. B. Eerdmans Publishing Co., 1959.

———. *Institutes of the Christian Religion*. Edited by John T. McNeill. Translated by Ford Lewis Battles. Philadelphia: Westminster Press, 1960.

Cleveland, Christena. *Disunity in Christ: Uncovering the Hidden Forces That Keep Us Apart*. Downers Grove, IL: InterVarsity Press, 2013.

Cone, James H. *A Black Theology of Liberation*. Maryknoll, NY: Orbis Books, 2010. First published 1970.

———. *Black Theology and Black Power.* Maryknoll, NY: Orbis Books, 1997. First published 1969.

———. *God of the Oppressed.* Maryknoll, NY: Orbis Books, 1975.

Congar, Yves. *I Believe in the Holy Spirit.* Rev. ed. Translated by David Smith. New York: Crosssroad Publishing Company, 1997.

———. *The Meaning of Tradition.* Reprint, San Francisco, CA: Ignatius Press, 2004.

———. *Tradition and Traditions: The Biblical, Historical, and Theological Evidence for Catholic Teaching on Tradition.* Reprint, San Diego, CA: Basilica Press, 1997.

Congregation for the Doctrine of the faith. "Declaration *Dominus Iesus* on the Unicity and Salvific Universality of Jesus Christ and the Church." (August 6, 2000), http://www.vatican.va/roman_curia/congregations/cfaith/documents /rc_ con_cfaith_doc_20000806_dominus-iesus_en.html.

Crossan, John Dominic, and Richard G. Watts. *Who Is Jesus? Answers to Your Questions about the Historical Jesus.* Louisville, KY: Westminster John Knox Press, 1996.

D'Costa, Gavin. "Christ, the Trinity, and Religious Plurality." In *Christian Uniqueness Reconsidered: Myth of Pluralistic Theology of Religions.* Edited by Gavin D'Costa. Maryknoll, NY: Orbis Books, 1990.

———. *Theology and Religious Pluralism.* Oxford: Oxford University Press, 1986.

Daly, Mary. *Beyond God the Father: Toward a Philosophy of Women's Liberation.* Boston: Beacon Press, 1973.

———. *The Church and the Second Sex.* New York: Harper & Row, 1968.

Davidson, Robert. *Genesis 1–11.* Cambridge: Cambridge University Press, 1973.

Darwin, Charles. *On the Origin of Species: By Means of Natural Selection or the Preservation of Favored Races in the Struggle for Life.* Reprint, New York: Cosimo Inc., 2007.

Dawkins, Richard. *The God Delusion.* Boston: Houghton Mifflin Company, 2006.

Day, John. *From Creation to Babel: Studies in Genesis 1–11.* London: Bloomsbury T. & T. Clark, 2013.

De La Torre, Miguel A. *Embracing Hopelessness.* Minneapolis, MN: Fortress Press, 2017.

———. *Genesis.* Louisville, KY: Westminster John Knox Press, 2011.

———. *Latino/a Social Ethics: Moving Beyond Eurocentric Moral Thinking.* Waco, TX: Baylor University Press, 2010.

———. "Liberation Theology." In *The Cambridge Companion to Christian Political Theology.* Edited by Craig Hovey and Elizabeth Phillips. Cambridge: Cambridge University Press, 2015.

———. *The Politics of Jesús: A Hispanic Political Theology.* Lanham, MD: Rowman & Littlefield, 2015.

Dennett, Daniel C. *Breaking the Spell: Religion as a Natural Phenomenon.* New York: Penguin, 2006.

Dillenberger, John. *God Hidden and Revealed: The Interpretation of Luther's Deus Absconditus and Its Significance for Religious Thought.* Philadelphia, Muhlenberg Press, 1953.

"Dogmatic Constitution on the Church: *Lumen gentium.*" Solemnly Promulgated by His Holiness Pope Paul VI (November 21, 1964), http://www .vatican.va/archive/ hist_councils/ii_vatican_council/documents/vat-ii_const _19641121_lumen-gentium_en.html .

Donovan, Mary Ann. *One Right Reading? A Guide to Irenaeus.* Collegeville, MN: Liturgical Press, 1997.

Dorrien, Gary. "The Future of Postliberal Theology." *The Christian Century* 118, no. 21 (July 18–25 2001): 22–29.

———. *The Remaking of Evangelical Theology.* Louisville, KY: Westminster John Knox Press, 1998.

Dreher, Rod. *The Benedict Option: A Strategy for Christians in a Post-Christian Nation.* New York: Penguin, 2017.

Dussel, Enrique. "From the Second Vatican Council to the Present Day." In *The Church in Latin America: 1492–1992.* Edited by Enrique Dussel. Maryknoll, NY: Orbis Books, 1992.

———. *A History of the Church in Latin America: Colonialism to Liberation (1492–1979).* Translated by Alan Neely. Grand Rapids, MI: Wm. B. Eerdmans Publishing Co., 1981.

Eliade, Mircea. *The Sacred and the Profane: The Nature of Religion.* San Diego, CA: Harcourt Brace Jovanovich, 1987.

Ellis, Marc H. *Revolutionary Forgiveness: Essays on Judaism, Christianity, and the Future of Religious Life.* Waco, TX: Baylor University Press, 2000.

———. *Toward a Jewish Theology of Liberation: The Challenge of the 21st Century.* 3rd exp. ed. Waco, TX: Baylor University Press, 2004.

Elton John. "Tower of Babel." From the album *Captain Fantastic and the Brown Dirt Cowboy.* MKA, 1975. Audio recording.

Emmanuel, Steven M. *Kierkegaard and the Concept of Revelation.* Albany, NY: State University of New York Press, 1996.

Engineer, Asghar Ali. "On Developing Liberation Theology in Islam." In *Voices from the Margin: Interpreting the Bible in the Third World.* New ed. Edited by R. S. Sugirtharajah. Maryknoll, NY: Orbis Books, 1995.

Escher, M. C. *The Tower of Babel.* 1928. Woodcut.

Evans, C. Stephen. *Passionate Reason: Making Sense of Kierkegaard's Philosophical Fragments.* Bloomington: Indiana University Press, 1992.

Feierman, Jay R., ed. *The Biology of Religious Behavior: The Evolutionary Origins of Faith and Religion.* Santa Barbara, CA: Praeger, 2009.

Feuerbach, Ludwig. *The Essence of Christianity.* Translated by George Eliot. New York: Harper Torchbooks, 1957.

Frei, Hans W. *The Eclipse of Biblical Theology: A Study in Eighteenth and Nine-teenth Century Hermeneutics*. New Haven: Yale University Press, 1974.
———. *The Identity of Jesus Christ: The Hermeneutical Basis of Dogmatic Theology*. Philadelphia: Fortress Press, 1975.
———. *Types of Christian Theology*. Edited by George Hunsinger and William C. Placher. New Haven: Yale University Press, 1992.
Freud, Sigmund. *Civilization and Its Discontents*. Edited and translated by James Strachey. New York: W. W. Norton & Company, 1989.
———. *The Future of an Illusion*. Translated by James Strachey. New York: W. W. Norton & Company, 1975.
———. *Moses and Monotheism*. Translated by Katherine Jones. New York: Vintage Books, 1955.
Friedman, Michael. *Reconsidering Logical Positivism*. New York: Cambridge University Press, 1999.
Gadamer, Hans-Georg. *Truth and Method*. 2nd rev. ed. Translated by Joel Weinsheimer and Donald G. Marshall. London: Bloomsbury, 2004.
Gandhi, Mahatma. *Gandhi's Experiments with Truth: Essential Writings by and about Mahatma Gandhi*. Edited by Richard L. Johnson. Lanham, MD: Lexington Books, 2006.
Geertz, Clifford. *The Interpretation of Cultures*. New York: Basic Books, 1973.
Gilkey, Langdon B. "Cosmology, Ontology, and the Travail of Biblical Language." *Concordia Theological Monthly* 33 No. 3 (March 1962): 143–54.
———. "Neoorthodoxy." In *New and Enlarged Handbook of Christian Theology*. Edited by Donald W. Musser and Joseph L. Price. Nashville, TN: Abingdon Press, 2003.
Gillespie, G. T. *A Christian View on Segregation*. Winona, MS: Association of Citizen's Councils, 1954.
Goffman, Daniel. *The Ottoman Empire and Early Modern Europe*. Cambridge: Cambridge University Press, 2002.
Goizueta, Roberto S. *Caminemos con Jesús: Toward a Hispanic/Latino Theology of Accompaniment*. Maryknoll, NY: Orbis Books, 1999.
González, Justo L. *Mañana: Christian Theology from a Hispanic Perspective*. Nashville, TN: Abingdon Press, 1990.
———. "Metamodern Aliens in Postmodern Jerusalem." In *Hispanic/Latino Theology: Challenge and Promise*. Edited by Ada María Isasi-Díaz and Fernando S. Segovia. Minneapolis, MN: Fortress, Press, 1996.
Gould, Stephen Jay. "Nonoverlapping Magisteria." In *Natural History* 106:16–22 (1997): 16–22.
Green, Clifford. "Introduction: Karl Barth's Life and Theology." In *Karl Barth: Theologian of Freedom*. Edited by Clifford Green. Minneapolis, MN: Fortress Press, 1991.
Griffiths, Devin. *The Age of Analogy: Science and Literature between the Darwins*. Baltimore, MD: Johns Hopkins University Press, 2016.

Gruchy, John W. de, with Steve de Gruchy. *The Church Struggle in South Africa.*
25th anniversary ed. Minneapolis, MN: Fortress Press, 2005.

Gunn, Steven. "War, Religion, and the State." 102–34 in *Early Modern Europe:
An Oxford History.* Edited by Euan Cameron. Oxford: Oxford University
Press, 1999.

Gutiérrez, Gustavo. *The God of Life.* Translated by Matthew J. O'Connell.
Maryknoll, NY: Orbis Books, 1991.

———. *A Theology of Liberation: History, Politics and Salvation.* Rev. ed. Edited
and translated by Sister Caridad Inda and John Eagleson. Maryknoll, NY:
Orbis Books, 1988.

———. *We Drink from Our Own Wells: The Spiritual Journey of a People.* Translated by Matthew J. O'Connell. Reprint, Maryknoll, NY: Orbis Books, 2003.

Gutiérrez, Gustavo, and Richard Shaull. *Liberation and Change.* Richmond, VA:
John Knox Press, 1977.

Hanfling, Oswald. *Logical Positivism.* New York: Columbia University Press,
1981.

Harari, Yuval Noah. *Sapiens: A Brief History of Humankind.* New York: Harper-
Collins, 2015.

Harris, Harriet. *Fundamentalism and Evangelicals.* Oxford: Clarendon Press,
1998.

Harris, Sam. *The End of Faith: Religion, Terror, and the Future of Reason.* New
York: W. W. Norton & Company, 2005.

Hauerwas, Stanley. *After Christendom? How the Church Is to Behave if Freedom,
Justice, and a Christian Nation Are Bad Ideas.* Nashville, TN: Abingdon Press,
1991.

———. *Character and the Christian Life: A Study in Theological Ethics.* South
Bend, IN: University of Notre Dame Press, 1994.

Hauerwas, Stanley, and L. Gregory Jones, eds. *Why Narrative? Readings in Narrative Theology.* Eugene, OR: Wipf & Stock Publishers, 1997.

Haught, John F. *God and the New Atheism: A Critical Response to Dawkins, Harris, and Hitchens.* Louisville, KY: Westminster John Knox Press, 2008.

———. *Making Sense of Evolution: Darwin, God, and the Drama of Life.* Louisville, KY: Westminster John Knox Press, 2010.

Hauser, Christine. "Solidarity with Islam at Christian College, Then Discipline."
In *The New York Times* (December 17, 2015), http://www.nytimes.com
/2015/12/17/us/ wheaton-college-professor-larycia-hawkins-muslim-scarf
.html?_r=0.

Hegel, G. W. F. *Phenomenology of Spirit.* Translated by A. V. Miller. Oxford:
Oxford University Press, 1977.

Heim, S. Mark. *The Depth of the Riches: A Trinitarian Theology of Religious Ends.*
Grand Rapids, MI: Wm. B. Eerdmans Publishing, 2001.

———. *Salvations: Truth and Difference in Religion.* Maryknoll, NY: Orbis
Books, 1995.

Helmer, Christine. *Theology and the End of Doctrine*. Louisville, KY: Westminster John Knox Press, 2014.

Hennelly, Alfred T., ed. *Liberation Theology: A Documentary History*. Maryknoll, NY: Orbis Books, 1990.

Heron, Alasdair I. C. *The Holy Spirit*. Philadelphia: The Westminster Press, 1983.

Heschel, Abraham J. *The Prophets*. Vol. 1. New York: Harper & Row, 1969.

Hesselink, John. "Calvin, Theologian of the Holy Spirit." In *Calvin's First Catechism: A Commentary*. Louisville, KY: Westminster John Knox Press, 1997.

Hiebert, Theodore. "Babel: Babble or Blueprint? Calvin, Cultural Diversity, and the Interpretation of Genesis 11:1–9." In *Reformed Theology, Identity and Ecumenicity*. Vol. 2, *Biblical Interpretation in the Reformed Tradition*. Edited by Wallace M. Alston Jr. and Michael Welker. Grand Rapids, MI: Wm. B. Eerdmans Publishing Co, 2007.

Hobbes, Thomas. *Leviathan*. Rev. student ed. Edited by Richard Tuck. Cambridge: Cambridge University Press, 1996.

Holcomb, Justin S. "Introduction: Mapping Theologies of Scripture." In *Christian Theologies of Scripture: A Comparative Introduction*. Edited by Justin S. Holcomb. New York: New York University Press, 2006.

Holmer, Paul. *The Grammar of Faith*. San Francisco: Harper & Row, 1978.

Holt, Mack P. *The French Wars of Religion, 1562–1629*. Rev. 2nd ed. Cambridge: Cambridge University Press, 2005.

Horn, F. W. "Holy Spirit." 260 in *The Anchor Bible Dictionary*. Vol. 3. Edited by David Noel Freedman. Translated by Dietlinde M. Elliot. New York: Doubleday, 1992.

Howard-Snyder, Daniel, and Paul K. Moser. "Introduction: The Hiddenness of God." In *Divine Hiddenness: New Essays*. Edited by Daniel Howard-Snyder and Paul K. Moser. Cambridge: Cambridge University Press, 2002.

Humphrey, Edith M. *Scripture and Tradition: What the Bible Really Says*. Grand Rapids, MI: Baker Academic, 2013.

Hunsinger, George. *How to Read Karl Barth: The Shape of His Theology*. Oxford: Oxford University Press, 1991.

———. "Truth as Self-Involving: Barth and Lindbeck on the Cognitive and Performative Aspects of Truth in Theological Discourse." *Journal of the American Academy of Religion* 61, no. 1 (Spring 1993): 41–56.

Huyssteen, J. Wentzel van. "Pluralism and Interdisciplinarity: In Search of Theology's Public Voice," *American Journal of Theology and Philosophy* 22, no. 1 (January 2001): 65–87.

———. *The Shaping of Rationality: Toward Interdisciplinarity in Theology and Science*. Grand Rapids, MI: Wm. B. Eerdmans Publishing Co., 1999.

John, Elton. See Elton John.

Johnson, Dominic D.P., Hillary L. Lenfesty, and Jeffrey P. Schloss. "The Elephant in the Room: Do Evolutionary Accounts of Religion Entail the Falsity of Religious Belief?" In *Philosophy, Theology and the Sciences* 1, no. 2 (2014): 200–231.

Johnson, Elizabeth A. *Ask the Beasts: Darwin and the God of Love.* London: Bloomsbury Publishing, 2014.

Johnson, William Stacy. *The Mystery of God: Karl Barth and the Postmodern Foundations of Theology.* Louisville, KY: Westminster John Knox Press, 1997.

Kant, Immanuel. "What Is Enlightenment?" In *Immanuel Kant: Philosophical Writings.* Edited by Ernst Behler. New York: Continuum, 1986.

Kärkkäinen, Veli-Matti. *A Constructive Christian Theology for the Pluralistic World.* Vol. 4, *Spirit and Salvation.* Grand Rapids, MI: Wm. B. Eerdmans Publishing Co., 2016.

———. *Pneumatology: The Holy Spirit in Ecumenical, International, and Contextual Perspective.* Grand Rapids, MI: Baker Academic, 2002.

Kaufman, Gordon D. *An Essay on Theological Method.* Rev. ed. Missoula, MT: Scholars Press, 1979.

———. *In Face of Mystery: A Constructive Theology.* Cambridge, MA: Harvard University Press, 1993.

Kierkegaard, Søren. *Attack Upon Christendom.* Translated by Walter Lowrie. Princeton: Princeton University Press, 1968.

———. *Concluding Unscientific Postscript to Philosophical Fragments.* Vol. 1. Edited and translated by Howard V. Hong and Edna H. Hong. 2nd printing, Princeton: Princeton University Press, 1992.

———. *Eighteen Upbuilding Discourses.* Translated by Howard V. Hong and Edna H. Hong. Princeton: Princeton University Press, 1990.

———. *Philosophical Fragments.* Edited and translated by Howard V. Hong and Edna H. Hong. 2nd printing, Princeton: Princeton University Press, 1987.

———. *For Self-Examination/Judge for Yourself!* Edited and translated by Howard V. Hong and Edna H. Hong. Princeton, NJ: Princeton University Press, 1990.

King, Martin Luther, Jr. "Letter from a Birmingham City Jail." In *A Testament of Hope: The Essential Writings of Martin Luther King, Jr.* Edited by James Melvin Washington. San Francisco: HarperSanFrancisco, 1991.

———. "A Time to Break Silence." In *A Testament of Hope: The Essential Writings of Martin Luther King, Jr.* Edited by James Melvin Washington. San Francisco: HarperSanFrancisco, 1991.

Kleinknecht, Baumgärtel, Bieder, Sjöberg, and Schweizer. "*Pneuma, pneumatikos.*" 332–455 in *Theological Dictionary of the New Testament,* Vol. 6. Edited by Gerhard Kittel and Gerhard Friedrich. Translated by G. W. Bromiley. Grand Rapids, MI: Wm. B. Eerdmans Publishing Co., 1968.

Konnert, Mark. *Early Modern Europe: The Age of Religious War, 1559–1715.* Toronto: University of Toronto Press, 2008.

Kuhn, Thomas S. *The Structure of Scientific Revolutions.* 50th anniversary ed. Chicago: The University of Chicago Press, 2012.

Labron, Tim. *Wittgenstein and Theology.* London: T. & T. Clark, 2009.

Landman, W. A. *Human Relations and the South African Scene in the Light of Scripture.* Cape Town: Dutch Reformed Church Publishers, 1976.

———. *A Plea for Understanding: A Reply to the Reformed Church in America.* Cape Town: NG Kerk-Uitgewers, 1968.

Lewis, Thomas A. *Why Philosophy Matters for the Study of Religion—and Vice Versa.* Oxford: Oxford University Press, 2015.

Lindbeck, George A. *The Nature of Doctrine: Religion and Theology in a Postliberal Age.* 25th anniversary ed. Louisville, KY: Westminster John Knox Press, 2009.

Lonergan, Bernard. *Method In Theology.* New York: Seabury, 1972.

Long, D. Stephen. *Divine Economy: Theology and the Market.* London: Routledge, 2000.

Luther, Martin. *Luther's Works.* Translated and edited by Jaroslav Pelikan and Helmut T. Lehmann. American ed. 55 vols. Philadelphia: Muhlenberg Press / Fortress Press; St. Louis: Concordia Publishing House, 1955–86.

MacIntyre, Alasdair. *After Virtue: A Study in Moral Theory.* 2nd ed. Notre Dame, IN: University of Notre Dame press, 1984.

Maimonides, Moses. *Guide of the Perplexed.* Translated by A.H. Freidlander. New York: Dover, 1956.

Marga, Amy. *Karl Barth's Dialogue with Catholicism in Göttingen and Münster: Its Significance for His Doctrine of God.* Tübingen: Mohr Siebeck, 2010.

Marsden, George M. *Fundamentalism and American Culture: The Shaping of Twentieth Century Evangelicalism, 1870–1925.* Oxford: Oxford University Press, 1980.

Marx, Karl. "Contribution to the Critique of Hegel's *Philosophy of Right.*" 16–25 in *The Marx-Engels Reader.* 2nd ed. Edited by Robert C. Tucker. New York: W. W. Norton & Company, 1978.

———. "Economic and Philosophic Manuscripts of 1844." 66–125 in *The Marx-Engels Reader.* 2nd ed. Edited by Robert C. Tucker. New York: W. W. Norton & Company, 1978.

———. "Manifesto of the Communist Party." 469–500 in *The Marx-Engels Reader.* 2nd ed. Edited by Robert C. Tucker. New York: W. W. Norton & Company, 1978.

———. "Theses on Feuerbach." 143–45 in *The Marx-Engels Reader.* 2nd ed. Edited by Robert C. Tucker. New York: W. W. Norton & Company, 1978.

McCormack, Bruce L. *Karl Barth's Critically Realistic Dialectical Theology: Its Genesis and Development 1909–1936.* Oxford: Clarendon Press, 1997.

———. *Orthodox and Modern: Studies in the Theology of Karl Barth.* Grand Rapids, MI: Baker Academic, 2008.

McDermott, Gerald R., and Harold A. Netland. *A Trinitarian Theology of Religions: An Evangelical Proposal.* Oxford: Oxford University Press, 2014.

McDonald, Jermaine M. "Ferguson and Baltimore according to Dr. King: How Competing Interpretations of King's Legacy Frame the Public Discourse on

Black Lives Matter." In *Journal of the Society of Christian Ethics* 36, no. 2 (Fall/Winter 2016): 141–58.

McFague, Sallie. *The Body of God: An Ecological Theology*. Minneapolis, MN: Fortress Press, 1993.

———. *Metaphorical Theology: Models of God in Religious Language*. Philadelphia: Fortress Press, 1982.

———. *Models of God: Theology for an Ecological, Nuclear Age*. Philadelphia: Fortress Press, 1987.

———. *Speaking in Parables: A Study in Metaphor and Theology*. Philadelphia: Fortress Press, 1975.

McGrath, Alister E. *The Future of Christianity*. Oxford: Blackwell Publishers, 2002.

Menocal, María Rosa. *The Ornament of the World : How Muslims, Jews, and Christians Created a Culture of Tolerance in Medieval Spain*. New York: Back Bay Books, 2002.

Migliore, Daniel L. *Faith Seeking Understanding: An Introduction to Christian Theology*. Grand Rapids, MI: Wm. B. Eerdmans Publishing Co., 1991.

Milbank, John. "Enclaves, or Where Is the Church?" In *The Future of Love: Essays in Political Theology*. Eugene, OR: Cascade Books, 2009.

———. "KNOWLEDGE: The theological critique of philosophy in Hamann and Jacobi." In *Radical Orthodoxy: A New Theology*. Edited by John Milbank, Catherine Pickstock, and Graham Ward. London: Routledge, 1999.

———. "The Programme of Radical Orthodoxy." In *Radical Orthodoxy? A Catholic Inquiry*. Edited by Laurence Paul Hemming. Burlington, VT: Ashgate Publishing, 2000.

———. "On Theological Transgression." In *The Future of Love: Essays in Political Theology*. Eugene, OR: Cascade Books, 2009.

———. *Theology and Social Theory*. 2nd ed. Oxford: Blackwell, 2006.

———. *Theology and Social Theory: Beyond Secular Reason*. Oxford: Blackwell Publishers Ltd., 1990.

———. *The Word Made Strange: Theology, Language, Culture*. Oxford: Wiley-Blackwell, 1997.

Milbank, John, and Catherine Pickstock. *Truth in Aquinas*. London: Routledge, 2000.

Milbank, John, Catherine Pickstock, and Graham Ward, eds. *Radical Orthodoxy: A New Theology*. London: Routledge, 1999.

Milbank, John, and Simon Oliver, eds. *The Radical Orthodoxy Reader*. London: Routledge, 2009.

Mitchell, Basil. *The Justification of Religious Belief*. Reprint, New York: The Macmillan Press, 1973.

Moltmann, Jürgen. *The Spirit of Life: A Universal Affirmation*. Translated by Margaret Kohl. Minneapolis, MN: Fortress Press, 1992.

Montague, George T. *The Holy Spirit: Growth of a Biblical Tradition*. New York: Paulist Press, 1976.

Moore, Gregory. *Nietzsche, Biology and Metaphor.* New York: Cambridge University Press, 2002.

Moritz, Joshua M. *Science and Religion: Beyond Warfare and Toward Understanding.* Winona, MN: Anselm Academic, 2016.

Nagel, Thomas. *The View from Nowhere.* Oxford: Oxford University Press, 1986.

Nasr, Seyyed Hossein, ed. *The Study Quran: A New Translation and Commentary,* Edited with the assistance of Caner K. Dagli, Maria Massi Dakake, Joseph E. B. Lumbard, and Mohammed Rustom. New York: HarperOne, 2015.

Nicholson, Hugh. *Comparative Theology and the Problem of Religious Rivalry.* Oxford: Oxford University Press, 2011.

Niebuhr, H. Richard. *Christ and Culture.* New York: Harper Torchbooks, 1951.

Nielsen, Kai. "Wittgensteinian Fideism." *Philosophy* 42, no. 161 (1967): 191–209.

Nietzsche, Friedrich. *The Antichrist.* In *The Portable Nietzsche.* Edited and translated by Walter Kaufmann. New York: The Viking Press, 1968.

———. *Beyond Good and Evil: Prelude to a Philosophy of the Future.* Edited and translated by Walter Kaufmann. New York: Vintage Books, 1989.

———. *On the Genealogy of Morality.* Edited by Keith Ansell-Pearson. Translated by Carol Diethe. Cambridge: Cambridge University Press, 1994, 2007.

Omar, Irfan A., ed. *A Christian View of Islam: Essays on Dialogue.* Maryknoll, NY: Orbis Books, 2010.

O'Shaughnessy, Thomas. *The Development of the Meaning of Spirit in the Koran.* (Rome: Pontifical Oriental Institute, 1953.

Ottati, Douglas F. *Theology for Liberal Protestants: God the Creator.* Grand Rapids, MI: Wm. B. Eerdmans Publishing Co., 2013.

Padgett, Tim. "El Salvador's New President Faces Gangs, Poverty and Instability." National Public Radio (March 19, 2014), http://www.npr.org/sections /parallels/2014/03 /19/291428131/el-salvadors-new-president-faces-gangs -poverty-and-instability.

Panikkar, Raimundo. *The Trinity and the Religious Experience of Man.* Maryknoll, NY: Orbis Books, 1973.

Pascal, Blaise. *Pensées.* Translated by A. J. Krailsheimer. Revised. New York: Penguin Books, 1995.

Pedraja, Luis G. *Jesus Is My Uncle: Christology from a Hispanic Perspective.* Nashville, TN: Abingdon Press, 1999.

Pelevin, Victor. *Babylon.* Translated by Andrew Bromfield. London: Faber and Faber, 2000.

Pew Research Center. "The Future of World Religions: Population Growth Projections, 2010–2050." April 2, 2015. http://www.pewforum.org/2015/04/02 /religious-projections-2010–2050/.

Phillips, Bernard S. *Beyond Sociology's Tower of Babel: Reconstructing the Scientific Method.* New York: Aldine de Gruyter, 2001.

Phillips, D. Z. *Faith after Foundationalism.* London: Routledge, 2013.

Pinnock, Clark H. *Flame of Love: A Theology of the Holy Spirit*. Downers Grove, IL: InterVarsity Press, 1996.

Plato. "Meno." In *Greek Philosophy: Thales to Aristotle*. 3rd ed. Edited by Reginald E. Allen. Translated by K. C. Guthrie. New York: The Free Press, 1991.

Pope Benedict XVI. "Saint Benedict of Norcia." Homily delivered at a General Audience in St. Peter's Square on April 9, 2008. http://w2.vatican.va/content /benedict-xvi/en/audiences/2008/documents/hf_ben-xvi_aud_20080409 .html.

Pope Francis I. *Evangelii Gaudium*. http://w2.vatican.va/content/francesco/en /apost_exhortations/documents/papa-francesco_esortazione-ap_20131124 _evangelii-gaudium.html.

Pseudo-Dionysius. *Pseudo-Dionysius: The Complete Works*. Translated by Colm Luibheid with Paul Rorem. New York: Paulist Press, 1987.

Rahner, Karl. *Foundations of Christian Faith: An Introduction to the Idea of Christianity*. Translated by William V. Dych. New York: Crossroad, 1999.

Rahner, Karl, with Paul Imhof and Hubert Biallowons. *Karl Rahner in Dialogue: Conversations and Interviews, 1965–1982*. Edited by Paul Imhof, Hubert Biallowons, and Harvey D. Egan. New York: Crossroad Publishing, 1986.

Ratzinger, Cardinal Joseph, Congregation for the Doctrine of the Faith. "Instruction on Certain Aspects of the 'Theology of Liberation' (Aug. 6, 1984)." In *Liberation Theology: A Documentary History*. Edited by Alfred T. Hennelly. Maryknoll, NY: Orbis Books, 1990.

Richardson, Alan, and John MacQuarrie. "Fideism." In *The Westminster Dictionary of Christian Theology*. Edited by Alan Richardson and John Bowden. Philadelphia: The Westminster Press, 1983.

Richardson, Cyril C., ed. and trans. "The So-called Letter to Diognetus." 33–73 in *Early Christian Fathers*. trans. and ed. New York: Collier Books, 1970.

Ricoeur, Paul. *The Symbolism of Evil*. Translated by Emerson Buchanan. New York: Beacon Press, 1967.

Robert, Dana L. "Shifting Southward: Global Christianity since 1945." *International Bulletin of Missionary Research* 24, no. 2 (April 2000): 50–58.

Rogers, Jack. *Claiming the Center: Churches and Conflicting Worldviews*. Louisville, KY: Westminster John Knox Press, 1995.

Rollefson, Richard Griffith. *Thinking with Kierkegaard and Wittgenstein: The Philosophical Theology of Paul L. Holmer*. Eugene, OR: Pickwick Publications, 2014.

Rorty, Richard. *Philosophy and the Mirror of Nature*. Princeton: Princeton University Press, 1980.

———. "Religion as Conversation-stopper." 168–74 in *Philosophy and Social Hope*. New York: Penguin Books, 1999.

Rosario Rodríguez, Rubén. *Christian Martyrdom and Political Violence: A Comparative Theology with Judaism and Islam*. Cambridge: Cambridge University Press, 2017.

————. "Liberating Epistemology: Wikipedia and the Social Construction of Knowledge." *Journal of Religion and Theology* 26, no. 2 (2007): 173–201.

————. *Racism and God-Talk: A Latino/a Perspective.* New York: New York University Press, 2008.

Rosin, Hanna. "Bush's 'Christ Moment' Is Put to Political Test by Christians: Act of Faith or Partisan Ploy, It Draws Faithful's Attention." In *The Washington Post* (Thursday, December 16, 1999).

Ruether, Rosemary Radford. *Sexism and God-Talk: Toward a Feminist Theology.* Boston: Beacon Press, 1983.

Salamun, Kurt. "Karl Jaspers on Human Self-Realization: Exintenz in Boundary Situations and Communication." In *Karl Jasper's Philosophy: Expositions and Interpretations.* Edited by Kurt Salamun and Gregory J. Walters. Amherst, NY: Humanity Books, 2008.

Sarna, Nahum M. *The JPS Torah Commentary: Genesis.* Philadelphia: The Jewish Publication Society, 1989.

Schleiermacher, Friedrich. *The Christian Faith: A New Translation and Critical Edition.* 2 vols. Edited Catherine L. Kelsey and Terrence N. Tice. Translated by Terrence N. Tice, Catherine L. Kelsey, and Edwina Lawler. Louisville, KY: Westminster John Knox Press, 2016.

————. *On Religion: Speeches to Its Cultured Despisers.* Translated by John Oman. Louisville, KY: Westminster John Knox Press, 1994.

Schloss, Jeffrey, and Michael J. Murray, eds. *The Believing Primate: Scientific, Philosophical, and Theological Reflections on the Origins of Religion.* Oxford: Oxford University Press, 2010.

Schmidt, W. H. "Dābhar." 122–25 in *Theological Dictionary of the Old Testament.* Vol. 3. Rev. ed. Edited by G. Johannes Botterweck and Helmer Ringgren. Grand Rapids, MI: Wm. B. Eerdmans Publishing, 1977.

Schrag, Calvin O. *The Resources of Rationality: A Response to the Postmodern Challenge.* Bloomington: Indiana University Press, 1992.

Schreiter, Robert J. *Constructing Local Theologies.* Maryknoll, NY: Orbis Books, 1985.

Segundo, Juan Luis. *The Liberation of Theology.* Translated by John Drury. Maryknoll, NY: Orbis Books, 1976.

Sells, Michael. "Spirit." 114–17 in *Encyclopedia of the Qur'ān.* Vol. 5, *Si-Z.* Edited by Jane Dammen McAuliffe. Leiden, NLD: Brill, 2006.

Shah-Kazemi, Reza. "Do Muslims and Christians Believe in the Same God." In *Do We Worship the Same God? Jews, Christians, and Muslims in Dialogue.* Edited by Miroslav Volf. Grand Rapids, MI: Wm. B. Eerdmans Publishing Co., 2012.

Smith, George Wayne. "Blood Cries Out from the Ground: Reflections on Ferguson." *Anglican Theological Review* 97, no. 2 (Spring 2015): 255–63.

Smith, Wilfred Cantwell. *What Is Scripture? A Comparative Approach.* 2nd ed. Reprint, Minneapolis, MN: Fortress Press, 1993.

Solzhenitsyn, Aleksandr. "Godlessness: The First Step to the Gulag." Templeton
    Prize Lecture, May 10, 1983 (London), http://orthodoxnet.com/blog/2011
    /07/men-have-forgotten-god-alexander-solzhenitsyn/.
————. *The Gulag Archipelago 1918–1956: An Experiment in Literary Investiga-
    tion*. 2 vols. Translated by Thomas P. Whitney. New York: Harper & Row,
    Publishers, 1973.
Sonderegger, Katherine. *Systematic Theology*. Vol. 1, *The Doctrine of God*. Min-
    neapolis, MN: Fortress Press, 2015.
Sorell, Tom. *Scientism: Philosophy and the Infatuation with Science*. Reprint, Lon-
    don: Routledge Books, 1991.
Squeeze. *Babylon and On*. A&M, 1987. Audio recording.
St. John of the Cross. "The Ascent of Mt. Carmel." In *The Collected Works of
    St. John of the Cross*. Translated by Kieran Kavanaugh and Otilio Rodriguez.
    Washington, DC: ICS Publications, 1964.
Steiner, George. *After Babel: Aspects of Language and Translation*. 2nd ed. Oxford:
    Oxford University Press, 1992.
Stout, Jeffrey. *Ethics after Babel: The Languages of Morals and their Discontents*.
    Princeton: Princeton University Press, 2001.
Stump, Eleonore. *The God of the Bible and the God of the Philosophers*. Milwau-
    kee, WI: Marquette University Press, 2016.
Taylor, Mark C. *Journeys to Selfhood: Hegel and Kierkegaard*. New York: Fordham
    University Press, 2000.
————. *Kierkegaard's Pseudonymous Authorship: A Study of Time and the Self*.
    Princeton: Princeton University Press, 1975.
Taylor, Mark Kline. "Introduction: The Theological Development and Contri-
    bution of Paul Tillich." In *Paul Tillich: Theologian of the Boundaries*. Edited
    by Mark Kline Taylor. Minneapolis, MN: Fortress Press, 1991.
————. *Remembering Esperanza: A Cultural-Political Theology for North Ameri-
    can Praxis*. Maryknoll, NY: Orbis Books, 1990.
Taylor, Mark Lewis. "Tracking Spirit: Theology as Cultural Critique in Amer-
    ica." In *Changing Conversations: Religious Reflection and Cultural Analysis*.
    Edited by Dwight N. Hopkins and Sheila Greeve Davaney. New York: Rout-
    ledge, 1996.
The Lutheran World Federation and the Catholic Church. "Joint Declaration
    on the Doctrine of Justification." (1999), http://www.vatican.va/roman_curia
    /pontifical_councils/ chrstuni/documents/rc_pc_chrstuni_doc_31101999_
    cath-luth-joint-declaration_en.html .
Thiselton, Anthony C. *The Hermeneutics of Doctrine*. Grand Rapids, MI: Wil-
    liam B. Eerdmans Publishing Company, 2007.
————. *New Horizons in Hermeneutics: The Theory and Practice of Transforming
    Biblical Reading*. Grand Rapids, MI: Zondervan, 1992.
————. *The Two Horizons: New Testament Hermeneutics and Philosophical
    Description*. Reprint, Grand Rapids, MI: William B. Eerdmans Publishing
    Company, 1993.

Thomas Aquinas. See Aquinas, Thomas.

Thurian, Max, ed. *Churches Respond to BEM*. Geneva: World Council of Churches, 1986.

Tilley, Terrence W. *Inventing Catholic Tradition*. Maryknoll, NY: Orbis Books, 2000.

Tillich, Paul. "Aspects of a Religious Analysis of Culture." In *Theology of Culture*. Edited by Robert C. Kimball. Oxford: Oxford University Press, 1959.

———. *Biblical Religion and the Search for Ultimate Reality*. Chicago: The University of Chicago Press, 1955.

———. *Dynamics of Faith*. Reprint, Grand Rapids, MI: Zondervan, 2001.

———. *A History of Christian Thought: From Its Judaic and Hellenistic Origins to Existentialism*. Edited by Carl E. Braaten. New York: Simon and Schuster, 1972.

———. "On the Idea of a Theology of Culture." In *Paul Tillich: Theologian of the Boundaries*. Edited by Mark Kline Taylor. Minneapolis: Fortress Press, 1991.

———. "The Present Theological Situation in Light of the Continental European Development." *Theology Today* 6, no. 3 (Oct. 1949): 299–310.

———. "The Significance of the History of Religions for the Systematic Theologian." In *Paul Tillich: Theologian of the Boundaries*. Edited by Mark Kline Taylor. Minneapolis, MN: Fortress Press, 1991.

———. *Systematic Theology*. 3 vols. Chicago: The University of Chicago Press, 1951, 1957, and 1963.

———. "What Is Wrong with the 'Dialectic' Theology?" In *Paul Tillich: Theologian of the Boundaries*. Edited by Mark Kline Taylor. Minneapolis: Fortress Press, 1991.

Tilson, Everett. *Segregation and the Bible*. New York: Abingdon Press, 1958.

Toulmin, Stephen. *An Examination of the Place of Reason in Ethics*. Cambridge: Cambridge University Press, 1950.

Tracy, David *The Analogical Imagination: Christian Theology and the Culture of Pluralism*. New York: Crossroad, 1981.

———. "Comparative Theology." 447 in *The Encyclopedia of Religion*. Vol. 14. Edited by Mircea Eliade. New York: MacMillan Publishing Co., 1987.

———. *Dialogue with the Other: The Inter-Religious Dialogue*. Louvain: Peeters Press, 1990.

———. "Lindbeck's New Program for Theology: A Reflection." *Thomist: A Speculative Quarterly Review* 49, no. 3 (July 1, 1985): 460–72.

———. *Plurality and Ambiguity: Hermeneutics, Religion, Hope*. Reprint, Chicago: The University of Chicago Press, 1994.

Vander Schel, Kevin M. *Embedded Grace: Christ, History, and the Reign of God in Schleiermacher's Dogmatics*. Minneapolis, MN: Fortress Press, 2013.

Vanhoozer, Kevin J. *Biblical Narrative in the Philosophy of Paul Ricoeur—A Study in Hermeneutics and Theology*. Cambridge: Cambridge University Press, 1990.

———. *The Drama of Doctrine: A Canonical-Linguistic Approach to Christian Theology*. Louisville, KY: Westminster John Knox Press, 2005.

Volf, Miroslav. *Allah: A Christian Response*. New York: HarperOne, 2011.

———. *Captive to the Word of God: Engaging the Scriptures for Contemporary Theological Reflection*. Grand Rapids, MI: Wm. B. Eerdmans Publishing Co., 2010.

———. *Exclusion and Embrace: A Theological Exploration of Identity, Otherness, and Reconciliation*. Nashville, TN: Abingdon Press, 1996.

———. *Flourishing: Why We Need Religion in a Globalized World*. New Haven, CT: Yale University Press, 2015.

———. "Wheaton professor's suspension is about anti-Muslim bigotry, not theology." In *The Washington Post* (December 17, 2015), https://www .washingtonpost.com/news/acts-of-faith/wp/2015/12/17/wheaton-professors -suspension-is-about-anti-muslim-bigotry-not-theology/.

Vonnegut, Kurt. *Breakfast of Champions*. Reprint, New York: Delacorte Press, 1973.

Wallace, Mark I. *The Second Naiveté: Barth, Ricoeur, and the New Yale Theology*. Macon, GA: Mercer University Press, 1995.

Ward, Graham. *Barth, Derrida and the Language of Theology*. Cambridge: Cambridge University Press, 1995.

———. *Cities of God*. London: Routledge, 2001.

———. *Politics of Discipleship*. Grand Rapids, MI: Baker Academic, 2009.

———. "In the Economy of the Divine: A Response to James K. A. Smith." In *PNEUMA: The Journal of the Society for Pentecostal Studies* 25, no. 1 (Spring 2003): 115–20.

Watson, Francis. "The Bible." 57–71 in *The Cambridge Companion to Karl Barth*. Edited by John Webster. Cambridge: Cambridge University Press, 2000.

Welker, Michael. *God the Spirit*. Translated by John F. Hoffmeyer. Minneapolis, MN: Fortress Press, 1994.

White House Petitions website, https://petitions.whitehouse.gov/petition /formally-recognize-black-lives-matter-terrorist-organization.

White, Curtis. *The Science Delusion: Asking the Big Questions in a Culture of Easy Answers*. Brooklyn, NY: Melville House, 2013.

Wilmore, Gayraud S., and James H. Cone, eds. *Black Theology: A Documentary History, 1966–1979*. Maryknoll, NY: Orbis Books, 1979.

Wink, Walter. *Jesus and Nonviolence: A Third Way*. Minneapolis, MN: Fortress Press, 2003.

Wittgenstein, Ludwig. *On Certainty*. Edited by G .E. M. Anscombe and G. H. von Wright. Translated by Dennis Paul and G. E. M. Anscombe. New York: Harper Torchbooks, 1969.

———. *Culture and Value*. Edited by G. H. von Wright. Translated by P. Winch. Rev. ed. Oxford: Basil Blackwell, 1998.

———. *Tractatus Logico-Philosophicus*. Translated by D. F. Spears and B. F. McGuinness. Reprint, London: Routledge Classics, 2001.

Wood, Susan K. "Communion Ecclesiology: Source of Hope, Source of Controversy." *Pro Ecclesia: A Journal of Catholic and Evangelical Theology* 2, no. 4
(Fall 1993): 424–32.

Wright, John, ed. *Postliberal Theology and the Church Catholic: Conversations
with George Lindbeck, David Burrell, and Stanley Hauerwas.* Grand Rapids,
MI: Baker Academic, 2012.

Wright, N. T. *Scripture and the Authority of God: How to Read the Bible Today.*
Rev. exp. ed. New York: HarperOne, 2013.

Wright, Robert. *The Evolution of God.* New York: Little, Brown, 2009.

Yong, Amos. *Beyond the Impasse: Toward a Pneumatological Theology of Religions.*
Eugene, OR: Wipf & Stock, 2003.

Young, Robert M. *Darwin's Metaphor: Nature's Place in Victorian Culture.* Cambridge: Cambridge University Press, 1985.

Young, Robin Darling. *In Procession before the World: Martyrdom as Public Liturgy in Early Christianity.* The Père Marquette Lecture in Theology 2001.
Milwaukee, WI: Marquette University Press, 2001.

Index of Subjects and Authors

Abrahamic religions, ix, 90n114, 110,
    131–36, 139, 148, 167–68, 176,
    182
Absolute Paradox, 13
academic theology, xi–xii, 1, 3, 13,
    21–22, 32, 35, 53, 70, 106, 109,
    142
African American liberationist theology,
    xii, xvii, 95, 171–73
    See also black liberation theology
aggiornamento, 177
Allen, Diogenes, 22n73, 26n89, 119, 130
Alves, Rubem, xiv, xvii, 177, 179n98,
    180, 184–85
analogia entis, 125
analogia fidei, 54, 125
analogical knowledge, 119–31
analogy of proportion, 121, 123
analogy of proportionality, 126
Anselm, xv, 127
anthropological approach, xiii, xvi,
    31–32, 50, 55, 72, 147
anthropological model. See anthropologi-
    cal approach
Apocalypse of John. See Revelation
    (book of)
apologetics, xvi, 31, 67, 90
apophatic theology, 81, 120
Aquinas. See Thomas Aquinas
Arabi, Ibn, 134
Aristotle, 114, 123, 187
atheism, xvii, 2, 38, 87, 97, 113, 113n10,
    114, 114n13, 133, 185
Augustine, 1, 50, 191

Babel, x, xi–xii, xiv–xv, 1, 80, 110, 168,
    187-94

Barth, Karl, xi, xiii–xiv, 6n12, 14–20,
    29n106, 32–33, 35–38, 41, 43, 46,
    51, 53–55, 58–61, 66, 84–86, 120,
    121, 124–26, 140, 146
Bauckham, Richard, 163, 164n41,
Bell, Daniel M., 83n83, 87n99, 101
Benedict of Nursia, 30, 30n112, 89
Benedict Option, 89, 93
black liberation theology, xii, xvii
Black Lives Matter, 170–74, 183
BLM. See Black Lives Matter
Bloesch, Donald G., 18, 19n60
Bonhoeffer, Dietrich, 17, 42, 97
Borges, Jorge Luis, xi
Boyarin, Daniel, 94
Brooks, David, 89
Brown, Delwin, 112–13
Brown, Michael, 170–71, 174
Bultmann, Rudolf, 6n12, 15, 16, 37, 43,
    128
Burrell, David B., xiii–xiv, 132n72

Calvin, John, 51–53, 182–83,
    190–93
capitalism, 88, 96, 101–2
Cartesian absolute certainty, 5, 26, 114,
    143
cataphatic theology, 81, 120
charismata, 160–61, 163, 183
Charismatic Movement, 146–47
Christ, xiii, 9–10, 16, 26, 28, 35, 39,
    45–46, 48–50, 54, 56, 58–59,
    61–63, 65, 70, 71, 79, 81–83, 87,
    90–91, 93, 96, 98, 101, 103, 105,
    125–26, 138–39, 141–43, 158–59,
    160–64, 177–80, 182, 187, 194
    See also Jesus

civil rights movement, 171, 173, 189, 193
Climacus, Johannes, 10. 13
comparative theology, ix, 31, 49, 59, 61, 65, 70, 107–108, 110, 131, 135–36, 139, 141, 143, 148, 168, 182, 185
Cone, James, xvii, 88, 92, 100
constructive theology, 20, 30, 45, 50, 51, 57, 62n110, 65, 71–72, 74, 107–8, 114, 148n11, 164
contextual theology, xvii, 50, 65, 142
correlational method, xiii, 31, 55, 124
creation, 3, 23, 48, 61, 63, 78–79, 81–82, 86, 123, 135, 142, 149–50, 158, 165, 188–190, 192–93
    doctrine of, 119–20, 124–26, 132–33, 149–50
    ex nihilo, 119
Crossan, John Dominic, 6n12, 117

Darwin, Charles, 113, 117–19
Dawkins, Richard, 113, 113n10
De La Torre, Miguel, 70, 95–105, 107, 142, 189, 192–93
de Lubac, Henri, 85, 97
democratic liberalism, 95, 101, 138
Descartes, René, 2–3, 127
Deus absconditus, 48, 132, 134, 168
    See also hiddenness of God
diástasis, 32
divine agency, xviii, 18, 46, 85, 139, 146, 150–51, 156, 166, 175–76, 183
divine essence, 120–21, 125, 127
divine initiative, 18, 139, 142–43
divine self-communication, 7, 46, 55, 75, 132, 140, 143, 176, 182
divine self-revelation. *See* divine self-communication
doctrine, xv–xviii, 2, 4, 6, 16–17, 25–29, 31, 33, 35, 38, 41, 52, 54, 57, 60–65, 79, 92, 95, 98, 108, 110, 112, 119, 125, 128, 136, 165, 167, 168, 181, 183, 184, 193
    of creation, 119-120, 124–26, 132–33, 149-150
    of God, 163–64

of revelation, 131–32, 140–43
of the Spirit, 148nn10 11
dogma, 7, 13, 80, 147, 148
dogmatics, xi, xiii, 17–20, 24, 32–33, 37, 39, 43–44, 48, 65, 67, 169
Dorrien, Gary, 17n55, 18n58, 20–21
Dostoevsky, Fyodor, 18, 18n57, 128
Dreher, Rod, 89

ecclesia, 172, 178, 185, 195
ecclesial authority, 1–2
ecclesial praxis. *See* ecclesial theology
ecclesial theology, xvii, 38, 71, 87, 95, 102, 104, 105, 183
Ellis, Marc, 175, 182n109
Enlightenment, xvi, 1–4, 6, 6n12, 14, 23–24, 33, 35, 60, 65, 66n2, 73, 87–88, 90, 94, 99, 102–3, 109, 112, 119n31, 146, 151
Enlightenment rationalism, 2, 6n12, 60, 109, 146
essence, 47, 123, 134, 172
    See also divine essence
Eucharist, 79, 93–94, 129–30, 176, 178, 180

feminist theology, xii, xvii, 74, 76, 80, 83, 95
Feuerbach, Ludwig, xvi, 18, 82, 124, 146
fideism, xviii, 7, 13, 112, 128, 131, 184, 186
First World War, 6n12, 14, 35–36, 45, 109, 140
foundationalism, 29, 41–42, 114
Frei, Hans W., xiii–xiv, 20, 23, 83, 88, 128
Freire, Paulo, 96
Freud, Sigmund, xvi, 36, 70n21

Gandhi, Mahatma, 187
Geertz, Clifford, xviii, 27, 110–111
Gegenständlichkeit, 37, 66
Gilkey, Langdon, 15n47, 19, 73
God, ix–xix, 2, 4–5, 7–13, 16–19, 24–32, 35–63, 65–86, 88, 101, 103, 107, 109, 111–12, 119–43, 145–69, 172, 174–76, 178–79, 181–86, 188–94

God as friend, 97–99
God as lover, 97–99
God as mother, 97–99
Goizueta, Roberto S., 88
González, Justo L., xvii, 88
Gould, Stephen Jay, 133
Gutiérrez, Gustavo, xvii, 96–97, 100,
 103–104, 142, 145–46, 177–79,
 181, 183–85, 194–95

Harari, Yuval Noah, 115–17
Harris, Sam, 113
Hauerwas, Stanley, xiii–xiv, 84, 97, 101,
 103, 109, 141
Hebrew Bible, 3, 62, 70, 133, 147–52,
 156–59, 163–64, 166–68, 175, 182
Hegel, G. W. F, 4, 6–7, 9–12, 14, 17, 24,
 41, 146
Heim, Mark, 61–62, 140–41, 147
Helmer, Christine, xv, xvii–xviii, 24, 30,
 168
hiddenness of God, ix, 110, 124, 131–36,
 143, 172, 175,
Hobbes, Thomas, 87
Holy Spirit, 2, 18, 33, 45, 51–53, 57,
 61–63, 65, 80, 90, 138–39, 141–
 43, 146–48, 156–61, 165–66, 177,
 179, 183, 190, 194
 See also Spirit
Homo narrativus, 116–17

imago Dei, xix, 78, 101, 150–51
incarnation, 7, 9–10, 25–26, 46, 48, 62,
 79–80, 82, 85, 91–93, 139, 141
Islam, ix–x, xii, 32–33, 108, 110, 131–
 32, 134–35, 137, 139, 141, 148,
 164–68, 183

Jaspers, Karl, 172
Jesus, xiii, 1n3, 4–6, 10, 17, 19, 23, 26,
 35, 39, 45–46, 48–52, 54, 56,
 58–59, 61–63, 65, 71, 74–75,
 78–83, 90–93, 98–100, 103,
 125–26, 138, 142, 146, 148, 155,
 158–66, 179–80, 187
Jesús, 95–96, 99–100
 See also Christ

Jesus of history. See Quest for the historical Jesus
Job, 51, 104, 133, 152
joder, 98, 104
Johnson, Elizabeth, 117–18
Judaism, ix, 33, 62, 90n21, 91, 108, 131–
 32, 135, 137, 139, 141, 147–57,
 182, 191

Kaiser Wilhelm, 14
Kant, Immanuel, 3–4, 13–14, 18, 111,
Kantian epistemology, 39–41, 72, 86, 111
Kantian "turn to the subject," 4, 112
Kärkkäinen, Veli-Matti, 148n11, 194
Kaufman, Gordan D., xii–xiii, 39–40, 72
Kierkegaard, Søren, 4–5, 7–15, 17–18,
 24–26, 41, 51–53, 57, 86, 111,
 120, 124, 127–29, 131, 181–82,
 184–85
King, Martin Luther, Jr., 170–71
Knitter, Paul, 145
koinōnia, 160
Kuhn, T. S., 28, 80

Latino/a liberationist theology, xvii, 68,
 98–101, 188
Letter to Diognetus, 162
liberal theology, xii, xiv, xvi, xviii, 3, 14,
 16–21, 29–32, 37–40, 72–73
liberalism, xvi, xviii, 14, 17–21, 31, 33,
 37–39
liberation theology, xii, xvii, 13, 66n2,
 68–70, 83, 85–86, 92, 94–105,
 106–7, 109, 141–42, 147, 167–69,
 172, 175, 177–85
liminality, 170, 172
Lindbeck, George A., xiii, xviii–xiv, 20,
 26–31, 33–34, 60, 83, 88, 90, 128,
 139, 173, 181
logical positivism, 127
Lonergan, Bernard, 69
Long, D. Stephen, 83n83, 86, 88, 92
Luther, Martin, 132n72, 134
Lyotard, Jean-François, 68, 90

MacIntyre, Alasdair, 21, 30, 68, 84, 89
Maimonides, Moses, 126, 132n72, 137

Marion, Jean-Luc, 84
Marx, Karl, xvi, 85, 97
McFague, Sallie, xiii, 70–83, 92, 107
metanarrative realism, 84, 88, 90
metaphorical theology, 20, 56, 71–77, 82,
    107, 119
Milbank, John, xiv, 29n106, 70, 83–94,
    98, 100–103, 107, 141–42
modernism, 87, 89, 92, 96, 99, 109, 147,
    181
Moltmann, Jürgen, 60, 143, 145, 164,
    168
Muhammad, 148, 165, 183
mysterium tremendum et fascinans,
    82–83

narrative theology, 3–4, 14, 19–22, 24,
    26–27, 29, 50, 53, 88, 112–13,
    119, 128, 169, 183
natural sciences, 28, 75, 80, 107, 111,
    113, 117
natural theology, 37, 47, 119–125
Nazism, 16
neoliberalism, 101
    See also democratic liberalism
neo-orthodoxy, xvi, xviii, 6n12, 14–17,
    19–20, 31–32, 37, 83–86, 88, 91,
    109–10, 181
neo-scholasticism, 86
nephesh, 149
neshamah, 149
New Testament, 6, 54, 56, 62–63, 70, 74,
    138, 148, 154, 157–64, 167, 182,
    189, 193
Nietzsche, Friedrich, xvi–xvii, 18, 98,
    184–85
nineteenth-century liberal Protestantism.
    See liberal thelogy
non-overlapping magisteria, 113–14
nouvelle théologie, 84–85

objective truth, 7, 8, 12–13, 23, 28, 37,
    59, 99
Orthodox Pluralism, 89
orthodoxy, xiii, 1n3, 13, 17, 19–20, 32,
    88–89, 92, 98, 165–66, 184
orthopraxis, 13, 33, 98

Ottati, Douglas F., xii
Ottoman Empire, 2

panentheism, 79, 81
Pascal, Blaise, 132, 134
Pedraja, Luis G., 188–90, 193
Pentecost, xiv–xv, 158, 159, 189–90
Pentecostalism, x, 57, 60, 146–47
perichoresis, 178
Pickstock, Catherine, 29n106, 83
Plato, 11
Platonic theory of recollection, 11, 32
Platonic thought, 23
pneuma, 149, 149n12, 157–59, 164, 181,
    182
pneumatology, 65, 145–47, 158–59, 163,
    165
pneumatological, 51, 60–61, 71, 164
postfoundationalism, 114
postliberal antifoundationalism, 29
postliberal theology, xiii, xviii, 20–21, 30,
    53, 83–84
postliberalism, xvi, 29–30, 83, 85, 88, 91,
    110, 128, 181
postmodernity, 42, 68
preferential option for the poor, ix, 33,
    66, 97, 100–101, 194
Pseudo-Dionysius, 120, 124

Quest for the historical Jesus, 5–6, 17, 19,
    50–51
Qur'an, 134, 137, 139, 148, 164–67,
    175, 182–83

Radical Orthodoxy, 29–30, 53, 83–95,
    97, 100–101, 103, 105–107, 109
rational religion of immanence, 7, 10–13
religious faith understood as subjectivity,
    7–8, 12–13, 36, 41, 124, 131, 146,
    150, 186
religious pluralism, xii, 31, 58, 61, 65–66,
    68–70, 107, 110, 138, 140–43,
    176, 181, 185
Renaissance humanism, 1
ressourcement, 84–85
revelation, xiii, xv, xvii, 4, 7, 9–14,
    16–19, 24–25, 28, 31–33, 35,